DATE DUE

DEMCO 38-297

FROM RICHARDSON TO PINERO

FROM RICHARDSON
TO PINERO

SOME INNOVATORS AND IDEALISTS

By

FREDERICK S. BOAS

M.A.(Oxon); Hon. LL.D.(St. Andrews); Hon. D.Lit.(Belfast)
FELLOW AND PROFESSOR OF THE ROYAL SOCIETY OF LITERATURE

Essay Index Reprint Series

Originally published by
COLUMBIA UNIVERSITY PRESS

BOOKS FOR LIBRARIES PRESS
FREEPORT, NEW YORK

First Published 1937
Reprinted 1969

Reprinted from a copy in the collections
of the Brooklyn Public Library

LIBRARY OF CONGRESS CATALOG CARD NUMBER:
69-17563

PRINTED IN THE UNITED STATES OF AMERICA

CONTENTS

PAGE

I INTRODUCTION 1

II RICHARDSON'S NOVELS AND THEIR INFLUENCE . 6

III THACKERAY ON THE EIGHTEENTH-CENTURY HUMOURIST
AS HERO 47

IV WORDSWORTH'S PATRIOTIC POEMS AND THEIR
SIGNIFICANCE TO-DAY 60

V EDMUND KEAN IN HIS HEROIC PARTS . . . 85

VI ROBERT BROWNING'S *PARACELSUS*, 1835–1935 . 122

VII ELIZABETH BARRETT BROWNING : IN HER VERSE AND
HER PROSE 145

VIII ARTHUR HENRY HALLAM AND *IN MEMORIAM* . 192

IX TENNYSON AND THE ARTHURIAN LEGEND . . 210

X MATTHEW ARNOLD IN HIS LYRIC VERSE . . 230

XI SIR ARTHUR PINERO : DRAMATIST AND STAGE-
CHRONICLER 250

INDEX 281

v

PREFATORY NOTE

OF the studies collected in this volume those on Elizabeth Barrett Browning, on Edmund Kean, and Sir Arthur Pinero appear in print for the first time. Those on Richardson's Novels and on Wordsworth's Patriotic Poems were English Association publications; and those on Tennyson and the Arthurian Legend and on Matthew Arnold appeared in the *Transactions of the Royal Society of Literature*. All of these are now out of print. Those on Thackeray's Humourists, Browning's *Paracelsus* and Arthur Henry Hallam are reprinted by permission, respectively from the *Contemporary Review*, the *Quarterly Review*, and *Queen's Quarterly* (Canada). All the studies in the volume have been revised and in some cases the titles have been modified. For the Index I am mainly indebted to my wife.

F. S. B.

I

INTRODUCTION

THE studies collected in this volume were written at considerable intervals and for different purposes. Most of them in their original form were lectures delivered before the Royal Society of Literature, the English Association and other bodies. These included several centenary addresses. Others appeared during the period of the World War. Their subjects were diverse—drawn from fiction, poetry, drama and (from some angles) biography.

But when I began to revise them and bring them together I found that they ranged consecutively over a period of about two centuries, from the publication of Richardson's first novel in 1740 to the death of Sir Arthur Pinero in 1934; and that their subjects were so far linked in that they manifested some form of innovation, independence, or idealism.

Thus Samuel Richardson begins with *Pamela* a new era in the English novel by using the epistolary method for the display of his minute sentimental analysis. In *Clarissa* the same method serves the higher purpose of presenting with the utmost elaboration a picture of noble womanhood, pursued, betrayed and martyred. *Sir Charles Grandison* furnishes what was in Richardson's eyes, if not in ours, the complementary and contrasted picture of triumphantly virtuous manhood.

When Thackeray lectured on the Eighteenth-century Humourists he probably thought that his title excluded Richardson, but in any case neither his sentiment nor his idealism could have appealed to him. To find the essentials of a " hero " in eighteenth-century men of letters Thackeray went to Steele and Pope, Fielding and Goldsmith, so different in many ways, but in whose genius he discovered both virile and tender elements akin to his own.

As the eighteenth century drew to its close the sentiment of the novelists from Richardson to Rousseau was transmuted into a dynamic social force that helped to set in motion the Revolution in France with its sequel of the Napoleonic wars. It was then that the spirit of Britain found heroic utterance in Wordsworth's *Poems Dedicated to National Independence and Liberty* and other patriotic verse. Their enduring appeal was proved again in the strikingly parallel conditions of 1914–18, and in to-day's testing time of the nations they retain much of their significance.

It was in the year before Waterloo that Edmund Kean, who had made a theatrical innovation with his natural methods of acting, attained his ambition of performing Shakespearian and other heroic parts on the boards of Drury Lane. When in this theatre the centenary of his death in May, 1833, was commemorated, the Shakespearian actor who paid the chief tribute to him, spoke of his performances in words that, as I have tried to show, could equally have been used of Wordsworth's Sonnets.

The year of Kean's death saw the publication by a new author of his first volume *Pauline*, followed in 1835 by a poetic work in dialogue form, *Paracelsus*. In an introduction to this the author, Robert Browning, made it clear that he was departing from traditional dramatic methods, and the division into five " parts " instead of " acts " was an indication that the work was not intended for the stage. But in disregarding " an external machine of incidents," and in giving preference to a display of a mood in its rise and progress Browning anticipated a leading trend of twentieth-century drama. In exposing the inevitable failure of a scheme of life resting solely on knowledge, and in interpreting the doctrine of development without materialist implications, the young poet was to prove himself truly prophetic.

His verse was to find an early admirer in Elizabeth Barrett Barrett, an invalid in her father's house, 50 Wimpole Street, who had commenced author with an epic on Marathon when she was fourteen. Some of her earlier poems and dramas have, I think, been undervalued ; and I have suggested that in the heroes of her girlhood's muse she partly found the inspiration to her own heroic defiance of a fanatical paternal despotism. I have not attempted to retell in detail what is now a familiar story. But I have taken advantage of the recent additions to the already large body of her correspondence to make something of a comparative estimate of her achievement in verse and prose. This has involved a reconsideration of some aspects of *Sonnets from the Portuguese*, *Poems before Congress* and *Aurora Leigh*.

The early 'thirties of the nineteenth century, when Robert Browning, Elizabeth Barrett Barrett and Alfred

Tennyson were beginning their careers, saw the untimely death in September, 1833, of Arthur Henry Hallam, whose youthful promise had dazzled the eyes of his contemporaries. His "Remains" in verse and prose, especially the latter, are still of interest, and serve as a prelude to *In Memoriam* in which Tennyson gave a novel scope to elegy, enlarging it from a personal threnody to a far-reaching inquisition into problems of God and Nature and Man.

In Memoriam appeared in 1850 and the first group of *Idylls of the King* in 1859. It was in the light of the spiritual conceptions that underlie *In Memoriam* that Tennyson gave his own interpretation of the Arthurian legend. I have attempted to justify that interpretation against its critics, but have noted some of the difficulties to which it inevitably gave rise.

Between the publication of *In Memoriam* and of *Idylls of the King* there appeared the early poems of an Oxford scholar whose naturally fastidious instinct had been further disciplined by the study of Greek models. Matthew Arnold's finely chiselled verse expresses a strikingly individual temper. He can find no satisfying solution of life's problems, but in spite of frustration and disillusion, at the centre of his being he remains stoically calm.

Among the cultural questions that drew Arnold away from poetry in his later life was the function of the theatre. A few years before his death in 1886 a new dramatist was beginning a career which was to provide the English stage with its most notable body of plays till the turn of the century. In farce, in sentimental comedy and in domestic drama Arthur Wing Pinero

4

was an innovator, independent in outlook and in treatment. He was not only a playwright ; he was a student of stage history from the eighteen-seventies to T. W. Robertson in the 'sixties, and still farther back to Edmund Kean. And in some parallels that I have suggested between his career and that of Ben Jonson we may even get a glimpse, at the close of this volume, of the greatest period of our theatrical history.

II

RICHARDSON'S NOVELS AND THEIR
INFLUENCE

HOWEVER great may be the debt of our
fiction to Lyly, Sidney, and Nash, to the
seventeenth-century romance-writers, or to
Bunyan, Defoe, and Swift, it is a commonplace of the
textbooks that a new era was begun by the publication
in November, 1740, of *Pamela, or Virtue Rewarded*,
from the pen of Samuel Richardson, master printer, who
thus commenced authorship at the mature age of fifty-
one. Gifted from boyhood with a talent for letter-
writing, he had already planned, and probably in part
composed, a series of *Familiar Letters*, with directions
"how to think and act justly and prudently, in the
common concerns of human life". Among these letters
were several dealing with the temptations to which girls
in service or without protection were exposed. Thus,
when he set out to handle the same theme more elaborately in the form of a story, he not unnaturally retained
the epistolary method. Hence *Pamela* appeared "in
a series of Familiar Letters from a beautiful Young
Damsel to her Parents. Now first published in order
to cultivate the Principles of Virtue and Religion in the
Minds of the Youth of both sexes."

6

The success of the work led Richardson to adopt the same method in his later novels. To those who wished that *Clarissa* " had been told in the usual narrative way " he retorted that he " had the good fortune to succeed in the epistolary way once before," and that he " perhaps mistrusted his talents for the narrative kind of writing." In *Sir Charles Grandison* he pleads that the advantages of the method more than atone for its lengthiness. " Mere facts and characters might be compressed in a much smaller compass, but would they be equally interesting ? "

A few words are therefore not amiss on the general aspects of the method to which Richardson was so constant. It is based upon the convention that man is primarily a letter-writing animal, and that pen, ink, and paper are his first needs. In the age of Lady Mary Montagu, Lord Chesterfield, and Horace Walpole, the theory was some degrees more plausible than in our own. But the world which it postulates of beings whose ruling passion (in the language of the day) is for interminable correspondence is a gigantic make-believe. Such a universal *cacoethes scribendi* would be fatal to any scheme of sane and ordered life. Thus in the case of Pamela her activity as a letter-writer can have left her scanty time to fulfil her duties as a servant, and we feel that her master, Mr. B——, is justified in speaking sarcastically of her constant scribbling. When she leaves his Bedfordshire house for his seat in Lincolnshire, Mr. Longman, the steward, offers her as parting gifts several yards of holland, a silver snuff-box, and a gold ring. But she asks in addition for what is more precious to her than dress materials or jewels—some

7

paper, and is gratified by receiving " above forty sheets of paper and a dozen pens, and a little phial of ink, which last I wrapped in paper and put in my pocket, and some wax and wafers." With these, as soon as she arrives at her new abode, she prepares to stand a siege in writing materials :

I set about hiding a pen of my own here, and another there, for fear I should come to be denied, and a little of my ink in a broken china cup, and a little in another cup, and a sheet of paper here and there among my linen, with a little of the wax, and a few wafers in several places lest I should be searched.

On her wedding-day she writes no less than six letters,[1] one of them containing a detailed account of the ceremony. She begins at 6 a.m., and continues at 8.30, near 3.0 p.m., and 8.0, 10.0, and 11.0 at night.

Clarissa looks upon correspondence as one of the first duties of women. "It was always matter of surprise to her that the sex are generally so averse as they are to writing, since the pen, next to the needle, of all employments, is the most proper and best adapted to their geniuses, and this as well for improvement as amusement." She was of opinion—and she is probably reflecting Richardson's own view—that

those women who take delight in writing excel the men in all the graces of the familiar style. The gentleness of their minds, the delicacy of their sentiments (improved by the manner of their education), and the liveliness of their imaginations qualify them to a high degree of preference for this

---

[1] Technically they are entries in her " journal," but they are indistinguishable from her letters.

employment, while men of learning, as they are called (that is to say of mere learning), aiming to get above that natural ease and freedom which distinguish this (and indeed every other kind of writing), when they think they have best succeeded, are got above, or rather *beneath*, all natural beauty.

It is characteristic of Clarissa that she had cultivated all the humdrum as well as the higher virtues of a letter-writer :

The hand she wrote, for the neat and free curl of her letters (like her mind, solid and above all *flourish*), for its firmness, evenness and swiftness, distinguished her as much as the correctness of her own orthography, and even punctuation, from the generality of her own sex. She was used to say, " It was a proof that a woman understood the derivation as well as sense of the words she used, and that she stopt not at *sound* when she spelt accurately."

Harriet Byron is so indefatigable a correspondent that between March 7 and 16 she writes twenty-two letters to her cousin, Lucy Selby, without waiting for a reply. A little later in the same month her pen is again equally active, and according to Leslie Stephen's calculation, she must have written for nearly eight hours a day.

It is with a sense of relief that we find one of the minor characters in *Clarissa*, Mr. Richard Mowbray, confessing in vigorous terms his hatred of correspondence :

I am tired of writing, I never wrote such a long letter in my life. My wrists and my fingers and thumbs ache damnably. The pen is a hundredweight at least. And my eyes are ready to drop out of my head upon the paper. The cramp but this minute in my fingers. Rot the goose and the goose-quill ! I will write no more long letters for a twelvemonth to come.

But not only are Richardson's personages, with this exception, constantly writing. They also forward, on the most trivial pretext, enclosures from other correspondents, and frequently intersperse these with comments of their own. The arrangement thus approximates at times to a Chinese puzzle, with bewildering results. Moreover, it is essential that the lines of communication between the correspondents should never be cut. Thus to whatever straits Pamela or Clarissa may be reduced, and however closely they may be sequestered, some device has to be manufactured by which they may get letters through to their friends.

But the conventions and artificialities of the epistolary type of novel are counterbalanced by one great advantage. The letter is of all forms of writing the most intimate and revealing. It mirrors emotions, moods, and events at the actual moment of their occurrence, while feelings have all their first poignancy and facts their original clearness of outline. The letter is the half-way house between speech and literature. It has the spontaneity and the freshness of the one combined with the permanence and the precision of the other. Every classical student, to take a familiar instance, feels in passing from the works of the historians of Rome to the letters of Cicero that he is for the first time in full touch with the motives and impulses of the men of the ancient world. And what is true of letters written by historical personages is equally true of letters written by fictitious characters. They subtly flatter the self-esteem of the reader by admitting him to revelations of personality which could not without impropriety be so fully or frankly made by any other means. They take us behind the scenes of life, and show us thoughts, and desires, and impulses, not tricked out and disguised for the contemplation of critical spectators, but in their native simplicity and ingenuousness. The instinct to which letters, real or feigned, thus appeal, though in certain aspects it may come under the ban of an austere morality, is a permanent one in human nature.

From these general considerations let us return to the novelist's own application of the method in *Pamela*. The story is in itself somewhat sordid and incredible, not seemingly suitable to be spun out through two volumes.[1] But in Dr. Johnson's trenchant phrase, "If you were to read Richardson for the story, your impatience would be so much fretted that you would hang yourself. But you must read him for the sentiment, and consider the story only as giving occasion to the sentiment." It is in delicate sentimental analysis, subtle delineation of progressive gradations of feeling, that the originality and charm of the work lie. By the skilful accumulation of minute stroke after stroke the complex character of Pamela is revealed. She, it is to be noted, writes almost every letter, and the Lincolnshire episodes are, in fact, related in her journal and not in strict letter form. In two points Richardson sacrifices dramatic truth of portraiture—in the second point, at any rate, intentionally. It is scarcely credible, except perhaps for her childish interest in clothes and finery, that she is

[1] I deal here with *Pamela* in its original form, and have not included the much inferior continuation in two further volumes.

little more than fifteen. And her letters in their style and spelling show no trace of the maidservant or the rustic. But it has to be remembered that Lady B. had given her an education above her place. As she writes to her parents :

My good lady, now in heaven, loved singing and dancing ; and, as she would have it, I had a voice, she made me learn both ; and often and often she has made me sing her an innocent song, and a good psalm too, and dance before her. And I must learn to flower and draw too, and to work fine work with my needle. . . . To be sure, I had better as things stand have learned to wash and scour, and brew and bake and such like. . . . I have read of a good bishop that was to be burnt for his religion ; and he tried how he could bear it, by putting his fingers into the lighted candle. So I, t'other day, tried, when Rachel's back was turned, if I could not scour a pewter plate she had begun. I see I could do 't by degrees ; it only blistered my hand in two places.

Her accomplishments even include a turn for versification, and there is nothing for which I find it so difficult to forgive Pamela as her metrical version of the 137th Psalm : " By the rivers of Babylon, there we sat down, yea, we wept, when we remembered Zion." It was bad enough that William Whittingham, one of the contributors to Sternhold and Hopkins, should paraphrase in pedestrian stanzas the most exquisitely cadenced of Hebrew lyrics :

> When we did sit in Babylon
>   The rivers round about ;
> Then in remembrance of Sion,
>   The tears for grief burst out.

We hang'd our harps and instruments
The willow trees upon;
For in that place, men, for that use
Had planted many a one.

But Pamela achieves the miracle of making the above
version sound relatively melodious and dignified :

When sad I sat in B——n hall,
All guarded round about,
And thought of ev'ry absent friend,
The tears for grief burst out.

My joys and hopes all overthrown,
My heart-strings almost broke,
Unfit my mind for melody,
Much more to bear a joke.

Nor is this composition intended by Richardson to be
a shocking example of a maidservant dabbling in verse.
For on the Sunday before the marriage the chaplain and
Mr. B—— read out alternately, stanza by stanza, the
two versions of the Psalm amidst the admiring comments of the assembled company.

But when Pamela writes in prose, she is mistress of a
vivid and perspicuous style. Bit by bit she lays bare
before us her singular character, with its mixture of
servile deference to rank, emotional susceptibility, and
genuine though self-conscious piety. All three are
combined in her description of Mr. B——, when he
gives her some of his mother's clothes, as looking " like
an angel." When he proves himself anything but an
angel, it is her piety that keeps her steadfast amidst
temptation. But it is a coarse-grained, alarmist piety

that makes her continually harp upon her " virtue " as if it were an external and acquired property instead of a spiritual essence, " closer than breathing, and nearer than hands and feet." And how hard it has to fight for supremacy is evident at every turn. When her libertine master, after insulting advances, summons her to an interview, her heart " fluttered about like a new-caught bird in a cage." On another similar occasion she " crept towards him with trembling feet, and my heart throbbing through my handkerchief." We see every flutter and throb of that heart, and learn its secrets before they are known to itself. When in Lincolnshire she thinks of drowning herself in the pond as an escape from the dangers that beset her, her meditations are in a whimsically blended vein of sentimentality and piety :

What hast thou to do, distressed creature, said I to myself, but throw myself upon a merciful God (who knows how innocently I suffer), to avoid the merciless wickedness of those who are determined on my ruin ?

And then thought I (and oh ! that thought was surely of the devil's instigation ; for it was very soothing, and powerful with me), these wicked wretches who now have no remorse, no pity on me, will then be moved to lament their misdoings ; and when they see the dead corpse of the unhappy Pamela dragged out to these dewy banks, and lying breathless at their feet, they will find that remorse to soften their obdurate heart, which now has no place there !—And my master, my angry master, will then forget his resentments, and say, Oh, this is the unhappy Pamela that I have so causelessly persecuted and destroyed ! Now do I see she preferred her honesty to her life, will he say, and is no hypocrite nor deceiver ; but really was the innocent creature she pretended to be ! Then, thought I, will he perhaps shed a few tears over the poor corpse of his persecuted servant . . . and the young men and maidens all around my dear father's will pity poor Pamela ! But oh ! I hope I shall not be the subject of their ballads and elegies ; but that my memory, for the sake of my dear father, may quickly slide into oblivion.

When she at last puts the thought of suicide away, we have one of Richardson's rare references to nature in personalized form.

What then, presumptuous Pamela, dost thou here ? thought I. Quit with speed these perilous banks, and fly from these curling waters, that seem, in their meaning murmurs, this still night to reproach thy rashness !

This episode is the περιπέτεια of the story, so far as it can be said to have one. On the same afternoon, on hearing that her master has escaped an accidental form of the death by drowning which she sought for herself, she makes the first direct confession of her feeling for him :

What is the matter that, with all his ill usage of me, I cannot hate him ? To be sure, I am not like other people ! He has certainly done enough to make me hate him ; but yet, when I heard his danger, which was very great, I could not in my heart forbear rejoicing for his safety ; though his death would have ended my afflictions . . . oh, what an angel would he be in my eyes yet if he would cease his attempts, and reform !

If reform be indulgently interpreted to mean that Mr. B———, having exhausted every illegitimate method of winning Pamela, offers her his hand in marriage, her prayer is fulfilled. Her piety is sufficiently robust to

15

keep her own virtue secure ; it does not presume to
exact penitence as the price of pardon from an offender
of rank. The first moment that he changes his tune,
she is ready to dance to his piping. Even though she
reasons with herself against trusting implicitly one who
has treated her so ill, she knows—as is shown in a
passage of really exquisite insight—that the surrender
of her deepest self has already been irrevocably made
to him :

Therefore will I not acquit thee yet, oh credulous, fluter-
ing, throbbing mischief ! that art so ready to believe what
thou wishest ! And I charge thee to keep better guard than
thou hast lately done, and lead me not to follow too implicitly
thy flattering and desirable impulses. Thus foolishly dia-
logued I with my own heart ; and yet, all the time, this heart
was Pamela.

Yet even if, with Pamela's character, her surrender
was inevitable, one feels that after all that has gone
before, it takes an unduly abject form.

When Mr. B—— points out to her the difficulties
that will beset her when she is elevated to the position
of his wife, she becomes dithyrambic in the expression
of her gratitude :

You may well guess, my dear father and mother, how
transporting these kind, these generous and condescending
sentiments were to me !—I thought I had the harmony of the
spheres all around me ; and every word that dropped from
his lips was as sweet as the honey of Hybla to me !

She assures him that she will be at no loss for occupation, even should she be unvisited by the ladies of

his acquaintance. In addition to domestic management and good works:

I will assist your housekeeper, as I used to do, in the making jellies, comfits, sweetmeats, marmalades, cordials; and to pot, candy, and preserve for the uses of the family; and to make, myself, all the fine linen of it for yourself and me.

Then, sir, if you will sometimes indulge me with your company, I will take an airing in your chariot now and then, and when you shall return home from your diversions on the green, or from the chase, or where you shall please to go, I shall have the pleasure of receiving you with duty, and a cheerful delight; and, in your absence, count the moments till you return; and you will, maybe, fill up some part of my time—the sweetest by far!—with your agreeable conversation, for an hour or two now and then; and be indulgent to the impertinent overflowings of my grateful heart, for all your goodness to me.

It is a fitting sequel that at the wedding ceremony, "when the bridegroom had done saying, *With this ring I thee wed*, &c." Pamela "made a curtsy, and said, 'Thank you, sir!'"

Not a highly impressive attitude, to our thinking, for a heroine, yet her marriage, we are told, so stirred the villagers at Slough, where the tale was read out by the local blacksmith, that they rang the church bells to celebrate it. Londoners were equally enthusiastic. In January, 1741, two months after the publication of the book, the *Gentleman's Magazine* stated that it was "judged in Town as great a Sign of Want of Curiosity not to have read Pamela as not to have seen the *French* and *Italian* Dancers." In February a second edition appeared, followed by others in March and May.

What gave the book its extraordinary vogue? Such a question can, in my opinion, never be fully answered. The secret of the meteoric popularity of certain plays, novels, and poems is one that in great part dies when that popularity is spent. Who can ever adequately explain why *The Spanish Tragedie*, or *Euphues*, or *Childe Harold* leapt into instant fame, and fired to such a degree the imaginations and sympathies of men? So it is with *Pamela*. Yet a partial explanation, at least, can be given. A new form of literature was needed in the interests of a newly arrived class of readers. The great growth of material prosperity among the citizens and traders after the Revolution settlement had largely multiplied the number of persons of leisure. Middle-class wives and daughters, in especial, had unlimited time and taste for reading. But what, unless they liked serious literature, were they to read? Addison, writing in 1711, could include in Leonora's library the high-flown pseudo-pastoral and pseudo-chivalric romances of the seventeenth century, La Calprenède's *Cleopatra and Cassandra*, D'Urfé's *Astræa*, Mdlle de Scudéry's *Grand Cyrus* and *Clelia*. But their day was past, and, indeed, the *Tatler* and the *Spectator* and their successors were partly designed to take their place with the female world. But a short essay, however attractive, could not fill many vacant hours, and it did not minister to the inextinguishable interest in affairs of the heart. Nor did this interest find gratification in the narrative master-pieces of Defoe and Swift. According to Pope, in the

Epistle to Augustus, written a few years before the publication of *Pamela,*

> Our wives read Milton, and our daughters plays.

But Milton is not an author to " lie in a lady's lap," and the only permanent *readers* of plays are prospective dramatists or professed students of literature.

Appearing under such circumstances, Richardson's novel was exactly suited to take the town by storm. It combined the sentimental interest of the heroic tale with accurate delineation of familiar characters and episodes, and with the moralizing tendency which the periodical essay had helped to make fashionable. It revealed to a delighted world of readers the latent romance, the neglected spiritual significance of humble and outwardly commonplace lives. The little duodecimo volumes in which it was printed, and which ladies held up to view at public assemblies, were as symbolic of its homely theme as the folios of an earlier day were of the adventures and amours of knights and high-born dames. But we must be careful not to read into the novel more than is really there. Richardson's psychological insight and evangelical piety combined make him recognize that a maidservant's soul is of equal importance to that of a princess, and that therefore there is nothing demeaning in a marriage between her and a fine gentleman. But he does not imply that the virtues of womanhood are only to be found outside the pale of conventional society. Some may recall the performance of Mr. Maugham's play, *Smith.* In this a well-connected Englishman, returning after a number of years' absence in the colonies, is so revolted by the insincerity and artificiality of the fashionable women whom he meets at his sister's house that he chooses as his wife the unsophisticated parlour-maid Smith. Such a play is inspired by a revolutionary social doctrine which, whatever we may think of it, has no place in Richardson's scheme. His aim was merely " to cultivate the principles of virtue and religion in the minds of the youth of both sexes." It is difficult to believe that the novel can have done much to advance these " principles." Pamela, it is true, resists temptation, but at what cost of delicacy and maidenly reserve ! She escapes burning, but she is not averse to playing with fire. And her whole story enforced the not very elevating doctrine that virtue, if circumspectly followed, proves in the end to be the best policy. Moreover, Richardson, though he had undertaken " not to raise a single idea throughout the whole that shall shock the exactest piety," found himself confronted with the dilemma which meets every writer who turns fiction or drama to moral uses. If he turns away his gaze from the evils against which he wishes to warn his readers, he can appeal only to the " fugitive and cloistered virtue " which overcomes the world by shunning it. If he paints scenes of depravity and temptation, his art may make them so lifelike that they may kindle a flame in the senses and imagination which his didacticism cannot afterwards extinguish. Rousseau, fervent admirer as he was of Richardson, said that in his novels he lit a fire that he might bring up the pumps and put it out. In *Pamela* it is highly questionable if he does put it out.

Clarissa, or The History of a Young Lady was apparently begun about 1744, and completed by October,

1746. It was published in a remarkably leisurely
fashion, even for a work of such bulk. Two volumes
appeared in November, 1747, two more in April, 1748,
and the three concluding volumes in December of the
same year. As with *Pamela*, through the use of the
epistolary form the interest of *Clarissa* is centred not in
the events but the personages, with their divergent
motives, reflections, and resolves. Like *Pamela* also it
has a declared moral aim. " To warn the inconsiderate
and thoughtless of the one sex, against the base arts and
designs of specious contrivers of the other ; to caution
parents against the undue exercise of their natural
authority over their children in the great article of
marriage ; to warn children against preferring a man
of pleasure to a man of probity "—these were among
the ends that Richardson sought to promote. But in
all other ways the two novels are as different as they
well could be.

Though *Clarissa* is about five times as long as *Pamela*,
it has far more organic unity. Long-winded as some
of the letters may seem at first sight, and redundant in
their details, they will almost invariably be found necessary to that minute revelation of character by almost
infinitesimal touches which is distinctive of Richardson's
art. The truth of this statement will be discovered by
any reader who, dismayed by the gigantic proportions
of the work, seeks to evade his full responsibilities by
" skipping." Views or observations thrown off apparently lightly by one of the correspondents, and perhaps
scarcely noticed at the time, are taken up later by another
character, and seen to be far more significant than
appeared at first. There is thus a constant interlacing

of phrases and of ideas throughout the work which reminds us of the repetition of the theme in a fugue. The author himself in an elaborate series of footnotes, like the critical apparatus to a classical text, frequently expounds the relations of one passage or letter to another and to the general scheme of the work. It is in its combination of infinitely detailed analysis with a structural unity sedulously kept in view that the peculiar impressiveness of *Clarissa* partly lies. In *Pamela* the interest is almost entirely focused on the heroine, and the letters, with few and unimportant exceptions, are written by her. In *Clarissa* there are not only four principal correspondents, the heroine and her bosom friend Miss Anna Howe, Lovelace and his intimate and confidant John Belford, but a variety of other letter-writers of different social classes. Even the subordinate personages are clearly individualized, and each of them has a distinctive epistolary style. There is nowhere in the later work the shy and tremulous grace of Pamela's maiden pen, but in range and variety Richardson's powers of expression have immeasurably increased. So strong indeed has his dramatic instinct become that it is intolerant at times of the epistolary convention, and some of the scenes are thrown into dialogue form, as if they were episodes in a play. The observation of life has widened to a surprising extent. Richardson remains essentially an anatomist of the heart, but the man who could paint with Hogarthian realism the episodes in Mrs. Sinclair's house, especially her hideously drawn-out death agony, or touch with a lighter brush the incidents in the King Street glove-shop, had a keener eye for " manners " than is usually allowed by his critics.

The least convincing group of characters in the novel is Clarissa's family circle. Her brother James and her sister Arabella are such monsters of cruelty and spite that they belong to the realm of fairy-tale. We can only believe in them and Clarissa as blood-relations on the same terms as we accept Cinderella and her sisters. There is nothing indeed to add to Clarissa's own cry: " How happy might I have been with any other brother in the world but James Harlowe; and with any other sister but his sister!" Mr. Harlowe, the father, is almost equally odious, but his gouty constitution and the rigour of eighteenth-century paternal despotism make his conduct at least credible. He has a short way with recalcitrant daughters:

In a strong voice, Clarissa Harlowe, said he, know that I will be obeyed.

God forbid, sir, that you should not!—I have never yet opposed your will.

Nor I your whimsies, Clarissa Harlowe, interrupted he. . . . I was going to make protestations of duty—No protestations, girl! No words! I will not be prated to! I will be obeyed! I have no child, I will have no child but an obedient one.

It is almost superfluous for Clarissa to add, "My father . . . has not . . . a kind opinion of our sex; although there is not a more condescending wife in the world than my mother." The struggles of this condescending wife between her feeling for her younger daughter and her abject submissiveness to the stern head of the house alone bring the Harlowe family within the range of human sympathy.

The suitor whom the family conspire to force upon Clarissa plays a passive rather than an active part, but his harshly-featured portrait is bitten in with a few mordant strokes which are further evidence of Richardson's close observation of externals :

There was the odious Solmes sitting asquat between my mother and sister with so *much* assurance in his looks. Had the wretch kept his seat, it might have been well enough, but the bent and broad-shouldered creature must needs rise, and stalk towards a chair, which was just by that which was set for me.

Again of a later interview :

The man stalked in. His usual walk is by pauses, as if . . . he was telling his steps : and first paid his clumsy respects to my mother, then to my sister, next to me, as if I were already his wife, and therefore to be last in his notice ; and sitting down by me told us in general what weather it was. Very cold he made it, but I was warm enough.

When Clarissa ignores his presence, " he fell to gnawing the head of his hazel ; a carved head, almost as ugly as his own." A description hard to match for its caustic terseness.

Similarly we might take in turn almost all the minor characters. Lord M——, Lovelace's splenetic, warm-hearted uncle, whose letters are crammed with proverbs, " a confounded parcel of pop-guns," as his nephew terms them ; the reverend Elias Brand, the officious and pedantic young clergyman, fond of " throwing about to a Christian and country audience scraps of Latin and Greek from the Pagan classics," who when sent to inquire about Clarissa in her last days puts the worst

possible interpretation upon all that he hears; Sally
Martin and Polly Horton, two of Mrs. Sinclair's crew—
who are sufficiently adroit to pose in Clarissa's company,
not without success for a time, as ladies of quality; Mrs.
Moore and the occupants of her Hampstead lodgings—
in the portraiture of all these Richardson shows a faculty
of exploiting the humours and foibles of both sexes for
which there was nothing to prepare us in *Pamela.*

But it is on the four principal letter-writers, distinguished in the prefatory list of names by capital letters,
that the novelist has massed the full powers of his genius.
In one case his success is only partial. The reformed
rake is never attractive, and Belford's letters of exhortation to Lovelace to give over his evil courses, though
intended by Richardson to be deeply impressive, seem
ponderously commonplace to-day. But his descriptions
of the death-beds of the libertine Belton, and the infamous Mrs. Sinclair, even if they have lost something
of their directly edifying quality, remain sombre genre-
pieces, the contemplation of which still works in us pity
and terror. And it is to Belford, as companion of
Clarissa in her last days and executor of her will, that
we owe the contrasted picture of the heroine's dying
hours.

But Clarissa's friend more than atones for any defici-
encies in Belford. Miss Anna Howe is, in my opinion,
though not the greatest, the most remarkable creation
in the novel. Remember what Richardson was—a
serious tradesman, intent on preaching moral lessons,
and with no knowledge of fashionable society from the
inside. One would have thought that the type most
foreign to his observation and his sympathy was a

woman of the finest breeding, with an airy, mocking gaiety that masks a penetrating judgement and a golden heart.   Yet such is the sister of Clarissa's soul, a woman essentially akin, amidst all that separates Richardson's prose from Shakespeare's poetry, to Portia, Rosalind, or Beatrice.   Might not Beatrice herself be speaking here ?

I think there is not one man in a hundred whom a woman of sense and spirit can either *honour* or *obey*, though you make us promise *both*, in that solemn form of words which unites or rather *binds* us to you in marriage . . .   Well do your sex contrive to bring us up fools and idiots, in order to make us bear the yoke you lay upon our shoulders ; and that we may not despise you from our hearts (as we certainly should, if we were brought up as you are) for your *ignorance*, as much as you often make us do (as it is) for your *insolence*.

It is in a retaliatory spirit for the general wrongs of her sex that she plays the part of Lady Disdain to the worthy Hickman, the " virtuous, sober, sincere, friendly " wooer, whom her mother urges upon her.   As she writes to Clarissa, " What, think you, makes me bear Hickman near me but that the man is humble, and knows and keeps his distance ? "   The triangular relations between her, Hickman, and her mother, with whom she keeps up an affectionate wrangle on equal terms, are exquisitely comic, and throw into sombre relief the domestic tyranny that drives Clarissa to her doom. One cannot spoil Miss Howe's final summing up of the story of her courtship :

Mr. Hickman was proposed to *me*.   I refused him again and again.   He persisted ; my mother his advocate.   My mother made my beloved friend his advocate too. I told him my dislike of all men—of him—of matrimony—still he persisted. I used him with tyranny . . . hoping thereby to get rid of him ; till the poor man (his character unexceptionably uniform) still persisting made himself a merit with me by his patience. This brought down my pride, and gave me at one time an inferiority in my own opinion to him, which lasted just long enough for my friends to prevail upon me to promise him encouragement and to receive his addresses. Having so done, when the weather-glass of my pride got up again, I found I had gone too far to recede.

I think that enthusiasts for the feminist cause might do worse than quarry in Miss Howe's letters, with their really remarkable note of modernity.

Of Clarissa herself it is difficult to speak. One can scarcely contemplate her character and fortunes without a reverential awe which forbids many words. Those who wish to know her as she is must seek her in Richardson's own pages. Nor must they be disappointed if at first she seems somewhat too formal and precise in her rectitude. Her day was distributed on unimpeachable principles. To rest she allowed six hours only. The first three morning hours were devoted to study and letter-writing. Two hours were given to domestic management, for she was a perfect mistress of the four principal rules of arithmetic. Five hours were spent in music, drawing, and needlework. Two hours were devoted to breakfast and dinner, one to visiting the poor, and the remaining four to supper and conversation. A life thus lived by methodical rule might have become priggish, and it cannot be denied that in the earlier part of the novel Clarissa's letters are frequently more like the formal dispatches of a diplomatist than the notes of a young lady to her relatives and friends. Richardson has sometimes been blamed for getting the story so slowly under weigh in the opening volumes of *Clarissa*. But he could not have done otherwise. It is only the minutely elaborated record of the successive humiliations and insults to which Clarissa is exposed that makes it in any degree credible that a girl who lives by rule and principle almost to a fault should take flight from her father's house with a notorious libertine. It needs a system of persecution relentlessly pursued in favour of the odious Solmes to waken in her virginal nature any warmth of feeling for Lovelace. As she writes to Miss Howe :

I cannot but say that this man—this Lovelace—is a man that might be liked well enough, if he bore such a character as Mr. Hickman bears ; and even if there were hopes of reclaiming him. And, further still, I will acknowledge that I believe it possible that one might be driven, by violent measures step by step, as it were, into something that might be called—I don't know what to call it—a *conditional kind of liking*, or so.

But she repudiates the word love, as having no pretty sound with it. It is her realization of the irrevocable and absolute stringency of the marriage bond, especially as it was interpreted in the eighteenth century, that constrains her to take any steps rather than enter upon it with a man whom she detests :

To be given up to a strange man, to be engrafted into a strange family ; to give up her very name, as a mark of her becoming his absolute and dependent property ; to be

28

obliged to prefer this strange man to father, mother, to every-body, and his humours to all her own, or to contend perhaps in breach of avowed duty for every innocent instance of free-will.   Surely, sir, a young creature ought not to be obliged to make all these sacrifices, but for such a man as she can love.   If she be, how sad must be the case.   How miserable the life, if it be called *life* !

It is even doubtful how far Clarissa's conditional kind of liking for Lovelace would under other circumstances have developed into love, and whether she could have whole-heartedly entered into the bond with him.   But when she has put herself into his power, she has in self-defence to assume a more reserved attitude than would otherwise have been necessary ; she has to " modesty away " in Miss Howe's phrase, her chances of winning his lawful love.   He, on the other hand, is now resolved to gain her on his own terms, and thus begins the long duel between them, which ends with his infamous stratagem.   Till then the issue has been in doubt, whether her purity and beauty would rouse his nobler nature ; and even in his own day Richardson had to meet the criticism of those who reproached Clarissa with undue coldness in her treatment of her wooer. But from the moment of his outrage, she becomes filled with a divine flame before which criticism shrivels. Lovelace's atoning proposal of marriage is as a worth-less offering at the shrine of a saint.   Henceforth her earthly days are but a *præparatio mortis* ; the white light of eternity falls over the scene.   Clarissa haled to prison on the information of Mrs. Sinclair, and dying at the lodgings in King Street, is one of the glorious martyr-figures of literature.   There are a few old-fashioned

touches of eighteenth-century evangelicalism, a few
jarring notes, like her purchase of her coffin, and its use
as a writing-desk, before her death. But if ever the pen
of a novelist can be called inspired, it is Richardson's in
these closing scenes of his greatest "history."

The man who could win even the conditional liking
of Clarissa was no ordinary libertine. Lovelace has
refinement, intellect, versatile energy, an imperial will.
He admires and quotes Shakespeare, refers familiarly to
classical and foreign authors, and chooses for Clarissa
an excellent library, containing, it may be noted, no
novels. He professes religion, calls the sabbath " a
charming institution," and accompanies Clarissa, much
against her will, to church. She is surprised at his
knowledge of Scripture—though his study of it has not
been in a devout vein :

O madam, I have read the Bible as a fine piece of ancient
history, but as I hope to be saved, it has for some few years
past made me so uneasy when I have popped upon some
passages in it that I have been forced to run to music or to
company to divert myself.

In spite of his cold-blooded accounts of his previous
amours, introduced incidentally to illustrate some point
or argument that he is pressing home, he is no mere
sensualist. It is the delight of " the most noble of all
chases " that enthrals him even more than the capture
of the victim. Women, in his philosophy, are creatures
of the field or of the air to be hunted, trapped, or caged.
Clarissa, struggling to escape, becomes transformed into
a " slippery eel," whom he must not let through his
fingers.

But his is not only the animal excitement of the sports-man ; he has the intellectual delight of the strategist in plans of campaign. Nothing pleases him better than when Belford charges him with having "the most plotting heart in the world." He revels in every detail of the complicated machinery which he sets in motion for Clarissa's ruin. He enjoys for their own sake, as well as for their object, the trickery by which he lures the heroine from her home, the misrepresentation of Mrs. Sinclair and her establishment, the pretence of a midnight fire at her house, the disguise in which he tracks his fugitive victim to Hampstead, even the gratui-tous piece of fooling with a customer at the King Street glove-shop where Clarissa finds her last refuge. But deeper in Lovelace than even the instincts of hunter, plotter, and actor is pride in the form of diseased self-love. It is this that drives him on to the ruin of Clarissa when he might have won her by honourable means. He sees in her virginal purity a challenge to his powers, and he is eager to humble through her the hated family of the Harlowes. It might have been thought that pride, even in its most debased form, would have re-strained Lovelace from the odious practices by which he finally brings about his victim's fall. The novelist fails to convince us that a man of birth and fashion, however profligate, would have stooped to such vile arts. But nothing could be more masterly than the working out of the nemesis that begins from the moment of the outrage. Lovelace has acted on his cherished maxim concerning the sex of "once subdued always subdued." He has reckoned confidently on making Clarissa his own for ever. But to his amazement he

31

finds that his weapons have turned against himself—
that the one woman who has stirred his higher nature
to fitful life is henceforth cut off by an impassable barrier.
He struggles against the acknowledgement of this, protests, entreats, curses, seeks to cheat himself by naming
her Clarissa *Lovelace*. The hunter has become the
quarry, and the avenging furies, set loose by his own
hand, track him relentlessly to his doom. It is, as in
all true tragedy, this long-drawn agony of soul that is
the sinner's expiation ; the avenging sword of Clarissa's
kinsman, Colonel Morden, is an instrument not of
punishment but of release.

The generation, however, that found in Tom Jones
a model hero looked indulgently upon Lovelace, and to
correct this perverted moral view Richardson resolved
to " produce into public view the character and actions
of a man of true honour." Between November, 1753,
and March, 1754, he issued in seven volumes *Sir Charles
Grandison*, to give the world " the example of a man
acting uniformly well through a variety of trying scenes,
because all his actions are regulated by one steady
principle."

This open proclamation by the novelist of his particular aim has tended to concentrate the attention of
readers and critics too exclusively upon the character
of the hero. It may therefore be of interest to deal
briefly with the technique of the work, and its general
relation to Richardson's previous novels. Like *Clarissa*,
it combines a serious (though not a tragic) main plot
with a subsidiary one in lighter vein. The main plot
is concerned with the remarkable triangular love-story

of Sir Charles Grandison, the Italian Lady Clementina della Poretta, and Miss Harriet Byron. The secondary plot, which occupies a much larger part of the novel than is generally recognized, revolves round Charlotte Grandison, the younger sister of Sir Charles, and her treatment, both before her marriage to him and after, of her humble adorer, Lord G——. But the two plots have not the same significant relationship as the corresponding ones in *Clarissa*, and they are set forth with far inferior art. Throughout *Clarissa* the reader has the overmastering sense of reading letters which have been actually interchanged, and which are stamped, in each case, with the individuality of the writer. But in *Sir Charles Grandison*, especially in the earlier volumes, Richardson reverts in part to the cruder method of *Pamela*, where the heroine writes what are virtually " epistles general," though they are nominally addressed to a particular correspondent. Thus Harriet Byron sends, day in, day out, letters to her cousin Lucy Selby without the slightest expectation of a reply. Fifteen successive letters are occupied with the early history of the Grandison family. Here the epistolary convention wears itself to the thinnest point, but this is at any rate preferable to the cumbrous machinery which Richardson sets in motion for revealing the details of Grandison's courtship at Bologna of the Lady Clementina. The story is told by Harriet Byron in letters to Lucy Selby, which enclose thirteen letters from Sir Charles's confidential friend, Dr. Bartlett, which in their turn enclose transcripts or translations of letters from Italy written either by Sir Charles himself or by Clementina's relatives and friends. Here Richardson comes near to a burlesque

33

of his chosen method, even apart from the awkward choice of Miss Byron as the exponent of her rival's love-story in its earlier stages. The later stages are mainly narrated by Sir Charles in letters to Dr. Bartlett, who leads a shadowy existence as a receiver of correspondence to which he never replies. Indeed, almost the only letters which create the illusion of a genuine exchange of confidences between friends are those which pass between Harriet Byron and Charlotte Grandison, afterwards Lady G——.

Her ladyship, though not quite such a ready writer as Miss Byron, has a livelier and more distinctive style. In his full-length portraiture of her, Richardson is evidently seeking to create a second Miss Howe, elevated in rank, and partnered (in the second volume) with a husband. He does not fall far short of success. This sprightly sister of Sir Charles is cast in the same mould as her predecessor. An inexhaustible flow of raillery and a spirit of militant feminism are united to keen perception and genuine loyalty of heart. In spite of his trying honeymoon experiences, Lord G—— (a titled Hickman, with a passion for collecting butterflies and china) is fortunate in securing such a prize. Yet Lady G—— lacks in an almost indefinable way the radiant charm of Miss Howe. Hers is a more riotous and hoydenish mirth, the gaiety of high animal spirits rather than of an exquisitely tempered nature. Nor is she called upon to bear a part in tragic issues wherein all that hides a heart from knowledge of its deepest self is shrivelled away. But though she thus suffers by contrast with her prototype, she is, on the whole, the most vital and attractive figure in the novel.

34

Other motives and situations already handled in *Clarissa* reappear in the later work. Sir Hargrave Pollexfen, whose abduction of Harriet Byron gives Sir Charles the opportunity of rescuing her, is a milk-and-water Lovelace, whose associates, Bagenhall and Merceda, are of the same kidney as Belton and Mowbray. In the irregular unions of the hero's brother, Sir Thomas Grandison (after his wife's death), his uncle Lord W——and his cousin Everard, the novelist gives further illustrations of one of his favourite themes—the evils of "keeping" as contrasted with the blessings of lawful marriage. Another of Richardson's recurrent subjects, which threatened to become something of an obsession, the self-interested or ambitious overriding of a girl's affections by her parents or a family council, is exemplified in Sir Thomas Grandison's tyrannical rejection of Lord L——'s proposal for the hand of his elder daughter. It enters also of course, in less reprehensible form, into the story of the Lady Clementina.

Here, at any rate, Richardson must be credited with the attempt to break new ground. It was a bold adventure for the English printer, with a limited knowledge of London fashionable society, to delineate the home life of an Italian of noble family. Later novelists like Marion Crawford have equipped themselves for such a task by years of residence in Rome or Florence, and by close study of the annals of the great houses of the peninsula. Little wonder therefore that Richardson fails to create Italian local colour or atmosphere. Yet up to a point he arouses interest in the fortunes of Clementina. The conflict between the claims of love and of religion and family tradition could not entirely fail of effectiveness when handled by such an expert in the analysis of emotion as Richardson. Clementina, torn between the strictest orthodoxy and her passion for the handsome Protestant " chevalier," who has taught her to read *Paradise Lost* and *Hamlet*, excites at first a measure of sympathy. But her delirium when Grandison refuses to be converted, and her ill usage by her spiteful and jealous cousin Laurana (who is Arabella Harlowe transplanted to Italy), branch off into melodrama. The various and varying attitudes of the members of the Poretta clan to Clementina's love-troubles are detailed with tedious prolixity, and the moment that the lady herself decides that she cannot marry Sir Charles without imperilling her soul she ceases to have further interest for the reader. There is no one to whom it can be of real concern whether she enters a nunnery or yields at last to the persistent suit of her countryman, the Count of Belvedere.

But the heaviest indictment to be laid against the long-drawn tale of Sir Charles's fruitless wooing of the daughter of the Porettas is that it makes Harriet Byron the least enviable and dignified of heroines. It was, of course, inevitable that, though courted by a band of suitors, she should fall hopelessly in love at first sight with her deliverer. She may perhaps be forgiven, when Richardsonian methods are taken into account, for her remarkably frank revelation of her feelings by raptures on Sir Charles's excellences or by arch protests against her expressions being misinterpreted. But what are we to think of her after she learns that Grandison is already pledged to a foreign rival? Was there ever a more pitiable effort at self-abnegation?

He ought to be, he must be, Clementina's; and I will endeavour to make myself happy, if I can maintain the second place in his friendship. . . . Nevertheless, at the time, do what I could, I found a tear ready to start. My heart was very untoward, Lucy; and I was guilty of a little female turn. When I found the twinkling of my eyes would not disperse the too ready drop, and felt it stealing down my cheek, I wiped it off.

Similar displays of ill-controlled emotion accompany Harriet's receipt of the varying tidings from Italy when Sir Charles pays court to Clementina for the second time. When it seems likely that the difficulties will be surmounted, " it is easy to see that this amiable creature's solitary hours are heavy ones. She has got a habit of sighing. She rises with swelled eyes: sleep forsakes her: her appetite fails." When news comes that Clementina has finally refused Grandison's suit she is so overcome that she is " not able to rise in two days and nights," and even has difficulty in carrying on correspondence ! Though she is full of genuine admiration for Clementina's sacrifice of love to conscience, she does not hesitate long in profiting thereby :

Shall your Harriet sit down and think herself happy in a second-place love ? Yet let me own to you, my cousin, that Sir Charles Grandison is dearer to me than all else that I hold most dear in this world : and if Clementina should not be unhappy, and he were to declare himself my lover, affectation be gone !

When the hoped-for declaration is made, through the unusual channel of the lady's grandmother, and Harriet is silent, while her kinswomen agree " that every point of female delicacy was answered," her free-spoken uncle Selby blurts out the truth of the situation :

Do you think if Harriet had *one* objection she would have been silent? I am for sending up for Sir Charles out of hand. Let him come the first day of next week, and let them be married before the end of it.

Though events do not march quite so quickly, and Harriet, after the fashion of the age, makes much ado about " naming the day," her eagerness to win the " second-place love " of " this glorious man," and her ecstasies when it is secured, make of her a curiously equivocal heroine.

Richardson really wins more sympathy for the subordinate figure of Emily Jervois, the ward of Sir Charles. In the delicate delineation of the emotions of the shy maiden who loves her guardian, as she thinks, with filial affection till the announcement of his contract with Harriet Byron reveals to her the true state of her heart, the novelist proves that the hand that drew Pamela was still cunning to explore the secrets of budding womanhood.

Such considerations, and they might be multiplied, may help to remind an age which leaves *Sir Charles Grandison* on the shelves that the character of the hero is far from being the only feature of interest in the work. On the well-worn topic of the presentation of Sir Charles himself it is difficult to add anything novel. But there are one or two general points on which a word may be said. It is not impossible, though it is difficult, for the art of the novelist to exhibit a man acting uniformly well through a variety of trying scenes, without making him appear a prig and a strait-laced pedant. Where the character of such a hero evolves naturally amidst the normal circumstances of life, the world will not be slow to acclaim the true μεγαλόψυχος. Let Henry Esmond bear witness to this. But where Richardson mars a conception that has in it real elements of nobility is in the artificial and fantastic way in which he develops it. Episodes and situations are invented merely to give Sir Charles an opportunity of displaying his miscellaneous assortment of virtues and accomplishments. He is equally expert in rescuing Harriet from abduction and arguing points of theology with Clementina ; he not only portions his sisters in the most generous way, but he is a benefactor to his father's mistress and her children, and reforms a libertine uncle ; he refuses to fight duels, and he does not dock his horses' tails. The catalogue might be extended indefinitely, but these samples will serve. It is enough to say in the classic formula, " people don't do these things "—at least no single person does them all. Life is but an imperfect machinery for the revelation of human virtues ; there is no one to whom it presents such incredibly frequent and diverse opportunities for their exercise as to Sir Charles Grandison.

Again, it was Richardson's misfortune that the epistolary method, so valuable for other purposes, was particularly ill-suited for the presentation of a faultless hero. Either the purely narrative method or the autobiographical, with its inevitable accompaniment of modest self-depreciation, would have served better. But as it is, Grandison's figure looms upon us, not in its true moral perspective, but in grandiose exaggeration through a distorting haze of universal panegyric. Even a man of abandoned character is forced by his example to cry, " I would rather be Sir Charles Grandison in this one past hour than the Great Mogul all my life ! " A bigoted Roman Catholic father has to confess, " I never saw a Protestant that I loved before. Your mind is still more amiable than your person." Lady G——'s caustic tongue drops honey when she speaks of this incomparable brother. Harriet Byron exhausts every superlative in his praise. " The Indies, my dear, ought to be his ! What a king would he make ! Power could not corrupt such a mind as his." Or again, " He is in all instances an imitator of the Almighty, an humbler of the impenitent and encourager of those who repent." Or finally, in the closing letter that she writes, " What is the boasted character of those who are called HEROES to the unostentatious merit of a TRULY GOOD MAN. In what a variety of amiable lights does such a one appear ! In how many ways is he a blessing and a joy to his fellow creatures ! "

But how few are the readers that ever reach these words. The great majority have long before been lulled into apathy concerning Sir Charles by an endless surfeit of sugared phrases. It is the tragi-comic fortune of Richardson's last novel, that, written to stimulate the world to lofty action, it has served rather as an opiate. *Habent sua fata libelli.*

The influence of Richardson upon the literature of the eighteenth century is even more noteworthy than the merits or defects of his art. Except Byron, there is no Englishman whose work has swept over Europe with such tempestuous force. The absence of " local colour " in the novels, their concern with that inner life which is common to men and women in all places, was largely responsible for this. Fielding and Smollett for the most part drew national types, which even in the days of continental " Anglomania " were not understood or appreciated. Moreover, as M. Texte has shown,[1] they were looked upon as being in the picaresque line of descent from Le Sage, whose mode in France was now outworn. On the other hand, Marivaux, in his *Vie de Marianne,* had in his detailed painting of scenes from humble life prepared the way for Richardson's ascendancy across the Channel. Marivaux has indeed before now been saluted as Richardson's master, but *Marianne,* though begun in 1731, was not finished till the year after the publication of *Pamela.* An English translation of part of it appeared in 1736, but there is no evidence that it came into Richardson's hands.[2] In any case he knew no French, and his method and technique, though akin to those of Marivaux, are independent in origin, while his genius was far more powerful. It was a novelist of a different school, Prévost, who did most to popularize Richardson in France by translating his works. His versions are adaptations rather than translations in the full sense, as he omits or modifies scenes, especially in *Clarissa,* which he thought too brutal for continental taste. As he says in his preface to his translation of *Sir Charles Grandison,* " J'ai supprimé ou réduit aux usages communs de

---

[1] In *Jean-Jacques Rousseau et les origines du cosmopolitisme littéraire* (1895).

[2] See *Richardson,* by B. W. Downs, pp. 165–6 (1928).

l'Europe ce que ceux d'Angleterre peuvent avoir de choquant pour les autres nations." Prévost's translations are of first-rate importance because it was through them that Rousseau became familiar with the novels. Diderot read them in the original. Their minute elaboration, their moralizing purpose, their exaltation of the infinite worth of the individual soul even among the lowly of the earth, appealed to different sides of his nature. In his novel, *La Religieuse* (1760), the influence of *Clarissa* is predominant. On Richardson's death in the following year he penned at once the passionate *Éloge*, which is the high-water mark of Richardson's worship in France :

> O Richardson, Richardson ! homme unique à mes yeux, tu seras ma lecture dans tous les temps. Forcé par des besoins pressants je vendrai mes livres ; mais tu me resteras ; tu me resteras sur le même rayon avec Moïse, Homère, Euripide et Sophocle.

There is reason to suppose that Diderot's dithyrambic periods, while perfectly sincere, were not without ulterior purpose. The exaltation of Richardson was probably intended to depreciate Rousseau, who had recently published *La Nouvelle Héloïse*. Whatever be the truth of this, the influence of Richardson's novels, especially *Clarissa*, upon Rousseau's romance is among the most interesting problems in the relations of French and English literature. Though he knew *Clarissa* only in Prévost's translation, he declared that " there was no novel in any language equal or even approaching to it," and that it contained " a complete picture of the human race." Both in subject-matter and in technique *La*

Nouvelle Héloïse borrowed largely from Richardson's masterpiece. Like Clarissa, Julie d'Étanges, though in love with her tutor St. Preux, is a victim of parental tyranny, and is forced into a marriage with M. de Wolmar. In a moment of passion she has given herself to her lover, but after her marriage duty conquers feeling. Even when St. Preux is a guest in her husband's house, she remains faithful to her vows, and finally, like Clarissa, she makes a sanctified end. The part of Miss Howe is played by Julie's cousin, Claire, who marries the worthy M. d'Orbe, a French Hickman, while milord Edward Bomston is the good genius of the piece, something after the fashion of Colonel Morden. The epistolary form is used throughout, and the letters that pass between Julie and Claire are evidently inspired by those between Clarissa and Miss Howe. Viewed as a novel, *La Nouvelle Héloïse* stands far below its English predecessor. It lacks the unity of scheme which, as I have indicated, makes *Clarissa*, with all its detail and diffuseness, an organic whole, and leads to the culmination of the interest in the final scenes. It is impossible to be deeply moved by the fortunes of Julie, who begins with a complete surrender to delirious passion, and afterwards turns into a pattern of morality. Digressions unrelated to the action of the story are constantly introduced, and what was begun as a romance ends almost as a tract. But the qualities that give Rousseau's work its eternal charm and significance are outside Richardson's range. They are the subtle, voluptuous melody of his prose, the lyrical ardour of his new glorification of nature, and the ecstasy of amorous passion which thrills through the earlier chapters

of *La Nouvelle Héloïse*. The sentiment that with
Richardson had drawn tears in the drawing-room, becomes in Rousseau a riotous outflow of individualistic
emotion, sweeping away in its rush all moral and social
barriers. From his writings it descended into the
market-place, and roused mankind against the oppression of a hard and soulless civilization. The electrical
spark lit in Richardson's back-parlour helped to kindle
the conflagration in which the Bastille disappeared.

Since the Revolution the French novel has had many
masters, and it has been swayed hither and thither by
varied tendencies. But the lesson of sentimental analysis, learnt in part from Richardson, has never been
lost. It is significant that *Marie-Claire*, which early in
this century repeated the instantaneous triumph of
Pamela, is the emotional autobiography of a girl of
much the same class as Richardson's first heroine.

In Germany the novelist found his first fervent
disciple in C. F. Gellert, who translated *Pamela* and
Grandison, and who imitated the spirit, though not the
epistolary form, of the earlier work in *Das Leben der
Schwedischen Gräfin* (1747–8). His poetical rhapsody
on Richardson's writings may be set beside Diderot's
prose pæan :

> Die Werke, die er schuf, wird keine Zeit verwüsten,
> Sie sind Natur, Geschmack, Religion.
> Unsterblich ist Homer, unsterblicher bei Christen
> Der Britte Richardson.

Wieland wrote a play on the subject of Clementina
(1760) ; Lessing's bourgeois tragedy, *Miss Sara Sampson* (1755), was strongly influenced by *Clarissa*. Goethe,

who in a famous passage in Book VI of *Dichtung und Wahrheit* shows an intimate insight into the essentials of Richardson's art, in Book XIII states that " he made the citizen world attentive to a more delicate morality." But his use of the epistolary form in *Werther* (1774), and his interpretation both of the sentimental temperament and of nature, are due to the influence of Rousseau rather than of Richardson at first hand.

In England Richardson's vogue was less enduring than abroad. The prose epic of Fielding outbid the epistolary novel in popular favour.[1] There is testimony to this out of Richardson's own mouth in some lines in one of the letters in *Grandison* : " The French only are proud of sentiments at this day ; the English cannot bear them : story, story, story, is what they hunt after, whether sense or nonsense, probable or improbable." Even those who still prized " sentiments " sought for them elsewhere, and in another kind, in the pages of *Tristram Shandy* or *The Man of Feeling*. The Gothic revival in romance, begun by Horace Walpole and transfigured by the genius of Scott, transported readers into an entirely different world, though Sir Walter, with his catholicity of appreciation, was one of Richardson's most illuminating critics. In the sphere of the domestic novel Miss Burney borrowed his epistolary method in *Evelina*, and Jane Austen owed something of her delicate analysis of emotion to her study of his works.

On the great Victorian masters of fiction he had

[1] A detailed comparison of the fluctuations in the fame of the two novelists in their own country has recently been made by Heinz Ronte in *Richardson und Fielding : Geschichte ihres Ruhms* (1935).

ceased to be a living influence. Thackeray took Fielding as his exemplar, and followed, in the main, his spirit
and technique. Dickens cannot be classed with any
school, but as far as he has affinities with his eighteenth-
century forerunners, they are with Fielding and with
Smollett.

But the influence of *Pamela* upon *Jane Eyre* has
been traced in a striking series of parallel incidents.[1]
And is it fanciful to suggest that in the twentieth century we are returning in some respects to the Richardsonian tradition? A number of present-day novelists,
both men and women, are pursuing the Richardsonian
path of sentimental analysis, though with the keener
perception of the interaction of body and spirit which
has been developed by the scientific habit of the age.
There are aspects of their work which seem to me more
closely related to the art of Richardson than to that of
any other of the classic masters of English fiction. But
however this may be, anyone who, undismayed by his
prolixity and his didacticism, comes to Richardson's
pages with an open mind, will, I believe, be surprised
to find how quickly he feels at home. A true transcript
of the inner life, at whatever period it is made, can never
become antiquated.

[1] See *Charlotte Brontë*, by Janet Spens, in English Association
Essays and Studies, vol. xiv (1929).

III

THACKERAY ON THE EIGHTEENTH-
CENTURY HUMOURIST AS HERO

THACKERAY'S lectures on *The English Humourists of the Eighteenth Century* were originally given in London, at Willis's Rooms, between May 21 and July 3, 1851, and were repeated in various towns in England and Scotland, and in the following year, in America. They were first published in 1853, and the issue of two elaborately annotated editions of them early in the present century testifies to their continued popularity. They were not intended to form a manual of literary criticism. They were an endeavour to re-create a number of representative figures against the background of the Augustan or the Hanoverian age. Except Hogarth, these humourists are all men of letters. But in Thackeray's eyes, throughout these lectures, the man of letters and the man of action are in essence the same. The happy warrior, whether he wields the pen or the sword, fights in the same spirit, is beset by kindred dangers, and in either case closes his career in victory or defeat.

Among the audience at the lectures in Willis's Rooms was Carlyle, and it is impossible to read *The English Humourists* without being struck by the remarkable

47

resemblance of Thackeray's critical "method of approach" to that of Carlyle, especially in the lectures on *Heroes and Hero-Worship.*

Thackeray chooses his group of English eighteenth-century notabilities because they are " humourists," and Carlyle his representative men of thought and action in all ages and countries because they are " heroes." But in each case the aim of the lecturer was to reveal the essential spirit of the men of whom he had chosen to speak. Thackeray himself took the precaution of warning his hearers at the outset that, though his subject was " Humourists," they must not expect to be entertained with " a merely humourous or facetious story."

Harlequin without his mask is a man full of cares and perplexities, like the rest of us, whose self must always be serious to him, under whatever mask or disguise or uniform he presents it to the public.

It is this " self " of which Thackeray is always in quest throughout his lectures; seeking to penetrate to it through the writer's works, through his letters, the records of his life, and his general environment. How closely his method approximates to that of Carlyle appears most clearly from the closing passage of the lecture on " Prior, Gay, and Pope."

In considering Pope's admirable career, I am forced into similitudes drawn from other courage and greatness, and into comparing him with those who achieved triumphs in actual war. I think of the works of young Pope as I do of the actions of young Bonaparte or young Nelson. In their common life you will find frailties and meannesses, as great as the vices and follies of the meanest men. But in the presence of the great occasion, the great soul flashes out and conquers transcendent. In thinking of the splendour of Pope's young victories, of his merit, unequalled as his renown, I hail and salute the achieving genius, and do homage to the pen of a hero.

The comparison of Pope's " young victories " to those of Napoleon and Nelson is exactly in the spirit of Carlyle's famous declaration that " the Hero can be Poet, King, Priest, or what you will, according to the kind of world he finds himself born into," and that the poet " could not sing the Heroic warrior, unless he himself were at least a Heroic warrior too." And when we remember Pope's physical infirmities, and the limitation of his interests to the salon, the boudoir, and the schools, we feel that in comparing his early achievements to those of the mighty conqueror and seaman, Thackeray has chosen the most challenging illustration of his thesis that could be found.

In another passage in the same lecture he again emphasizes the fundamental similarity of all heroic spirits :

Mind that there is always a certain stamp about great men ; they may be as mean on many points as you and I, but they carry their great air ; they speak of common life more largely and generously than common men do. . . . He who reads these noble records of a past age salutes and reverences the great spirits who adorn it.

And are there any words of Carlyle more saturated with the spirit of hero-worship than these ?

I should like to have been Shakespeare's shoe-black, just to have lived in his house, just to have worshipped him, to

have run on his errands, and seen that sweet, serene face.
I should like, as a young man, to have lived on Fielding's
staircase in the Temple, and after helping up to bed perhaps,
and opening his door with his latch-key, to have shaken hands
with him in the morning, and heard him talk and crack jokes
over his breakfast and his mug of small beer. Who would
not give something to pass a night at the club with Johnson,
and Goldsmith, and James Boswell, Esq., of Auchinleck?

Was it because he thought that no one should venture
to follow in the footsteps of James Boswell, Esq., that
Thackeray did not include Johnson among his
humourists? In any case, they are a dozen as they
stand. If *Vanity Fair* is a novel without a hero, *The
English Humourists* has no lack of them.

In his quest of eighteenth-century heroes, Thackeray
was naturally influenced by his own conception of what
constitutes heroic character. He realized that a man
may have " the great air " in spite of faults of passion,
hot blood, and improvidence. But where he found, or
thought he found, meanness, sentimentality, hypocrisy,
or lack of chivalry to women, his condemnation was
unsparing. That is why his treatment of the humourists
is so much less appreciative in some cases than in others.

The searching issues of the world-conflict in 1914–18
proved with startling vividness how nobly right was
Thackeray's conception of the heroic character, whether
in peace or war. When applied with complete knowledge and insight, it is a true touchstone. But if the
knowledge and the insight are imperfect, even such a
test may partly break down.

Take, for instance, the lecture on Swift. Thackeray
recognizes the lonely grandeur of his intellect and of his

personality. An "immense genius; an awful down-fall and ruin. So great a man he seems to me, that thinking of him is like thinking of an empire falling." An entirely apt and illuminating simile. Yet in the course of the lecture he brings charges against him which seem to me quite inconsistent with those lofty phrases:

If you had been his inferior in parts . . . his equal in mere social station, he would have bullied, scorned, and insulted you; if undeterred by his great reputation you had met him like a man, he would have quailed before you, and not had the pluck to reply, and gone home, and years after written a foul epigram about you—watched for you in a sewer, and come out to assail you with a coward's blow and a dirty bludgeon. If you had been a lord with a blue ribbon, who flattered his vanity or could help his ambition, he would have been the most delightful company in the world. . . . His servility was so boisterous that it looked like independence.

Or, again:

I know of few things more conclusive as to the sincerity of Swift's religion than his advice to poor John Gay to turn clergyman, and look out for a seat on the Bench. Gay, the author of the *Beggar's Opera*—Gay, the wildest of the wits about town—it was this man that Jonathan Swift advised to take orders, to invest in a cassock and bands, just as he advised him to husband his shillings and put his thousand pounds out at interest. The Queen, and the bishops, and the world were right in mistrusting the religion of that man.

Here Thackeray accuses Swift of servility and hypocrisy in the most vulgar acceptation of the terms. He is insensible to the irony which runs through the *Tale of a Tub*, and Swift's other religious and political tracts. He does not take into consideration his intellectual scorn

51

of fanaticism, his ambition to rise that he might serve great causes in Church and State, his idealism turned sour. The problem of Swift's inmost "self" is not one that can be probed in an hour's lecture to a miscellaneous audience, even by a Thackeray. And the treatment of the Dean's relation with Stella, vivid and moving though it is, is thrown out of perspective by the assumption that Stella, "one of the saints of English story," was a victim of Swift's ill-usage, only partly atoned for by his final sacrifice in her favour of "that young woman who lived five doors from (his) lodgings in Bury Street."

Similarly, Thackeray's acrid estimate of Sterne is due largely to the fact that, after twenty-five years of married life, Yorick, on his own confession, was "fatigatus et aegrotus de mea uxore," and was writing philandering letters to Eliza, otherwise Mrs. Elizabeth Draper, wife of Daniel Draper, Esq., Counsellor of Bombay. Far be it from us to defend such letters, whether from Prebendaries of York or other married gentlemen in less dignified positions. But Thackeray at once assumes that all the blame lies with Sterne, and that his amorous coquettings with Eliza and other ladies were the outcome of a diseased and lachrymose sentimentality.

I suppose Sterne had this artistical sensibility; he used to blubber perpetually in his study, and, finding his tears infectious and that they brought him a great popularity, he exercised the lucrative gift of weeping; he utilized it, and cried on every occasion. I own that I don't value or respect much the cheap dribble of those fountains. He fatigues me with his perpetual disquiet and his uneasy appeals to my risible or sentimental faculties.

Such a passage contains the proverbially dangerous half-truth. It ignores two things which are essential to a just appreciation of Sterne ; that his sentimentality is shot through and through with a subtle intellectuality which gives it a unique function and value ; and that this sentimentality was not merely a personal attribute of the author of *Tristram Shandy*, but was one of the predominant notes of eighteenth-century literature, from Richardson to Rousseau. If Thackeray had nothing better to say of Sterne, he would have done well to leave him alone.

Considering his harshness to Sterne, it is curious to find him so indulgent to Pope. It is true that Pope's tortuous proceedings about his correspondence had not been brought fully to light in 1851. Even so, one is scarcely prepared for the statement that, with some exceptions, including almost all his letters to women, " I do not know, in the range of our literature, volumes more delightful." There were two things that seem to have biased Thackeray in Pope's favour—" the constant tenderness and fidelity of affection " towards his mother, " which pervaded and sanctified his life "—and his merits as a literary artist. I have already quoted his tribute to Pope as a " hero," and without prejudice to the poet of Twickenham's commanding place in literature of the Augustan age, the estimate seems to me as over-generous as that of Sterne is the reverse.

But there is another group of Thackeray's portraits of which we feel that they give us the very men as they lived and moved. Addison and Steele, Fielding and Goldsmith—each of these he knew as intimately as if they had been his contemporaries. They all belonged

to the type of which he had intuitive understanding—
essential nobility marred by a measure, greater or less,
of human frailties. Addison, it is true, " the parson in
a tye-wig," stands somewhat apart from the others.
He must have been one of the " finest gentlemen the
world ever saw ; at all moments of life serene and
courteous, cheerful and calm. He could scarcely ever
have had a degrading thought." Yet even he had his
failing. " If he had not had that little weakness for
wine—why, we could scarcely have found a fault with
him, and could not have liked him as we do."

Nor does Addison's critical, quizzing attitude towards
the other sex satisfy Thackeray's exacting standard.
Here it was that Steele, the reckless and improvident
captain of Fusiliers, redressed the balance in his own
favour:

His heart seems to warm and his eye to kindle when he
meets with a good and beautiful woman ; and it is with his
heart, as well as with his hat, that he salutes her. About
children and all that relates to home he is not less tender, and
more than once speaks in apology of what he calls his softness.
He would have been nothing without that delightful
weakness. It is that which gives his works their worth and
his style its charm. It, like his life, is full of faults and careless blunders ; and redeemed like that by his sweet and
compassionate nature. . . . I own to liking Dick Steele the
man and Dick Steele the author much better than much better
men and much better authors.

It needed insight and courage to rehabilitate Steele in the
eyes of mid-Victorian respectability which had found in
Addison, chaperoned by Macaulay, a figure after its
own heart. It needed yet greater boldness to pro-

claim aloud the essential nobility of the author of
Tom Jones :

Stained, as you see him, and worn by care and dissipation,
that man retains some of the most precious and splendid
human qualities and endowments. He has an admirable
natural love of truth, the keenest instinctive antipathy to
hypocrisy, the happiest satirical gift of laughing it to scorn.
His wit is wonderfully wise and detective ; it flashes upon a
rogue and lightens up a rascal like a policeman's lantern. He
is one of the manliest and kindliest of human beings.

And beside him, akin in courage and kindliness, but
slighter and frailer, glides the gracious figure of Goldsmith. " Your love for him is half pity. You come
hot and tired from the day's battle, and this sweet
minstrel sings to you. . . . He carries no weapon save
the harp on which he plays to you, and with which he
delights great and humble, young and old."

Was it conscious or unpremeditated art by which
Thackeray, opening his lectures amidst the hurtle and
thunder of the falling empire of Swift's greatness, closes
them upon soft and low pastoral airs from Goldsmith's
limpid verse and prose ?

I have mentioned above that literary criticism as such
has an insignificant place in the volume. In the opening
sentence Thackeray announced that it was of the men
and of their lives rather than of their books that he
intended to speak. But where he incidentally plays the
critic, his judgement is, as a rule, as discerning as his
expression of it is terse and lucid. Take, for instance,
the few sentences which catch the very spirit of Steele's
style. " The great charm of Steele's writing is its natural-

ness. He wrote so quickly and carelessly, that he was forced to make the reader his confidant, and had not the time to deceive him. He has a small share of book-learning, but a vast acquaintance with the world." With this compare the passage in which he does homage to the craftsmanship of Pope—which is the exact antithesis of Steele's :

Men of letters should admire him as being one of the greatest literary artists that England has seen. He polished, he refined, he thought ; he took thoughts from other works to adorn and complete his own ; borrowing an idea or a cadence from another poet, as he would a figure, or a simile from a flower, or a river, stream, or any object which struck him in his walk, or contemplation of Nature.

It is curious to find Thackeray, in the middle of the nineteenth century, eulogizing Pope's style with such whole-hearted fervour. He seems serenely unconscious of Wordsworth's attack on the " poetic diction " of the Augustan age, or of the pre-Raphaelite crusade on behalf of nature and simplicity which had been begun in *The Germ*, in the year before his lectures were delivered. The conscientious finish, the urbanity, the allusiveness of Pope's art appealed to kindred qualities in the novelist's own literary methods. But his enthusiasm does not stop short this side of idolatry when he declares that in the final passage of *The Dunciad*, beginning,

> She comes, she comes, the sable throne behold,
> Of Night primaeval and of Chaos old,

Pope " reaches to the very greatest height which his sublime art has attained, and shows himself the equal of all poets of all times." And in quite a different field of literature, *Humphrey Clinker* gets something more than its deserts when it is voted to be " the most laughable story that has ever been written since the goodly art of novel writing began."

But to many readers the most delightful passages in the book are those in which, with a broad brush, Thackeray paints the social background against which his humourists played their parts. Here he characteristically relies not upon the historians and biographers, but upon the novelists, essayists, and caricaturists:

I take up a volume of Dr. Smollett, or a volume of *The Spectator*, and say the fiction carries a greater amount of truth in solution than the volume which purports to be all true. Out of the fictitious book I get the expression of the life of the time : of the manners, of the movements, the dress, the pleasures, the laughter, the ridicules of society—the old times live again, and I travel in the old country of England. Can the heaviest historian do more for me ?

" We arrive," he laments, " at places now, but we travel no more." If this could be said in 1851, what verb would the lecturer have substituted to-day ? And from the fiction and periodicals of our more complex age will some magician of the twenty-first century conjure up such a picture of Georgian London before the war as Thackeray does of the capital in the time of Queen Anne ?

The Maypole rises in the Strand again ; the churches are crowded with daily worshippers ; the beaux are gathering in the coffee-houses ; the gentry are going to the drawing-room ; the ladies are thronging to the toy-shops ; the chairmen are jostling in the streets ; the footmen are running with links before the chariots, or fighting round the theatre doors.

He stands beside Addison as he gazes out of his window " at Ardelia's coach as she blazes to the Drawing Room, with her coronet and six footmen, and, remembering that her father was a Turkey merchant in the City, calculates how many sponges went to purchase her ear-ring, and how many drums of figs to build her coach-box." He looks over the shoulder of Hogarth and sees " how the Lord Mayor dinès in state ; how the prodigal drinks and sports at the bagnio ; how the poor girls beats hemp in Bridewell ; how the thief divides his booty and drinks his punch at the night-cellar, and how he finishes his career at the gibbet."

As we read such passages, we are not merely catching vivid glimpses of the Capital two hundred years ago, we are being shown something of the process of Thackeray's development as a novelist. It is not an accident that the lectures on the Humourists were first delivered in the year before the publication of *Esmond*. Hitherto, especially in *Vanity Fair* and *Pendennis*, Thackeray had painted the life and manners of the early and middle nineteenth century. But his method was in lineal descent from that of Fielding, and by a natural impulse he turned, after a time, to the eighteenth century for a subject suited to his art in its grandest style. Here he could not rely solely on his own penetrating genius. With a lofty conception of the allegiance to truth to which the historical novelist is bound, he had set himself to master the documents which preserve the form and presence of the age of Queen Anne and her successors.

Of this study *The English Humourists* is the preliminary, and *Esmond* the crowning, outcome. The lectures are an imperishable possession on their own account, for their brilliant, if not always impartial portraiture, their social vignettes, their subtly modulated prose harmonies, and the light that they throw on Thackeray's conception of the heroic ideal in life and in art. But beyond this they are the antechamber through which we shall do well to pass into that glorious imaginative structure where real eighteenth-century figures—Marlborough and the Pretender, Addison and Steele—mingle for ever with the offspring of the novelist's creative genius, Beatrix, Henry Esmond and Lady Castlewood—

> Forms more real than living man,
> Nurslings of immortality.

IV

WORDSWORTH'S PATRIOTIC POEMS AND THEIR SIGNIFICANCE TO-DAY

WORDSWORTH'S pre-eminence as a poet of nature and of rural life has somewhat overshadowed the part of his work devoted to the larger issues, national and international, of his time. It is sometimes forgotten that the lyrist of the Daffodils and the Daisy, the chronicler of the humble fortunes of Michael and of Ruth, could turn, with equal success of poetic intuition, to the causes that make or mar the greatness of kingdoms and of peoples. It may therefore be useful to consider once again the poems of Wordsworth that were inspired by the conflict with Napoleon, and to see what bearing they may have on the strikingly parallel European situation between 1914 and 1918. But to grasp fully the significance of these poems, and to realize the stern passion for liberty which both weights them and gives them wing, it is necessary to trace briefly Wordsworth's attitude towards the French Revolutionary movement in which Napoleonism had its birth.

Wordsworth's first direct contact with the Revolution took place while he was an undergraduate at Cambridge. During his third summer vacation, he set out with a friend on a continental tour, and landed at Calais on the

eve of July 14, 1790, the anniversary of the fall of the
Bastille, which was celebrated by the festival of the Oath
of Federation.   He noted the widespread joy that marked
the occasion, the general atmosphere of "benevolence and
blessedness."   But on this journey, which extended to
Switzerland and the Italian Lakes, he was more occupied
with scenery than with politics.   His active interest in the
Revolution dates from the following year, when, in
November, France again "lured" him "forth."

Much had happened since his former visit—the death
of Mirabeau, the flight to Varennes, the Convention of
Pilnitz at which foreign Powers determined to resist
French aggression, and the meeting of the Legislative
Assembly.   After a brief stay in Paris, he moved to
Orleans, and thence in the spring of 1792 to Blois.   It
was here that he first became an adherent of the revolutionary doctrines in their extreme form.   Hitherto, as he
states in an interesting passage of autobiography,[1] he
had taken democratic equality much as a matter of course:

> For, born in a poor District, and which yet
> Retaineth more of ancient homeliness,
> Manners erect, and frank simplicity
> Than any other nook of English Land,
> It was my fortune scarcely to have seen,
> Through the whole tenor of my School-day time,
> The face of one, who, whether Boy or Man,
> Was vested with attention or respect
> Through claims of wealth and blood.

[1] *The Prelude*, ix, 215 ff.   The quotations that follow in the
next few pages are from Books ix–x in the original 1805–6 version
(as printed by Dr. E. de Selincourt), which is here used in preference to the text of 1850.

At Cambridge he had been in a practically Republican society

> Where all stood thus far
> Upon equal ground, that they were brothers all
> In honour, as in one community,
> Scholars and Gentlemen.

One trained thus, and reared in the tradition of mountain liberty, was bound to hail

> As best the government of equal rights
> And individual worth.

Thus if his enthusiasm for the Revolution had at first been lukewarm, it was because the events

> Seemed nothing out of nature's certain course,
> A gift that rather was come late than soon.

But at Blois his chief associates were a band of Royalist officers, whose fanatical opposition to the Revolution drove Wordsworth into the other extreme. Amongst them was one of a different type, Captain Michael Beaupuy, a member of a noble family of Périgord and about fifteen years Wordsworth's senior. In the course of his military service Beaupuy had traversed much of France and seen the evils under which the country was groaning. He had thus become an enthusiastic advocate of the Rights of Man. " Man he loved as man." His eloquence and high character deeply impressed the young Englishman, and they discoursed together in the spirit of Rousseau of

> Man and his noble nature, as it is
> The gift of God and lies in his own power.

The outbreak of war between France and the allied
Powers in the summer of 1792 led to the separation of
the two friends. On July 27 Beaupuy left Blois with
his regiment to fight on the Rhine. Wordsworth soon
afterwards moved to Orleans, where he heard of the
September Massacres on the 2nd and the proclamation
of the Republic on the 21st of the month. In his joy
at this latter event, it seemed that the lamentable crimes
just committed

> were past,
> Earth free from them for ever, as was thought,
> Ephemeral monsters, to be seen but once;
> Things that could only show themselves and die.

In this optimistic spirit, so bitterly to be mocked by
coming events, he returned to Paris in October,

> and ranged
> More eagerly than I had done before,
> Through the whole city, and in progress pass'd
> The Prison where the unhappy Monarch lay
> Associate with his Children and his Wife
> In bondage.

It was the period when the struggle between the
Girondins and the Jacobins was beginning, and Wordsworth felt moved to throw himself into it on the Girondin
side :

> An insignificant Stranger and obscure,
> Mean as I was, and little graced with power
> Of eloquence even in my native speech,
> And all unfit for tumult or intrigue,
> Yet would I willingly have taken up
> A service at this time for cause so great,
> However dangerous.

But an effectual though prosaic obstacle intervened : his friends at home stopped his supplies and he had to return to England in December, 1792, dragged, as it then seemed, by a chain of harsh necessity, but really, as he afterwards acknowledged, providentially delivered from the possibility of a fruitless martyrdom.

Even after his return the Revolution monopolized his interest, and his sympathy with its progress was not diminished by the execution of Louis XVI on January 21, 1793, or by the outbreak of war between France and England which followed on February 11. But the spectacle of the conflict between his native country and the land with which he thought the hopes of humanity bound up caused him bitter anguish. When England gained victories and thanksgivings were offered in the churches,

> I only, like an uninvited Guest
> Whom no one own'd sate silent, shall I add,
> Fed on the day of vengeance yet to come ?

But the fall of the Girondins, and the accession of the Jacobins to power, brought disillusion. Robespierre in especial, the chief of the " Atheist crew," was to Wordsworth the incarnation of the evil spirit of the Terror, and he gives a vivid picture of the joy with which in August, 1794, as he was crossing the sands at Morecambe, he heard from a band of travellers that the Jacobin leader was dead. In a transport of gratitude he poured forth a hymn of triumph at the advent of " golden times " which he felt certain had now indeed come. With renewed belief in the saving mission of France he opposed more and more bitterly the policy of Pitt, who

was conducting an energetic campaign against the
English friends of the Revolution, and had even procured the suspension of the Habeas Corpus Act for this
purpose.

> Our Shepherds . . . at that time
> Thirsted to make the guardian Crook of Law
> A tool of Murder.

During the early days of the Directorate Wordsworth
still retained his faith in France, but the beginning of
Napoleon's campaign in Italy in 1796 proved to him
beyond all doubt that the Revolution had turned into an
aggressive movement against the rights of others :

> Become oppressors in their turn
> Frenchmen had changed a war of self-defence
> For one of conquest, losing sight of all
> Which they had struggled for; and mounted up,
> Openly in the view of earth and heaven
> The scale of Liberty.

The conquest of Lombardy was followed by the over-
throw of the Venetian Republic, and its cession to Austria
at the Treaty of Campo Formio (October, 1797). In
the spring of the following year Switzerland was invaded,
its ancient constitution overthrown, and a new Helvetic
Republic instituted on the French model.

For a time Wordsworth, with his faith in France
shattered by these events, sought to find a new basis for
his political creed in the abstract individualistic doctrines
of William Godwin. But this was a passing phase, and
the liberty of which he finally became the golden-
mouthed apologist was not that of the *Contrat Social* or
of *Political Justice*, but the liberty rooted in national

character and history. His championship thereof is the
more significant and arresting, because it was the outcome of bitter mental and emotional travail. Perhaps
it has never been possible, even for lifelong students of
his poetry, to realize fully till 1914 all that this meant to
Wordsworth. History has proved the most illuminating of commentators. For his disillusionment, which
was shared by Coleridge and Southey, in the French as
apostles of liberty had its parallel in the equally bitter
disillusionment of those who had looked upon the
Germans as apostles of culture and not of *Kultur*. The
contrast between the France of Mirabeau and Beaupuy
and that of Robespierre and Napoleon was as poignant
to the English champions of the Revolution as the
contrast between the Germany of Goethe, Kant, and
Beethoven and that of Nietzsche, Treitschke, and Bernhardi to twentieth-century English devotees of German
literature, philosophy, and music.

It was Coleridge who first gave trumpet-tongued
voice to the anguish with which he and his friends gazed
on the incredible spectacle :

When France in wrath her giant-limbs upreared,
 And with that oath, which smote air, earth and sea,
 Stamped her strong foot and said she would be free,
Bear witness with me how I hoped and feared !
With what a joy my lofty gratulation
 Unawed I sang, amid a slavish band . . .
For ne'er, O Liberty ! with partial aim
I dimmed thy light or damped thy holy flame ;
 But blessed the pæans of delivered France,
And hung my head and wept at Britain's name.

Forgive me, Freedom ! O forgive those dreams !
 I hear thy voice, I hear thy loud lament,
 From bleak Helvetia's icy caverns sent—
I hear thy groans upon her blood-stained streams.

So sang Coleridge in February, 1798, immediately
after the invasion of Switzerland. But with Wordsworth it was not emotion in the moment of its experience, but emotion remembered in tranquillity, that gave
birth to his finest verse. Hence it was not till some
four or five years afterwards that he began to give poetic
utterance to the feelings which had been aroused in him
by the fate of Venice and of Switzerland.

It was in August, 1802, a few months after the signing
of the Treaty of Amiens, which gave Europe a truce
from warfare for little more than a year, that Wordsworth
began the series of " Poems Dedicated to National
Independence and Liberty." The series, which contains forty-six pieces, of which the latest is the Thanksgiving Ode on January 18, 1816, has the characteristic
inequality of Wordsworth's work. But some of the
sonnets included in it are amongst his most consummate
achievements. The rigorous limitations of this poetic
form were a curb to his faults of diffuseness and pedes-
trianism. Within its narrow room he found the truest
liberty for his muse. In his hand, as in that of his great
exemplar, Milton,

> The thing became a trumpet ; whence he blew
> Soul-animating strains.

Even Milton, though he had put the sonnet to a new use
as a poetic mouthpiece on public affairs, had not crystal-

67

lized in it the record of a nation's fortunes, as Wordsworth does in the lines " On the extinction of the Venetian Republic " :

> Once did She hold the gorgeous East in fee ;
> And was the safeguard of the West : the worth
> Of Venice did not fall below her birth,
> Venice the eldest Child of Liberty.
> She was a maiden City, bright and free ;
> No guile seduced, no force could violate ;
> And, when she took unto herself a Mate,
> She must espouse the everlasting Sea.

It is not necessary to ask here whether the facts of Venetian history entirely justify this magnificent eulogy. However this may be, the sestet of this sonnet is an incomparable elegy upon the final disappearance of fallen greatness in whatever form :

> And what if she had seen those glories fade,
> Those titles vanish, and that strength decay ;
> Yet shall some tribute of regret be paid
> When her long life hath reached its final day :
> Men are we, and must grieve when even the Shade
> Of that which once was great is passed away.

But if the fate of Venice could stir reflective sorrow, that of Switzerland begot more poignant emotions which found utterance in verse as austere and majestic as her Alpine heights :

> Two Voices are there ; one is of the sea,
> One of the mountains ; each a mighty Voice :
> In both from age to age thou didst rejoice,
> They were thy chosen music, Liberty !
> There came a Tyrant, and with holy glee ;

Thou fought'st against him; but hast vainly striven:
Thou from thy Alpine holds at length art driven,
Where not a torrent murmurs heard by thee.

If Liberty had thus been exiled from her mountain
home, the more imperative was it that she should cling
to her other ancient habitation:

Of one deep bliss thine ear hath been bereft:
Then cleave, O cleave to that which still is left;
For high-souled Maid, what sorrow would it be
That Mountain floods should thunder as before,
And Ocean bellow from his rocky shore,
And neither awful Voice be heard by thee!

Greece, Venice, England—on their shores and ships
Liberty had in turn made her dwelling-place. Was she
to be driven from her English haunts as she had been
driven from her Alpine holds? Was it to prove in
vain that "Nature herself," as Wordsworth wrote in
1809 in his prose pamphlet, *The Convention of Cintra,*
" by encircling with the Ocean the country we inhabit,
has proclaimed that this mighty nation is to be for ever
her own ruler, and that the land is set apart for the home
of immortal independence "?

Two main dangers, in his eyes, had to be resolutely
faced. One was that of foreign invasion. In August,
1802, he had taken advantage of the Peace to pay another
visit to the north of France. As he halted on his return
near Dover he was alarmed as he looked across the
Channel to the shores that he had just left.

Inland, within a hollow vale, I stood;
And saw, while sea was calm and air was clear,
The coast of France—the coast of France how near!

Drawn almost into frightful neighbourhood.
I shrunk; for verily the barrier flood
Was like a lake, or river bright and fair,
A span of waters.

If this could be written in 1802, what intensity of
meaning has it gained in an age of Dreadnoughts,
Zeppelins, and Submarines? Even in the day of sailing-
vessels Wordsworth's fears were not unjustified, for in
the following year, after the renewal of hostilities in
May, Napoleon established his camp at Boulogne, with
the object of transporting his troops to our southern
shores in flat-bottomed boats. The scheme failed, as
we trust and believe that all later schemes to cross " the
barrier flood " will fail. But even had the troops
effected a landing, they would have had to do battle
not only with the regulars but with thousands of
volunteers whom the crisis had called to the colours.
To " the men of Kent," who would have had to
bear the first brunt of the attack, the poet addressed a
stirring call:

> Vanguard of Liberty, ye men of Kent,
> Ye children of a Soil that doth advance
> Her haughty brow against the coast of France,
> Now is the time to prove your hardiment !
>
> . . . .
>
> No parleying now. In Britain is one breath;
> We all are with you now from shore to shore;
> Ye men of Kent, 'tis victory or death !

And in the lines on the expected invasion, written
in 1803 though not published till nearly forty years
afterwards, he summoned men of all parties to

sink their differences and unite against the common foe :

> Come ye—who, if (which Heaven avert !) the Land
> Were with herself at strife, would take your stand,
> Like gallant Falkland, by the Monarch's side,
> And, like Montrose, make Loyalty your pride—
> Come ye—who, not less zealous, might display
> Banners at enmity with regal sway,
> And like the Pyms and Miltons of that day,
> Think that a State would live in sounder health
> If Kingship bowed its head to Commonwealth—
>
> .   .   .   .
>
> Come ye—whate'er your creed—O waken all,
> Whate'er your temper, at your Country's call ;
> Resolving (this a free-born Nation can)
> To have one Soul, and perish to a man,
> Or save this honoured Land from every Lord
> But British reason and the British sword.

But party spirit was not the internal danger that Wordsworth really feared. It was the growth of materialism due to the rapid increase of national and individual wealth caused by the Industrial Revolution :

> The wealthiest man among us is the best :
> No grandeur now in nature or in book
> Delights us. Rapine, avarice, expense,
> This is idolatry ; and these we adore :
> Plain living and high thinking are no more :
> The homely beauty of the good old cause
> Is gone ; our peace, our fearful innocence,
> And pure religion breathing household laws.

A degenerate England would prove unequal to the stern ordeal with which she was faced, and a note of

unwonted passion thrills in the lines in which the poet
invokes his mighty predecessor who had inspired his
countrymen in an earlier, simpler day :

> Milton ! thou shouldst be living at this hour :
> England hath need of thee : she is a fen
> Of stagnant waters : altar, sword, and pen,
> Fireside, the heroic wealth of hall and bower,
> Have forfeited their ancient English dower
> Of inward happiness. We are selfish men ;
> Oh ! raise us up, return to us again ;
> And give us manners, virtue, freedom, power.

In the lonely elemental grandeur of his life smaller
men would find an uplifting force.

> Thy soul was like a star, and dwelt apart ;
> Thou hadst a voice whose sound was like the sea :
> Pure as the naked heavens, majestic, free.

And Milton was only the chief of a goodly company :

> The later Sidney, Marvel, Harrington,
> Young Vane, and others who called Milton friend.

As he thought of these and their like, Wordsworth's
confidence in his country returned. He felt assured
that the " famous stream " of British freedom would not
perish in bogs and sands.

> In our halls is hung
> Armoury of the invincible knights of old :
> We must be free or die, who speak the tongue
> That Shakespeare spake ; the faith and morals hold
> Which Milton held. In everything we are sprung
> Of Earth's first blood, have titles manifold.

And in a sonnet of curiously intimate self-revelation,

the poet pleads pardon for his momentary doubts and fears :

> When I have borne in memory what has tamed
> Great Nations, how ennobling thoughts depart
> When men change swords for ledgers, and desert
> The student's bower for gold, some fears unnamed
> I had, my Country—am I to be blamed ?
> Now, when I think of thee, and what thou art,
> Verily, in the bottom of my heart,
> Of those unfilial fears I am ashamed.

It will be noted that Wordsworth's heroes in these sonnets are all of one type. Except Shakespeare, who figures as the representative of English speech rather than of English faith and morals, they are austere republicans. It is characteristic of Wordsworth that he should choose as an exemplar of English manhood Algernon Sidney, the visionary revolutionist, rather than Sir Philip, the flower of Elizabethan chivalry, who died fighting for the freedom of the Netherlands against the Spanish oppressor.[1]   And why not a word of Chatham, or Wolfe, or Burke, or Wesley, who, in their different spheres, inspired eighteenth-century England with " ennobling thoughts," and anticipated the Wordsworthian doctrine,

> That by the soul
> Only, the nations shall be great and free ?

But the course of events, public and private, was soon

[1] Wordsworth, however, does full justice to Sir Philip some years later in *The Convention of Cintra,* where he mentions him with Washington, Nelson, and Lord Peterborough amongst those in whom courage is consummated by principle.

to lead the poet to find patterns of heroic manhood outside the circle of seventeenth-century political idealists.
On February 5, 1805, his beloved younger brother, John,
captain of an East Indiaman, was lost with his ship,
which struck on the Shambles, off the Bill of Portland.
A few minutes before the ship went down he " was seen
talking to the first mate, with apparent cheerfulness, and
he was standing on the hen-coop, which is the point
from which he could overlook the whole ship, the
moment she went down—dying, as he had lived, in the
very place and point where his duty stationed him."

The fate of his brother brought home to Wordsworth
with peculiar poignancy the pathos and the glory of the
fate of the mightier seaman who on October 21 of the
same year also died " where his duty stationed him."
In the brooding reflection of the poet during the winter
days that followed, the highest qualities of Nelson and
his sailor brother were combined into the " Character
of the Happy Warrior." " This short poem," as
Frederic Myers has truly said, " is in itself a manual of
greatness : there is a Roman majesty in its simple and
weighty speech."

It opens with the arresting question forced upon
Wordsworth, himself essentially a pacificist, by the
events of the year of Trafalgar :

Who is the happy Warrior ?   Who is he
That every man in arms should wish to be ?

In him the child must be father to the man :

It is the generous Spirit, who, when brought
Among the tasks of real life, hath wrought
Upon the plan that pleased his boyish thought.

74

But boyish instincts have now developed into self-conscious resolves.   It is the peculiar glory of the happy warrior to wring good out of evil, to gain strength from the struggle with circumstances :

> Who, doomed to go in company with Pain,
> And Fear, and Bloodshed, miserable train !
> Turns his necessity to glorious gain :
> In face of these doth exercise a power
> Which is our human nature's highest dower ;
> Combats them and subdues, transmutes, bereaves
> Of their bad influence and their good receives.

He will not lie in wait for wealth or honours ; they must seek out him.   He needs no external sources of happiness.   The votary of Duty has, like the stern Lawgiver herself, a smile upon his face ; he has a joy that the world cannot give or take away.

> Who if he be called upon to face
> Some awful moment to which Heaven has joined
> Great issues, good or bad for human kind,
> Is happy as a Lover ; and attired
> With sudden brightness like a man inspired,
> And, through the heat of conflict, keeps the law
> In calmness made, and sees what he foresaw.

In many of the letters written by soldiers from the front during the World War we can recognize shining through their rough and colloquial phraseology the spirit of these lines.   One passage may be quoted from the letter of a young officer, who was afterwards killed in action : " I cannot tell you how much I enjoy it all. There is something so noble and so great about the whole show which places it on a far higher plane than any other scene in which one has acted in this life." And as national armies, whether volunteer or conscript, more and more replace the professional soldiers of Wordsworth's day, his picture of the " happy warrior," comforted even in the hour of storm and turbulence by the inward vision of serener hours, bids fair to have an ever wider significance.

> He who, though thus endued as with a sense,
> And faculty for storm and turbulence,
> Is yet a Soul whose master-bias leans
> To homefelt pleasures and to gentle scenes ;
> Sweet images ! which, whereso'er he be,
> Are at his heart ; and such fidelity
> It is his darling passion to approve ;
> More brave for this, that he hath much to love.

We all now know that with Nelson's victory the issue of the world-conflict was really decided, that England's sea-power shattered Napoleon's dreams of universal conquest. But it was a long way from Trafalgar to Waterloo, and the allies were to pass through many an hour of deepest darkness. Within little more than a month of Trafalgar, Austerlitz (December 2) laid Austria at the invader's feet, and in the following year, on October 14, Prussia was overthrown at Jena. Wordsworth realized how stern was the responsibility thus laid on England :

> Another year !—another deadly blow,
> Another mighty Empire overthrown !
> And we are left, or shall be left, alone ;
> The last that dare to struggle with the Foe.
> 'Tis well ! from this day forward we shall know

That in ourselves our safety must be sought;
That by our own right hands it must be wrought,
That we must stand unpropped, or be laid low.
O dastard whom such foretaste doth not cheer !

England was, however, not completely isolated till
June, 1807, when by the Treaty of Tilsit Russia made
peace with Napoleon, and agreed to adopt his blockade-
system against this country, proclaimed in the famous
Berlin decrees.

Portugal was the only country which now stood outside the system. Her territory was invaded by a French
army under Junot, and her Prince-Regent driven into
exile. A similar fate was prepared for Spain, but when
Napoleon in June, 1808, forced King Charles IV and his
son Ferdinand to resign their claims to the crown, and
proclaimed his brother Joseph king, the Spanish people
rose in righteous fury against this foreign yoke. Napoleon's unprovoked aggression on the ancient liberties
of Spain aroused much the same feeling throughout
Europe as the German violation of Belgian neutrality
has done in our own day.

To Wordsworth, the spectacle of a nation, forsaken
by its rulers, rising spontaneously in defence of its freedom, was of most joyful augury. Henceforth the conflict with France entered, in his eyes, upon a new and
more auspicious phase. Hitherto, he declares in *The
Convention of Cintra*,

a deliberate and preparatory fortitude—a sedate and stern
melancholy, which had no sunshine and was exhilarated only
by the lightnings of indignation—this was the highest and
best state of moral feeling to which the most noble-minded

77

among us could attain. But from the moment of the rising
of the people of the Pyrenean peninsula, there was a mighty
change; we were instantaneously animated; and from that
moment the contest assumed the dignity, which it is not in
the power of anything but hope to bestow.

But the Muse will often consort with " stern melancholy," and fight shy of " hope." Though the exploits
of the Spaniards in the Peninsular War, especially of the
guerrilla leader Palafox at the siege of Saragossa, drew
from Wordsworth a number of sonnets, none of them can
take rank with those inspired by the earlier phases of the
struggle against Napoleon. Perhaps the finest is that
entitled "Indignation of a high-minded Spaniard,"
written in 1810:

> We can endure that He should waste our lands,
> Despoil our temples, and by sword and flame
> Return us to the dust from which we came;
> Such food a Tyrant's appetite demands;
> And we can brook the thought that by his hands
> Spain may be overpowered, and he possess,
> For his delight, a solemn wilderness
> Where all the brave lie dead. But, when of bands
> Which he will break for us he dares to speak;
> Of benefits, and of a future day
> When our enlightened minds shall bless his sway;
> *Then*, the strained heart of fortitude proves weak;
> Our groans, our blushes, our pale cheeks declare
> That he has power to inflict what we lack strength to
>   bear.

It is difficult to believe that these lines were written
about Spain in 1810 and not about Belgium in 1914.
Belgium was made into " a solemn wilderness," with

her lands wasted and her temples despoiled. But though Napoleon affected the rôle of the liberator of oppressed peoples, he had at least not formulated a theory like Treitschke and Bernhardi, that small States are incapable of a high civilization and that the blessings of an alien *Kultur* must be forced upon them at the sword's point.

While the struggle in the Peninsula was at its height, another national uprising took place which awakened Wordsworth's keenest sympathy. This was the revolt of the Tyrolese, headed by the inn-keeper, Andreas Hofer, against the Bavarians to whom they had been subjected by Napoleon. These mountain peasants were champions of liberty after the Cumberland poet's own heart, but when he cries:

Advance, come forth from thy Tyrolean ground,
Dear Liberty! stern Nymph of soul untamed;
Sweet Nymph, O rightly of the mountains named,
Through the long chain of Alps from mound to mound,
And o'er the eternal snows, like Echo, bound;

we feel that though the thought is akin to that of the octave of the sonnet " On the Subjugation of Switzerland," the expression of it is fancifully pretty instead of sublime.

Napoleon's invasion of Russia was a subject less suited to Wordsworth's muse, yet it is surprising that the tragedy of the retreat from Moscow should not have wrung from him more poignant verse. One rubs one's eyes when here, of all places, the assailant of " what is usually called poetic diction," reintroduces such outworn figures as " Frost's inexorable tooth," or calls upon the " mild Seasons " to whisper to the " billows of the main " and " the aerial zephyrs "

> That old decrepit Winter—*He* hath slain
> That Host which rendered all your bounties vain !

Even Waterloo drew from the poet no truly inspired strain. The two sonnets " occasioned " by the battle are undistinguished. So in the main is the " Thanksgiving Day " ode, though in some ringing lines it sums up the spirit in which this country had fought and won.

> Who paints how Britain struggled and prevailed
> Shall represent her labouring with an eye
>   Of circumspect humanity ;
> Shall show her clothed with strength and skill
>   All martial duties to fulfil ;
> Firm as a rock in stationary fight ;
> In motion rapid as the lightning's gleam ;
> Fierce as a flood-gate bursting at mid-night,
> To rouse the wicked from their giddy dream—
> Woe, woe to all that face her in the field !
> Appalled she may not be, and cannot yield.

But if Wordsworth failed to sing worthily of Waterloo, so did Scott, whose poem on the battle never rises to heroic strain. Byron's glittering stanzas in Canto III of *Childe Harold* count among the triumphs of rhetoric rather than of poetry, but they can claim to be the only contemporary verse suggested by Waterloo that has for a century kept its hold on the popular imagination.

It was the earlier phases of the great European conflict that, not only in Wordsworth's case, were the more fruitful in poetic inspiration. Campbell's battle-songs,

Ye Mariners of England (1801) *Hohenlinden* (1803), and *The Battle of the Baltic* (1809), in spite of an occasional false note, are noble lyrics of patriotism and of the martial spirit in exalted mood. Scott's glorious recital in *Marmion* (1808) of the death-struggle of Scotland's chivalry around her king at Flodden burns with the fire of the heroic struggle that was being waged by Britain while he wrote the lines. They make an appeal to the man-at-arms that will never die. As they inspired Wellington's troops behind the lines of Torres Vedras, so more than a century later they were recited to encourage our soldiers in the trenches of Northern France.

It is impossible to think of Wordsworth's sonnets being put to such a purpose. Even when he wrote of war, the moving accident was not his trade. The pageantry of arms made no appeal to him. Nor did the swaying fortunes of a world-struggle such as he saw, and as on a yet vaster scale we have witnessed in our own day, with its tragic suspense, its grandeur, its pathos, its irony, inspire his muse. Why, nevertheless, has it been truly said that these sonnets [1] " are worthy of comparison with the noblest passages of patriotic verse and prose which all our history has inspired—the passages where Shakespeare brings his rays to focus on ' this earth, this realm, this England '—or where the dread of national dishonour has kindled Chatham to iron glow, or where Milton rises from the polemic into the prophet and Burke from the partisan into the philosopher " ?

It is because Wordsworth keeps his gaze steadily fixed on those elements in the history and character of England

[1] F. W. H. Myers, *Wordsworth*, p. 79.

and of those who fought with her, which justified and ennobled their feats by land and sea. In the earliest days of the conflict with France, when he thought that English victories were blows to freedom, he had even bent his head in shame. But once he recognized that his country and her allies were the champions of "national independence and liberty," his voice rose on their behalf with the austere and solemn grandeur of a Hebrew prophet. France turned to tyranny was as Ephraim joined to idols, to be denounced with holy wrath.

In the twentieth century we have seen another great nation that has forsaken its true mission, and that is joined to idols, to the worship of naked Force. May we not cry to Wordsworth, in his own words, "Thou shouldst be living at this hour"? The causes for which the war was fought, the validity of "a scrap of paper" when it has the seal of British honour, the right of existence of small States, the claims of individual liberty against military autocracy, the preservation of the principle of nationality against the subversive domination of a ravenous world-power—all these would have been dear to Wordsworth's heart. He who sang of Venice and of Switzerland in their downfall, and of Touissant, dispossessed and imprisoned, could have given immortal utterance to Belgium's agony and faith, and the heroism of her King:

> Thou hast great allies,
> Thy friends are exaltations, agonies,
> And love, and man's unconquerable mind.

His moving relation of Spain's appeal to England

might have been written of Belgium's appeal to her in a later hour.[1]

A people whose government had been dissolved by foreign tyranny, and which had been left to work out its own salvation by its own virtues, prayed for our help. . . . They had spoken of unrelenting and inhuman wrongs . . . of the blessed service of freedom chosen; of heroic aspirations; of constancy, and fortitude and perseverance; of resolution even to the death; of gladness in the embrace of death; of weeping over the graves of the slain by those who had not been so happy as to die; of resignation under the worst final doom; of glory, and triumph and punishment. This was the language which we heard, this was the devout hymn that was chanted; and the responses, with which our country bore a part in the solemn service, were from her soul and from the depths of her soul.

Thus it is always with great literature. It transcends the conditions which gave it birth; it gains with the flight of time new and more pregnant significance. In the hundred and twenty years since the Napoleonic conflict the " famous stream " of British freedom has run deeper in its channels, and has immeasurably broadened. It was possible for the poet, though his gaze in the sonnets is backward rather than forward, to foresee something of the democratic development that has taken place within these islands since 1815. But he could not anticipate that growth of the British dominions beyond the sea, which has carried our national ideals and forms of polity to all corners of the world. British liberty means more, and for a far vaster section of humanity,

[1] *The Convention of Cintra*, pp. 111–12, in vol. i of Grosart's edition of his prose works. Also published separately, with an introduction by A. V. Dicey (1915).

than in Wordsworth's day. But its inmost spirit is unchangeable, and it has never found more august, serene, and fortifying utterance than through his lips. By such utterance he has himself become the peer of the mighty spirits whom he invoked in England's name, and stands by their side in the *sursum corda* of a younger, fierier apostle of freedom.[1]

All our past acclaims our future : Shakespeare's voice and
    Nelson's hand,
Milton's faith and Wordsworth's trust in this our chosen and
    chainless land,
Bear us witness : come the world against her, England yet
    shall stand.

[1] Swinburne, *England : An Ode.*

V

EDMUND KEAN IN HIS HEROIC PARTS

EDMUND KEAN died on May 15, 1833. The centenary of his death was celebrated on May 15, 1933, at Drury Lane theatre, where Sir Frank Benson gave a commemorative address and Dame Madge Kendal, whose father had acted with Kean, laid a wreath at the foot of his statue. Shortly afterwards there appeared a biography of Kean by an American scholar, Dr. Harold N. Hillebrand, based upon documentary researches by himself and others, including, on this side of the Atlantic, Dr. W. J. Lawrence and Mrs. Gabrielle Enthoven. Dr. Hillebrand's volume also makes use of the previous *Lives* of Kean, by B. W. Procter (Barry Cornwall) in 1835, by F. W. Hawkins in 1869, and by J. F. Molloy in 1888, but it has now superseded them as an authoritative presentation of the facts of his career.

It is improbable that much will be added to these facts, and it seems therefore opportune, in the light of our present knowledge, to consider again Edmund Kean's place in the history of the English stage, and more particularly the chief parts with which his name is identified. These will be found to have been drawn from four dramatic groups: (1) Shakespearian tragedies;

(2) other Elizabethan plays, in especial, Massinger's *A New Way to Pay Old Debts*; (3) Restoration and eighteenth-century heroic dramas, ranging from Otway's *Venice Preserved* to George Colman's (Junior) *The Mountaineers*; (4) Plays written during Kean's lifetime, among which C. R. Maturin's *Bertram* had the leading place.

This seems at first sight to be a somewhat motley collection. Their merits, literary or dramatic, are singularly diverse. But an examination of the place that they successively took in Kean's theatrical career, will show that they one and all included roles specially suited to the display of his genius as an actor. They had in them, using the word in its wider sense, an element of the heroic. They showed men, often stained with crime or driven by passion, but of larger mould than their fellows, torn by contending forces of good or evil, and when foiled by destiny, going with heads bloodied but unbowed to their doom.

The date of Kean's birth and his parentage have been the subjects of much discussion, and the evidence has been sifted anew by Dr. Hillebrand. As between the two dates mentioned by Procter and Hawkins, March 17, 1789 and November 4, 1787, the latter, or, at any rate, some date in 1787 is the more likely. With regard to his parents the evidence is in favour of Edmund Kean and Nancy Carey. This elder Edmund was a surveyor's clerk and afterwards an architect. He was a speaker in debating clubs, and an occasional imitator on the stage of public men. The last days of his short life were clouded by madness. Nancy Carey was the granddaughter of Henry Carey, author of *Sally in Our Alley*, and daughter of George Savile Carey, a theatrical imitator. She was herself an actress of small parts, chiefly in provincial companies. She left the child to the care of Mrs. Price, a widowed sister of his father and to Miss Charlotte Tidswell, who was for forty years a minor member of the Drury Lane company. She probably introduced little Edmund, who had a very irregular schooling, to the Drury Lane Theatre. According to his own account in later days he took a humble part in the production of *Macbeth*, with Kemble and Mrs. Siddons in the chief roles, with which Drury Lane was reopened on April 21, 1794, after a fire. He was one of the little goblins that came dancing on the stage in Act IV. But the first documentary evidence of his appearance in a name part is on playbills recently recovered, now in the Enthoven collection and at Harvard. They announce the performance at Drury Lane on June 8, 1796, of three pieces, including the *Merry Wives of Windsor*, in which the part of Robin, Falstaff's page, is played by Master Kean. The occasion was the benefit of four members of the Company, including Miss Tidswell. It is of interest that Kean's earliest theatrical association, however humble, was with Shakespeare.

It was probably about two years later, in 1798, that Edmund, " a slender, pale, diminutive boy, really eleven years of age, but not taller than nine," came under the care of a rich woman of good social position, Mrs. Clarke. The authority for this is an unsigned and undated MS. now in the Victoria and Albert Museum, which Hillebrand thinks was probably drawn up by a friend of Mrs. Clarke for Procter, when he was writing his *Life*. She took the boy into her house and encouraged him to

act for her friends till on one occasion he ran away—
apparently to offer himself as a sailor at Portsmouth.
She then put him in charge of Captain Miller, stationed
at Windsor Castle, but first let him give a public recital
at the Rolls Rooms in Chancery Lane.   At Windsor he
performed for the officers, became acquainted with
Eton boys, and recited twice before George III and his
queen.   He then paid a visit to Oxford with a letter of
introduction, and was welcomed by the scholars.   He
appears to have been back in London between 1800 and
1802, acting with amateurs or in minor playhouses.
But there is little doubt that he trod the boards of a
major theatre on May 18, 1802.   A Covent Garden
playbill announces on that date " (for this night only)
Recitations by the celebrated Master Carey (his first
appearance on this stage)."   Procter states that he
recited Rolla's address to the sun, from Sheridan's
Pizarro, whereby he is first associated with heroic
drama, but that he was hoarse and did not make much
impression.   It is curious that he should have appeared
under his mother's surname, but it can scarcely be any
other than he.

So ends the first, early London, chapter in Kean's life.
For the next dozen years he was " on the road."   Our
first certain news of him is with the company of Samuel
Jerrold (father of Douglas) at Sheerness, on Easter
Monday, 1804.   It is a sign (as Hillebrand thinks) that
it cannot have had much standing that a boy of seventeen
played principal parts, including Rolla in *Pizarro*, and
George Barnwell, the evil apprentice, in Lillo's
domestic tragedy of *The London Merchant*.   Though
neither Rolla nor Barnwell became a standing role

in Kean's repertory he revived them from time to time.

A playbill happily preserved shows that he was back from Sheerness for a time in London by February, 1805, for on the 15th he acted at the Theatre, Wivell's Billiard Room, Camden Town, the part of Octavian, in the younger George Colman's musical melodrama, *The Mountaineers*. During the next ten years this was one of his favourite roles. He appeared in it at Swansea on September 4, 1809, for his benefit; at Exeter on January 20, 1813; in Guernsey where he opened with it on Easter Monday, 1813; at Dorchester on November 15, 1813; and at Drury Lane (for the Theatrical Fund) on July 4, 1815, and on July 7 to close the season.

The scene of *The Mountaineers* is laid in Spain in the mediæval period when it was largely in the occupation of the Moors with their capital at Granada. From slavish captivity there the noble Count Virolet, and a more or less comic Irishman, Captain Kilmallock, escape with Zorayda, the daughter of their Moorish master, to the Sierra del Ronda, a mountainous district of Andalusia. To the same district comes travelling in man's attire Virolet's sister Floranthe. She had been betrothed to Don Octavian, but had been charged by her father to love another, whom Octavian had run through the body, and left at the time for dead, but who had recovered and married " a rich one-eyed widow of Salamanca." Octavian had fled in despair to the woods of the Sierra del Ronda, where Floranthe has come to seek him. We see him entering from the cave, which he has made his home, and hear him salute the rising sun.

Tis dawn—
Thou hot and rolling sun ! I rise before thee !
For I have twice thy scorching flames within me,
And am more restless. Now to seek my willow,
That droops his mournful head across the brook :
He is my Kalender ; I'll score his trunk
Within one more long, long day of solitude !
I shall lose count else, in my wretchedness :
And that were pity.

We hear him, too, declaiming to some of the fugitives
from Granada who have discovered his lonely retreat :

O wander, boundless love, across the wild !
Give thy free passions scope, and range the wilderness !
Crib not thyself in cities . . .
Gain is the old man's god : he offers up
His issue to 't—and mercenary wedlock
Murders his offspring's peace. They murdered mine—
They tore it from my bosom by the roots,
And with it pluck'd out hope !

So when Floranthe, in her male disguise, comes before
him he thinks it is a mocking vision :

What art thou—speak—that face—yet this attire—
Floranthe ! No—it cannot—Oh, good Heaven !
Vex not a poor creature thus ! Floranthe !
How my sight thickens—speak—
   Flor. Octavian.
   Oct. That voice ! It is—So long too—let me clasp thee.
   (*Runs to meet her, staggers, and falls on his face.*)

But he recovers to find " 'tis real," and is not only
reunited to his own beloved but saves her brother
Virolet's Moorish flame Zorayda from the scimitar of
her incensed sire. *The Mountaineers* is not of much

account as literature, but it gave Kean effective opportunities for emotional acting, and the role of Octavian
was at a later date to have a decisive influence on his
fortunes.

There followed a visit to Belfast, where the season
opened on March 27, 1805. Round this visit, in which
Kean played chiefly small parts, a number of stories have
gathered, but most of them have not survived Dr.
Lawrence's expert analysis. One, however, related by
Procter concerning him and Mrs. Siddons, who was
paying her farewell to Belfast, may well be true. She
asked the company to run through one of the plays at
her lodgings. She noted one " little man who was to
play one of the secondary characters," who "although he
had not a great deal to do, endeavoured to do his best."
When he had finished she cried " Very well, sir—very
well. I have never heard that part given in the same
way before." So early was Kean to show himself an
innovator in the actor's art.

But something more than the approval of a Siddons
was needed to give him an opportunity in London. It
is true that he had a season at the Haymarket, beginning
in June, 1806. But it was one of very small parts. He
who had played Octavian at Camden Town was now
reduced to the part of a goatherd in the same play. In
Hamlet he was Rosencrantz, and after July 18 his name
is frequently missing from the bills. He saw, in Hillebrand's words, that " in the closed circle of the London
theatres there was as yet no place for him. His way led
out again towards the circumference, the provinces,
where if he had to starve he could at least starve as
Octavian and not as a goatherd."

It certainly was an abrupt transition in September, 1806, from the Haymarket to Mrs. Baker's company, which acted in her theatres in some of the chief towns in Kent. She was a " character," illiterate and domineering, but shrewd and kind-hearted. She took all the gate money herself, and then went to bed with the cash in a large front pocket. She kept her money for many years in boxes, jars and canisters.

With her Kean was promoted to two leading parts, Hastings in *Jane Shore*, and Young Norval in Home's *Douglas*, both of which he acted at Tunbridge Wells. They were parts which he continued to act for a number of years.

Jane Shore is one of the best of Nicholas Rowe's plays —a blend of historical and domestic drama. It deals with the fortunes of the beautiful mistress of Edward IV, after his death, and the rise to power of her enemy, the Duke of Gloster, afterwards Richard III. The fortunes of Jane herself, especially her tragic wandering as an outcast through the snowy streets, and her reunion at the point of death with her forgiving husband, are the most effective elements in the play. But the part of Lord Hastings, who deserts the nobly-born Alicia for love of Jane, and even seeks to force her to his will, gave opportunities to Kean. We can imagine him declaiming the lines :

> How fierce a fiend is passion. With what wildness,
> What tyranny untamed it reigns in woman !
> Unhappy sex ! whose easy yielding temper
> Gives way to ev'ry appetite alike;
> And love in their weak bosoms is a rage,
> As terrible as hate, and as destructive.

Or in a softer key the words of Hastings when he is sent
by Gloster at an instant to his doom :

> Let necessity
> Supply the place of time and preparation
> And arm me for the blow. 'Tis but to die,
> 'Tis but to venture on that common hazard
> Which many a time in battle I have run ;
> 'Tis but to close my eyes, and shut out daylight,
> To view no more the wicked ways of men.

In John Home's *Douglas* as in *Jane Shore,* the finest
part is that of the heroine—Lady Randolph. In the
days when Scotland was threatened by the sword of the
invading Danes, Lady Randolph had lost in battle her
first husband, Douglas, to whom she had been secretly
married for only a few weeks. She had made a second
loveless marriage with Lord Randolph, whose heir
Glenalvon pursues her with unlawful passion. The
infant child of her union with Douglas is thought to have
been drowned with his nurse. But he had been saved
by a peasant who brings him up as his own son. When
he is of an age to bear arms the Douglas blood within
him urges him to seek service with the Scottish King
against the invaders. On his way he rescues Lord Randolph from an ambush set by the villainous Glenalvon.
The words in which he describes himself to Randolph
are familiar even to those who know nothing else of the
play :

> My name is Norval. On the Grampian hills
> My father feeds his flocks : a frugal swain,
> Whose constant cares were to increase his store

And keep his only son, myself, at home.
For I had heard of battles, and I long'd
To follow to the field some warlike lord.

From old Norval, who has gone in pursuit of the youth,
Lady Randolph learns the true story, and she reveals to
Douglas the secret of his birth and that she is his mother.
To tell him more she bids him meet her at midnight
in the wood near the Castle. Glenalvon persuades
Randolph that it is a guilty assignation, makes him
draw his sword against Douglas, and then treacherously
stabs the youth from behind. With what defiant
melancholy must Kean have breathed forth the young
hero's dying words to his mother :

Too soon we part : I have not long been Douglas.
O destiny ! hardly thou deal'st with me.

          *   *   *

O had I fallen as my brave fathers fell,
Turning with fatal arm the tide of battle,
Like them I should have smiled and welcomed death ;
But thus to perish by a villain's hand,
Cut off from nature's and from glory's course
Which never mortal was so fond to run !

We do not now endorse Sir Walter Scott's verdict
that *Douglas* is " one of the best acting plays going."
But it has something of true native quality, and its
romantic plot gave opportunities for the display of some
of Kean's most distinctive powers.

Apart from Hastings and Douglas and Bob Acres in
The Rivals he played minor parts under Mrs. Baker's
management. This he attributed to the hostility of
her manager, Mr. Long, who (appropriately to his name)
objected to small men. As Kean wrote to Mrs. Clarke,

"Mr. Long kept me in the background as much as possible and frequently gave those characters, which undoubtedly were mine, to fellows who certainly would have adorned the handles of a plough, but were never intended for the stage, but these met Mr. Long's approbation because they were *taller* than me."

So after a year he rejoined the Jerrold company at Sheerness in September, 1807, when he acted Hastings again, and the name part in Nathaniel Lee's *Alexander the Great*, and in *The Rival Queens*. At the production of this an officer in a stage-box kept exclaiming "Alexander the little," till Kean withered him with a haughty look and the retort—"Yes, with a great soul."

He thought it a mark of this great soul when under his next management in 1808, that of Beverley at Gloucester and Stroud, he refused to play second to the infant phenomenon, Master Betty—"to any man except John Kemble." But it was against a woman in the company, not a man, of whom, as the future proved, Kean should have been on his guard. Two sisters from Waterford, Mary and Susan Chambers, were acting at Gloucester, with little stage experience and small talent. Kean and Mary fell in love and were married at Stroud on July 17, 1808. She was of an affectionate and clinging nature, and was a tender mother to their sons, Howard, born September 13, 1809 (who died aged four), and Charles, January 18, 1811. But she had not a powerful enough personality to keep in the straight path a man of genius and of strong passions, who was always too ready to find a refuge from the trials and vicissitudes of his career in drink. And judged by

95

her letters she had the common Irish habit of making the worst of things.

The first year after their marriage was spent under the reputable management of J. B. Watson, whose company had its headquarters at Cheltenham, but which from October, 1808, till the summer of 1809 performed at Birmingham, where, as extant playbills show, Kean acted in a great variety of more or less important parts, including Joseph Surface in the *School for Scandal*. But there was little opportunity for the display of his tragic or higher romantic qualities.

In June, 1809, he and Mary transferred themselves to the company of Andrew Cherry, who had a theatrical circuit including towns in South Wales and Waterford, Mary's birthplace. It is difficult to understand why they were in such low water that, if Procter is to be trusted, the pair had to tramp the 180 miles from Birmingham to Swansea, Kean carrying a bundle of clothes and four swords, and Mary dragging after him. It was a strange odyssey for a man who was leaving after a year one recognized company, to spend, as it turned out, two years in another. With Cherry he was able to act again in some of his favourite parts, Rolla, Octavian and Douglas. He appeared too, in Shakespearian parts: Edgar in *King Lear* (when he also acted Friday in *Robinson Crusoe*); Petruchio in Garrick's adaptation of *The Taming of the Shrew*, and no less a role than Hamlet. This he acted at Waterford during the visit which began in the middle of April, 1810. He was there seen in the last Act of the play by a young subaltern, T. C. Grattan who at that time was interested in little but the fencing match between Hamlet and Laertes.

Hamlet was a little pale, thin man, who seemed a mere pigmy beside the very tall Laertes in high-heeled boots. But Grattan was struck by " his quiet gracefulness of manner, while he parried the cut and thrust attacks of his adversary, and by the carriage and action of a practised swordsman when he began to return the lounges." [1] On inquiry Grattan was told that his name was Kean, actor of first-rate talent, chief tragic hero of the company; and also the principal singer, stage-manager and getter up of pantomimes, and one of the best harlequins in Wales or the West of England.

Thus began the long friendship between Kean and Grattan, and at the same time his intimacy with Sheridan Knowles. A playbill for May 10, 1810, shows that Kean and Knowles were acting together in Frederick Reynolds's play, *The Exile*. On the company's second visit to Waterford early in 1811 the association was still closer, for they appeared together in two early plays by Knowles, *Brian Boroihne* and *Leo, or the Gipsy*, in both cases Kean acting the name part. Neither of these pieces was included by their author in his published works, but they are, I think, the first contemporary plays in which Kean appeared.

From a letter in the *Hibernian Magazine*, dated May 7, 1811, and signed Thespian (discovered by Dr. W. J. Lawrence) we learn that Jaffier in Otway's *Venice Preserved* was another of Kean's successful impersonations at Waterford. The play is Otway's masterpiece

[1] Grattan would have been interested to read Professor Dover Wilson's technical discussion of the sword-play in *Hamlet* in his introduction to G. Silver's *Paradoxes of Defence*, 1599 (1933).

and was admirably adapted for the display of Kean's powers. Jaffier, the devoted husband of the lovely Belvidera, whom he has married in defiance of her tyrannous father, the Senator, Priuli, is drawn, at the lowest depths of his fortune, by his friend Pierre into a conspiracy against the Republic. But he reveals the secret to his wife :

> Lock this within thy breast,
> I've bound myself by all the strictest sacraments
> Divine and human.
>
> *Bel.* Speak !
> *Jaff.*   To kill thy father
> *Bel.*   My father !
> *Jaff.* Nay, the throats of the whole Senate
> Shall bleed, my Belvidera : he amongst us
> That spares his father, brother, or his friend
> Is damned. How rich and beauteous will the face
> Of ruin look, when these wild streets run blood
>   Whilst thou far off in safety
> Smiling, shall see the wonders of our daring ;
> And when night comes with praise and love receive me.

But yielding to her entreaties he is persuaded to betray the conspiracy and Pierre :

> Must I betray my friend ? Ah, take me quickly,
> Secure me well before that thought's renewed.
> If I relapse once more, all's lost for ever,
> *Bel.* Hast thou a friend more dear than Belvidera ?
> *Jaff.* No ; thou'rt my soul itself ; wealth, friendship, honour,
> All present joys and earnest of all future,
> Are summed in thee ; methinks, when in thy arms.
> Thus leaning on thy breast, one minute's more

Than a long thousand years of vulgar hours.
Why was such happiness not given me pure?
Why dashed with cruel wrongs and bitter wantings.

He tries to salve his conscience by extracting from the Senators an oath to spare the lives of his friends, but by an equivocation the oath is disregarded, and Pierre is led forth to be executed publicly on the wheel. To save him from this disgrace Jaffier, at Pierre's whispered entreaty, stabs him to death, and then plunges the dagger into his own breast. The struggle between love and friendship, with its tragic close for both Jaffier and Pierre, gave Kean a magnificent opportunity, and Jaffier was for long one of his favourite roles.

It is strange in the light of Kean's success with his company, that Cherry should have let him leave (if the story is true) rather than raise his salary from twenty-five to thirty shillings a week. And it is still more strange to find the Keans again completely "down and out." They wandered from one northern town to another in the greatest straits. At Richmond in Yorkshire, according to Mary, "A gentleman who kept a large establishment for the education of young gentlemen, was very kind and the young gentlemen called next day with their pocket money and left it with the landlady directed to Mr. Kean, the sum amounting, I think, to eleven shillings and sixpence." Even when they got to London and Kean, early in 1812, received an offer from John Hughes to join his Exeter company, he had to write a letter to him, still extant, begging for an advance of £10 to enable him to get down to the West Country.

This was a humiliating prologue to what was to prove

the most fateful of his provincial engagements. It is
with Hughes's company that we have the first documentary record from playbills of his appearance in most of
his great Shakespearian parts. We have already heard
of his Hamlet at Waterford. But it is at Totnes on
August 6, 1812, when he took his benefit, that we have
the first bill announcing him as Shylock, " after which
he will dance a new Pas de Deux," followed by a Pantomime in which he played a noble savage. At Exeter he
played Othello on December 14, Macbeth on December
16, Hamlet on December 21, Richard III on January 18,
1813.

In April 1813 the company went over to Guernsey
and opened a season at St. Peterport. One of the
most valuable sections of Hillebrand's biography is that
in which he explodes, from an examination of local
papers, some of the legends which have gathered round
this visit, and which represent that Kean in his chief parts
was very badly received by the islanders. Their real
attitude is represented by the following quotation from
Le Miroir Politique (May 29, 1813) :

We cannot but approve of the manner in which Mr. Kean
fills most of his tragic characters. His attitudes are easy, his
action judicious, and his tones as good as the badness of his
voice will allow.

In a later issue his Othello is specially praised.
" Dignified, feeling, and impressive throughout, he
drew forth our admiration—our sympathy—our tears."
But his friendly critic warns him against " occasional fits
of languor and negligence," and he had twice to apologize
for not appearing when his name was billed. He was

probably drunk, and in any case the Guernsey visit ended in a quarrel with Hughes, and once again the Keans were at a loose end. In a letter from Exeter, discovered by Dr. Lawrence, Mary writes to a friend on September 5 : " I am now with two lovely boys pennyless, friendless. He is gone to London." But in response to her entreaties he returned, and probably under the management of Henry Lee of Taunton, acted at Barnstaple in October. A bill is extant for October 28, announcing Kean as Jaffier in *Venice Preserved*, and as Chiron in a Ballet with Master Howard Kean (a child of three years old) as the infant Achilles. When, less than a month later, on November 22 Howard, who was idolized by his parents, died at Dorchester, Mary, in a letter to her sister, expressed something akin to remorse. " O Dear Susan, tell me I have no sin to answer for in exposing his innocence, his angel form to gain a dinner for his parents, the thought sometimes harrows up my soul."

It was an irony of fate that this tragic blow should fall upon the couple on the very eve of an almost miraculous revolution in their professional fortunes. Even so, this was wellnigh prevented by a curiously malicious stroke of fate. When Kean had gone off to London, leaving Mary at Exeter, it was probably to try to get a place at a small London theatre, the Olympic, which Robert William Elliston was re-opening in Wych Street. While he was at Barnstaple Kean received a definite offer from Elliston at three guineas a week salary, and wrote accepting it on October 2. He did so, as Mary wrote to her sister, " very reluctantly, knowing he could never get into either of the great theatres after mumming there ;

but not seeing any other resource." At the Olympic he would have been debarred from acting in any of the tragedies of which Drury Lane and Covent Garden theatres had the London monopoly.

But at this, of all moments, one of them was in a totally unforeseen way holding out a hand to him. Dr. Drury, Headmaster of Harrow, and a friend of several of the Committee of Drury Lane, which included Byron, had been spending the summer near Exeter, and had heard the praises of Kean. At his instigation, on November 15, two days after Kean had still more definitely closed with Elliston, Arnold, the Drury Lane manager arrived at Dorchester, saw Kean in the part of Octavian, and a day or two later as Alexander the Great, and offered him an engagement for three years at a commencing salary of eight pounds. Kean at once accepted this, without mentioning Elliston who, he trusted, would release him from his contract. This he refused to do, while the Drury Lane managers after Kean's arrival in London, declined to engage him, or pay him his salary, till he could show them a warrant of release from his previous contract. Again for some weeks the Keans were in the direst financial straits, but at last matters were adjusted, and late in 1814 Kean entered as the leading tragedian the service of the theatre where twenty years before he had, by his own account, made his début as a goblin in *Macbeth*. It was all-important for Drury Lane to find a tragedian who could compete with Kemble and Young at Covent Garden. Yet the only preliminary announcement of Kean's forthcoming appearance on January 26 was in an " omnibus " advertisement in *The Times* on the Saturday, January 22, 1814, which gives a good idea of the varied theatrical fare provided at the leading theatre :

THEATRE ROYAL : DRURY LANE

This Evening : *Illusion.* After which *Two Strings to Your Bow.* To which will be added the new splendid comic pantomime called *Harlequin Harper*, or *A Jump from Japan.* On Monday, *Othello*, with the Pantomime. On Tuesday, the *Castle of Andalusia*, with the Pantomime. On Wednesday Mr. Kean, from the Theatre Royal, Exeter, will make his first appearance at this theatre as *Shylock* in *The Merchant of Venice.*

There was only one morning rehearsal, and at this the acting manager, Raymond, and the company were completely upset by Kean's original conception of his part. Raymond protested against the " innovation." " Sir," answered Kean, " I wish it to be an innovation." " It will never do, depend upon it," retorted Raymond. " Well, sir, perhaps I may be wrong ; but if so, the public will set me right." It was an appeal to Cæsar.

What was Kean's innovation ? It was a challenge to the so-called " classical " school of acting which had held sway since the rise to fame of J. P. Kemble in 1783 and of his sister, Mrs. Siddons. Kemble, possessed of a fine figure and of a resonant voice, aimed primarily in his Shakespearian impersonations at formal declamation and imposing still-life effects. To these he sacrificed nature and passion. As Hazlitt summed it up, " He was the statue of perfect tragedy, not its living soul." Mrs. Siddons, though she had more of natural genius and grandeur, was cast in similar mould.

What a contrast did Kean present when he stepped upon the stage in a black wig instead of the red one

which had become traditional in the part of Shylock.
"There came on," wrote a spectator, "a small man
with an Italian face and fatal eyes which struck all."
And the acting of this small man was alive, not only in
every glance of the eyes, but in every gesture of the
body and in every tone of the voice. The effect on
the audience, though the house was only a quarter full,
was electrical. "How the devil so few of them kicked
up such a row," said William Oxberry, who acted
Gobbo, listening from the green-room, "was something
marvellous." At the fall of the curtain there was no
mistaking the verdict, and Kean rushed home to his wife
with the cry, "Mary, you shall ride in your carriage,
and Charley shall go to Eton."

The London Press had not realized that January 26,
1814, was to be an historic "first night," and it was
represented at Drury Lane by only two papers, the
Morning Post and the *Morning Chronicle*.

The *Post* paid a tribute to Kean's expressive counten-
ance, to the management of his clear and articulate voice,
and the mastery of his art in the Trial scene. But it
criticized his "too great activity," which would not
commend itself to anyone accustomed to the classical
tradition.

The *Chronicle* spoke in more decided tones. By
singular good fortune its representative on that eventful
night was William Hazlitt, as fearless a romanticist in
criticism as Kean was in acting. As he stated later, "I
had been told to give as favourable an account as I
could. I gave a true one. I am not one of those who
when they see the sun breaking from behind a cloud
stop to ask others whether it is the moon."

Thus his " true account " in the *Morning Chronicle* of January 27 began :

Mr. Kean (of whom report had spoken highly) last night made his appearance at Drury Lane Theatre in the character of Shylock. For voice, eye, action and expression, no actor has come out for many years at all equal to him. The applause from the first scene to the last was general, loud and uninterrupted.

Hazlitt always maintained that he had not " written up " Kean in the *Chronicle* and that the actor's later career had ratified his verdict. Indeed in this first notice he prophesied that other plays than *The Merchant of Venice* would give him fuller opportunities for his special powers :

Notwithstanding the complete success of Mr. Kean in the part of Shylock we question if he will not become a greater favourite in other parts. There was a lightness and vigour in his tread, a buoyancy and elasticity of spirit, a fire and animation which would accord better with almost any other character than with the morose, sullen, inward, inveterate, inflexible malignity of Shylock.

And so it was to prove. On February 12 he appeared in another Shakespearian part, Richard III, which had been inseparably associated with the name of Garrick. Though he was hampered with a severe cold, he again achieved a triumph. The box-office receipts had risen from £164 on the first night of *The Merchant of Venice* to £720. In addition to the *Morning Post* and the *Morning Chronicle* there were now present the dramatic critics of *The Times*, the *Examiner*, the *Scots Magazine* and the *Champion*. But again it was Hazlitt who contributed the most notable interpretation of the performance:

Mr. Kean's manner of acting this part has one peculiar advantage; it is entirely his own, without any traces of imitation of any other actor. He stands upon his own ground, and he stands firm upon it. Almost every scene had the stamp and freshness of nature . . .

The concluding scene, in which he is killed by Richmond, was the most brilliant. He fought like one drunk with wounds: and the attitude in which he stands with his hands stretched out, after his sword is taken from him, had a preternatural and terrific grandeur, as if his will could not be disarmed, and the phantoms of his despair had a withering power.

" A preternatural and terrific grandeur " ! Hazlitt's words help us to understand what Coleridge meant when he said that to see Kean act was like reading Shakespeare by flashes of lightning.

His next appearance at Drury Lane was as Hamlet on March 12. It will be remembered that four years previously T. C. Grattan had described him in that part at Waterford as a " mere pigmy " compared with the Laertes. Hillebrand has pointed out that Kean's " insignificant stature, hitherto cloaked on the Drury Lane boards by the gaberdine of Shylock and the deformity of Richard, would be revealed to the full in Hamlet's solemn black." Moreover, Hamlet's role is one of meditation rather than of passion and action in which Kean excelled. Thus, though his performance was very successful, we do not specially link his name with the part.

It is otherwise with *Othello* in which he achieved an overwhelming triumph on May 5. Hazlitt called Kean's *Othello* " the finest piece of acting in the world," and to Leigh Hunt it was " the masterpiece of the living stage." His Iago, of whom he gave a novel rendering as " a jocund elastic villain," was similarly acclaimed. Within a few years he was to find a rival in both these parts in C. M. Young, an actor of the statuesque Kemble school, who appears to have captivated feminine theatre-goers. In a letter to Miss Marianne Neaill, dated October 24, 1822, the poet-critic, George Darley, draws a trenchant contrast between the two performers :

I knew also that Young would be the God of your Idolatry —he is just a lady's tragedian. . . . There is some excuse however for you, as you've never seen Kean. Young's Othello is a maudlin piece of work—very sweet and pretty and elegant and all that, but the man can't *feel* the character . . . Young is a mere declaimer—or rather the echo of a declaimer—for he professes to imitate Kemble ; all of whose attributes he reaches but his energy. Kean is not an orator, he feels too intensely—he is all ardour, passion, vehemence, enthusiasm, with more capability of expressing tender and pathetic feelings than any tragedian, male or female, I have ever seen—indeed I think he excells in pathos. But he has not that flowing eloquence, that rolling volubility, which delights the petticoat part of an audience, and which Young is too happy in. In short, I am positive you would still prefer Young, tho' Kean were to outdo himself—and in this I can only say your sex is in fault, 'tis pity you're a woman.[1]

[1] *The Life and Letters of George Darley*, edited by Claude Colleer Abbott, p. 22. This letter has escaped the notice of Kean's biographers.

Kean's second Drury Lane season, preceded by a visit to Dublin in July and August, 1814, saw his appearance in other Shakespearian parts. They included Macbeth in a semi-operatic version of the play; Romeo, with Mrs. Bartley as Juliet, and Richard II, but in none of these did he repeat the triumphs of his first season. One great Shakespearian part was barred to him during the lifetime of George III, that of King Lear. The authorities would have viewed with disfavour the representation of a mad old King. But in January, 1820, George III died, and on April 24 Kean appeared as Lear, though in the garbled version by Nahum Tate, in which all ends happily for Lear and Cordelia, the latter being married at the close to Edgar. Even with this handicap Kean's genius again triumphed, though on this occasion he did not satisfy Hazlitt, who was angered by the use of the Tate version and who partly shared Lamb's view that it was impossible to act Lear. Later, in the season 1822–3, Kean restored for some nights the original ending. " The London audience," he had declared, " have no notion of what I can do till they see me over the dead body of Cordelia." It was the last of his services to Shakespeare, but it was marred by his physical inability to support Cordelia in his arms, and he had to return to the Tate version.

But Kean did not confine himself among the Elizabethans to Shakespeare. He had taken his first London benefit on May 25, 1814, in the character of Luke in Sir John Burgess's adaptation of Philip Massinger's play, *The City Madam*. It was in another of Massinger's plays, *A New Way to pay Old Debts*, that in his third

season at Drury Lane, on January 12, 1816, he achieved
his greatest triumph in a non-Shakespearian play.   This
drama has kept the stage while other Elizabethan plays
more famous in their own day have been laid on the
shelf.   A memory of my boyhood is of the Irish
tragedian, Barry Sullivan, in the play at the old Belfast
Theatre Royal.   Its principal character, the heartless
and ambitious usurer, Sir Giles Overreach, who plays
a fiendish form of Galsworthy's " Skin-game," and is
finally overthrown and goes mad, has always attracted
actors by its opportunities for passionate display.   In
Kean's hands the effect was electrical.   Scream after
scream rang through the house otherwise awed into
stillness.   Hysterical women had to be removed.   Lord
Byron, who was present, was seized with a sort of con-
vulsive fit.   If J. C. Hawkins is to be trusted, one of
the actresses in the play fainted on the stage ; another
staggered to a chair and wept aloud ; and the actor
Munden was so transfixed with terror that he had to be
taken off by the armpits, and when once behind the
scenes exclaimed, " My God, is it possible ? "   Again,
as after *The Merchant of Venice,* Kean rushed home to
Mary, who cried, " Well, Edmund, and what did Lord
Essex say ? "

"Damn Lord Essex, the pit rose at me."

Bolder, but less successful, was Kean's revival on
April 24, 1818, of Marlowe's *Jew of Malta.*   The part
of Barrabas, the Jew of Malta, naturally attracted the
actor who in Shylock, the Jew of Venice, had achieved
fame in a night.   It was easy to pass from " My daughter
and my ducats " in *The Merchant of Venice* to " O girl,
O gold," in *The Jew of Malta,* which, we are told,

Kean uttered with "an absolute delirium of drunken joy." Changes were, however, made in Marlowe's tragedy: "The heaviness of the fourth act was finely relieved by a song warbled by the tragedian in the disguise of a harper. It was executed *à merveille* and produced a powerful effect." Even with such an incongruous addition Kean must have the credit of paying a tribute to Marlowe by reviving after a century and a half of theatrical neglect one of his plays. It was not till near the end of the nineteenth century that another and greater play, *Doctor Faustus*, was staged by William Poel.

As Kean was led from *The Merchant of Venice* to *The Jew of Malta* so he had been led from the part of the Moor in *Othello* to that of another Moor, Zanga, in the now almost forgotten play of *The Revenge* by Edward Young. It was the main piece in the performance on his second benefit night, May 24, 1815. But of greater interest was his appearance on the same night as Abel Drugger in *The Tobacconist*, an adaptation of Ben Jonson's comic masterpiece, *The Alchemist*. Drugger is a young tobacconist, who hopes to prosper in business by getting mystic hints from the pseudo-alchemist, Subtle. It is a minor part, but it is associated with great names. David Garrick had acted it, and his widow did not approve of Kean appearing in it. She wrote to him, "Dear Sir, you can't play Abel Drugger, yours, Eva Garrick"; and with unusual modesty Kean replied, "Dear Madam, I know it, yours, Edmund Kean". Those who saw Mr. (now Sir) Cedric Hardwicke in the part of Drugger at the Malvern Theatrical Festival in August, 1932, will know what opportunities

this comparatively minor part in *The Alchemist* offers
to an actor who can take advantage of them. But Kean
was much better fitted in another part which was powerfully acted by Mr. Ralph Richardson at the same festival.
This was Oroonoko, the enslaved African prince in the
heroic late seventeenth-century tragedy of that name,
by Thomas Southerne, based on a novel of Mrs. Aphra
Behn. Oroonoko, lured treacherously to captivity in
Surinam, where he helps the planters to beat off an attack
by Indians, finds himself reunited to his white bride
Imoinda who had been brought by evil fortune before
him to the same fate. The Lieutenant-Governor seeks
to force her to his love, though she has been bought
for the household of the Lord-Governor, who is soon
expected from England. The planters listen with
amazement while Oroonoko cries to Imoinda:

> Take, take me all: inquire into my heart,
> (You know the way to every secret there)
> My heart the sacred treasury of love:
> And if, in absence, I have misemploy'd
> A mite from the rich store: if I have spent
> A wish, a sigh, but what I sent to you;
> May I be curs'd to wish, and sigh in vain,
> And you not pity me.

The fear of the fate that may be in store for Imoinda
and their unborn child leads Oroonoko against his better
judgement to plan a rising to free his fellow-slaves.
Again he is the victim of treachery, and Imoinda to
save them from the planters' vengeance begs him to
kill them both. But his love for her at the last moment
stays his hand, and she has to stab herself and die in

his arms. He then follows her example, but first kills the Lieutenant-Governor :

> 'Tis as it should be now. I've sent his ghost
> To be a witness of that happiness
> In the next world which he deny'd us here.

Kean's affecting portrayal of the conflict of emotions in this " noble savage," when *Oroonoko* was produced at Drury Lane on January 10, 1817, appealed strongly to the critics, though the play had a short run.

But after the triumph of *A New Way to Pay old Debts* Kean's most outstanding success was in a contemporary play. On May 9, 1816, he appeared in the name part of *Bertram*, a tragedy by a Dublin curate, Charles Robert Maturin. It had been recommended by Scott to Byron, at whose instigation it was produced at Drury Lane, and to whom its melancholy and misanthropy must have appealed. It may well have had a peculiar attraction for Kean because Bertram reproduces in a more tragic form that role of Octavian in *The Mountaineers* which had been a favourite in his repertory since 1805, and in which Arnold had seen him on the fateful evening at Dorchester on November 15, 1813. But *The Mountaineers* was a farrago of melodrama and comedy ; *Bertram* is steeped throughout in the gloom and mystery of Kotzebrue's German drama and of the Gothic romances of Horace Walpole and Monk Lewis.

The scene is laid in Sicily. Count Bertram has in youth loved and been loved by Imogine. But St. Aldobrand, a rival suitor and a favourite at Court, had procured his exile and had forced Imogine into a hated

marriage with himself. Bertram becomes a social out-
law and a pirate chief. The play opens in a night of
hurricane, when his vessel is wrecked on the rocky coast
near St. Aldobrand's castle, and the neighbouring Gothic
Convent, where the monks give him shelter after his
rescue from the waves. But to the questions of the
Prior Bertram gives curt, evasive answers :

> *Prior.* Tell us thy name. *Bertram.* A man of woe.
> *Prior.* Look not so wild—can we do aught for thee ?
> *Bertram.* Yes, plunge me in the waves from which you
> snatched me.
> *Prior.* I'll question not with him—his brain is wrecked.
>
> *   *   *
>
> Food and rest will restore him—lead him in.
> *Bertram (dashing off the monks).*   Off—ye are men
> —there's poison in your touch.   (*Sinking back.*)
> But I must yield, for this has left me strengthless.

It was the custom of St. Aldobrand to give shelter in
his castle for certain days to all shipwrecked mariners.
Though he is absent with St. Anselm's knights at
Palermo his wife maintains the custom, and thus Bertram
finds himself at moonlight in the home of his arch-foe
and in presence of Imogine, from whose lips he learns
that she is Aldobrand's wife. His last link with humanity
is snapped :

> In want, in war, in peril,
> Things that would thrill the hearer's blood to tell of,
> My heart grew human when I thought of thee—
> Imogine would have bound my leechless wounds—
> Imogine would have sought my nameless corse,
> And known it well—and she was wedded—wedded.
> Was there no name in hell's dark catalogue

113

To brand thee with, but my mortal foe's ?
And did I 'scape from war and want and famine
To perish by the falsehood of a woman ?

(*He curses her and turns to go.*)

Imo. Stay. *Ber.* No. *Imo.* Thou hast a dagger.
Ber. Not for woman.
Imo. It was my prayer to die in Bertram's presence,
But not by wounds like these. (*Falls down.*)
Ber. (*turning back*). On the cold earth !
I do forgive thee from my inmost soul.

Bertram wins Imogine to a guilty love, of which the
reaction is despairing remorse. In her passionate appeal
to her confidante, Clotilda, there are a haunting rhythm
and a sombre imagery that show Maturin's verse at its
highest :

Imo. O hang me shuddering on the baseless crag—
    The vampire's wing, the wild-worm's sting be on me,
    But hide me, mountains, from the man I've injured.
Clot. Whom hast thou injured ?
Imo. Whom doth woman injure ?
    Another daughter dries a father's tears,
    Another sister claims a brother's love,
    An injured husband hath no other wife,
    Save her who wrought him shame.

In vain she seeks to save St. Aldobrand on his return from
the sword of her lover. Then crazed with horror she
flies with her child to the woods where once again she
comes face to face with Bertram, who is being led in
chains by knights and monks to his doom. He catches

her in his arms as she sinks to death, and cries to his custodians :

I loved her, yea, I love, in death I loved her—
I killed her—but I loved her—
What arm shall loose the grasp of love and death.

Then snatching one of the Knights' swords he cries :

Bertram hath but one fatal foe on earth
And *he is here*

and falls dead upon the blade.

The psychology of the play is weak. Bertram's constant passion is regarded as redeeming his crimes. But its sombre lyric quality gives its author still a place in the notable line of Anglo-Irish playwrights, and the intensity of its passion made it peculiarly suitable for the display of Kean's genius.

Another much inferior contemporary play in which, however, Kean scored a considerable success, was *Brutus* or *The Fall of Tarquin* by J. H. Payne, the American author of *Home, Sweet Home.* It was largely concocted from plays by earlier dramatists, but when it was produced on December 3, 1818, it had a run of thirty-nine consecutive performances.

Very different was the fate on February 15, 1819, of *Switzerland*, a play by Jane Porter, author of *The Scottish Chiefs.* Kean had not been in favour of producing it—it was a poor piece—and he killed it by transforming himself " into an almost motionless automaton, while the audience cried, ' Shame, Kean ! ' "

One cannot help speculating on what he might have made in that year, 1819, of the Count's part in *The Cenci*, had the manuscript come into his hands before publication, and had it been possible during the Regency to produce a play with such a plot, though Shelley appears to have had Eliza O'Neill of Covent Garden in view for the role of Beatrice.   But in that year an equally great poetic name came nearer to being linked with that of Kean, though his biographers seem to have overlooked this. When Keats wrote his tragedy, *Otho the Great*, at Shanklin in the summer of 1819, he designed the part of the hero, Ludolph, for Kean.   He wrote to his brother George in September : " Mine, I am sure, is a tolerable tragedy ; it would have been a bank to me, if, just as I had finished it, I had not heard of Kean's resolution to go to America.   That was the worst news I could have had.   There is no actor can do the principal character besides Kean."   And though he wrote to a friend in December, " 'Twould do one's heart good to see Macready in the part," yet in the same month he assured his sister :

It is accepted at Drury Lane with a promise of bringing it out in the next season ; as that will be too long a delay we have determined to get Elliston to bring it out this season or transfer it to Covent Garden.   This Elliston will not like, as we have every motive to believe that Kean has perceived how suitable the principal character will be for him.   My hopes of success in the literary world are now better than ever.

But Keats was too sanguine.   *Otho the Great* never appeared at Drury Lane, or elsewhere.

With the departure of Kean to America on October 7, 1820, the creative period of his career, covering fifteen years, from his first appearance as Octavian in

February, 1805, may be said to end. The last dozen years of his life, though they are of interest to his biographer, added but little to his range or reputation as an artist. In New York, Philadelphia, Baltimore and Boston he appeared in the chief plays of his repertory, and though he had to contend with the established popularity of Thomas Cooper, an American actor of the classic Kemble School, he achieved widespread success, till an incident at Boston, on May 25, 1821, turned popular feeling against him. There was so thin a house, owing to the lateness of the season, for his *Richard III* that he refused to play and left Boston next morning. On July 23, after recrossing the Atlantic, he consoled himself for the insult to one of his favourite parts, by making his reappearance in it before an enthusiastic Drury Lane audience. But in the following year he had most unwillingly to tolerate a rival in the Drury Lane company, C. M. Young, whom Elliston, now manager at Drury Lane, had acquired from Covent Garden, and of whose competition with Kean as Othello, Darley's account has already been quoted.

Yet as in the West Country in 1808 Kean's real danger, and now in sordid form, was not from a man but from a woman. From 1820 or earlier he had carried on an intrigue with Charlotte Cox, wife of a banker, whose acquaintance he had first made in Dorchester or Taunton. Cox had played a contemptible part in the affair, and Kean seems to have been genuinely astonished when he brought an action against him early in 1825 and secured £800 damages. In the face of furious popular indignation, fanned by *The Times*, Kean, a week afterwards, on January 24, 1825, appeared as Richard III, which was performed almost in dumb show amidst a pandemonium. *Othello* followed on the 28th to a similar accompaniment, and after the fall of the curtain Kean reappeared with the challenging words, " I stand before you, ladies and gentlemen, as the representative of Shakespeare's heroes, and by the public voice I must stand or fall."

Eight years were to follow, with successful episodes, but, in the main of declining powers—including a second visit to America, now extended to Canada ; a season, May and June, 1828, in Paris ; engagements in the provinces and in London, not only at Drury Lane but at the Coburg, the Haymarket, and Covent Garden. It was there on March 25, 1833, that his performance of *Othello* was arrested by a more implacable adversary than the howling mob at Drury Lane eight years ago. With words of the Moor broken on his lips he threw his arms round his son Charles, the Iago, and whispered, " I am dying, speak to them, for me." Seven weeks later, on May 15, he lay dead at Richmond.

" Speak to them, for me." If we may give those words a wider interpretation, how are we a century after his death, to speak for and of Kean ? Let us remember first his other words : " I stand before you as the representative of Shakespeare's heroes." He was addressing an audience to whom not the play, but the " hero," and the actor impersonating him, was " the thing." Since the time of Garrick theatregoers, especially in the matter of tragedy, were less concerned with the merits of the piece, new or old, than with the comparison of one star actor or actress with another in the chief roles. This was the atmosphere in which Kean was bred, and in which from first to last he was at home. I have not found in his letters a word of critical opinion about the merits of any play in which he appeared. The investigations of our own day into the textual transmission of Shakespearian tragedies or into the problems of Elizabethan staging would have left him cold. Indeed, Shakespeare and Massinger, Otway and Home, Colman and Maturin were, in one sense, the same to him so long as they provided heroes whom he could impersonate.

The worst effect of this was seen in Kean's inability to show anything of "team" spirit. His words in a letter to Elliston on October 13, 1822, are significant. "The throne is mine and I will maintain it . . . even if I sail to another quarter of the globe. No man in this profession can rob me of the character of the first English actor." As Othello he deliberately played J. B. Booth's Iago off the stage. He took in bad part the association with Young. And what is even more striking he never acted for any length of time with a leading lady of the highest class.

On the other hand, his intense concentration upon roles which gave the fullest scope to his powers as an actor has given him almost a legendary pre-eminence in the annals of the modern theatre. Though he did so much to standardize the "star" system, otherwise, as Raymond had protested before his appearance as Shylock at Drury Lane on January 26, 1814, he was an innovator. On that night he broke the domination of the classical school of acting, and became the forerunner of a long line of romantic tragedians, including Macready and Phelps, Irving and Martin Harvey.

And it is not a mere coincidence that the years in which Kean was creating his chief heroic roles were those in which England was engaged in a life-and-death struggle with Napoleon. Sir Frank Benson in his centenary address at Drury Lane made this a cardinal point :

Kean's work came at a very critical moment in England's history, and somehow or other, with that wonderful art of the actor, he seemed to represent all the might and the courage and the determination of our land in those days when he was acting on the stage ; singing the songs of our race to the accompaniment of the great deeds of a mighty people.

The last words would be equally applicable to Wordsworth's contemporary *National Poems Dedicated to Independence and Liberty.*

Dame Madge Kendal at the Drury Lane commemoration formed, through her father, as has been already said, a personal link with Kean. She was present also when later in the centenary year I spoke on Kean to the Royal Society of Literature. And on this occasion the *Morning Post,* the only surviving paper that sent its dramatic critic to Kean's first London performance of Shylock, was represented by the present holder of that office, Mr. S. R. Littlewood. And it so happened that Mrs. Thomas Hardy had come up direct from Dorchester where Kean's future fate had been virtually decided when he was seen there by the Drury Lane manager in the part of Octavian on November 15, 1813. And to complete these links with the actor's own days Sir Arthur Pinero, who had always been deeply interested in Kean's career,[1] sent me the following note :

Irving once asked Mrs. Brown, who lived with the Baroness Burdett-Coutts as companion for many years, and who had been an ardent playgoer in her younger days, to tell him what she thought of Kean as an actor. " He had moments of passion and intensity," said the old lady, " that almost lifted you out of your seat." " And for the rest of the time ? " asked Irving. " For the rest of the time," was the reply, " he was like a stroller in a booth." I had this from Irving himself.

Mrs. Brown's memories were probably of Kean in his later days, though even in 1813 a friendly Guernsey critic, as has been seen, noted in him " occasional fits of languor and negligence." Yet at his zenith, there is overflowing testimony that he had more than " moments " of passion and intensity. The two words are, however, significant. Kean had passion and intensity in more overwhelming measure than any English actor since the days of Richard Burbage and Edward Alleyn. He had within him a demonic energy that triumphed over physical limitations, an elemental quality that found its fit interpreter in the kindred romantic genuis of a Hazlitt and a Coleridge. And as we look back on his career, with its kaleidoscopic vicissitudes of triumph and disaster, we may apply to him the lines written in an earlier day, and with another purpose :

> A fiery soul which, working out its way,
> Fretted the pigmy body to decay :
> And o'er-informed the tenement of clay.

[1] See below, p. 270.

VI

ROBERT BROWNING'S *PARACELSUS*, 1835–1935

IT was a happy though probably undesigned coincidence that the publication of Mr. T. J. Wise's collection of *Letters of Robert Browning* in 1933 coincided with the centenary of the appearance of his first slender volume *Pauline*. Some of the most interesting passages in the *Letters* refer to that early work, which we now know to have been an attempt by the youthful poet, aged twenty, at something in the nature of a spiritual autobiography. It was the anonymous venture of one quite unknown to fame. It is, therefore, not surprising, as Browning a half-century later wrote to Mr. Wise on July 6, 1886, that " no single copy of the original edition of *Pauline* found a buyer : the book was undoubtedly stillborn—and that despite the kindly offices of many friends who did their best to bring about a successful birth." One of these friends was probably John Forster, to whom Browning presented an inscribed copy of the poem on October 30, 1833. In this copy, now preserved at South Kensington, John Stuart Mill pencilled a number of comments, of which the most important are reproduced by Mr. Thurman L. Hood in his valuable notes to the Letters. Mill had intended to make these comments the basis of an article in *Tait's Magazine*, but found that he had been forestalled by a flippant line in this Review, where it was called " a piece of pure bewilderment." This was unfortunate for Browning. Though Mill had jotted down some caustic criticisms he had also written : "A cento of most beautiful passages might be made from this poem—and the psychological history of himself is powerful and truthful, *truthlike* certainly all but the last stage." Another friend to whom the young poet presented a copy of *Pauline* was the Rev. W. Johnson Fox, who wrote an appreciative review of it in the *Monthly Magazine*, Vol. VII, 1833. An anonymous critic in the *Athenæum*, April 6, 1833, wrote : " There is not a little true poetry in this very little book," and spoke of its defects as " a grain of sand in a cup of pure water." As late as June 13, 1876, Browning writing to Norman MacColl declared that this notice " gratified me and my people far beyond what will ever be the fortune of criticism now." Even at that date he did not know that his discerning critic was Allan Cunningham. But these few voices did not carry far, and it was not till 1850 that Dante Gabriel Rossetti coming upon *Pauline* in the British Museum was so carried away that he " copied the whole of it from its not being otherwise procurable." Rossetti also (as Browning relates in a letter to William Sharp) wrote to him in Florence to make sure if the poem were by him.

Browning himself appears to have retained only two copies of the original edition of *Pauline*, which were stowed away upstairs in an old leather trunk that had once belonged to his father. When he unearthed these early in 1886, in the presence of Mr. Wise and F. J. Furnivall, he presented one to James Dykes Campbell to complete his Browning collection and the other he kept for his son. Thus, when Mr. Wise, on March 10, 1886, made an offer for one of the copies he was too late, and he had to spend nearly two years in hunting for another, for which, as Browning wrote to him on January 31, 1888, he had to give " above two-thirds of the price paid for printing the whole edition fifty-five years ago." Meanwhile in 1886 Mr. Wise had produced for the members of the Browning Society a type-facsimile reprint, to the number of four hundred copies, of the original edition of *Pauline*.

One is tempted to repeat the classical tag, *ex pede Herculem*. The fate of *Pauline* in the half-century after its publication is, broadly speaking, typical, as allusions in the *Letters* show, of the fortunes of Browning's poetry as a whole during the same period. There is something almost pathetic in the expressions of gratitude by so lofty and independent a spirit to the few, personal friends or strangers, who in the earlier years showed their appreciation and understanding of his work. Among them are Richard Hengist Horne, himself " an unappreciated man," who wrote a generous article on Browning in the *Church of England Quarterly*, October, 1842; the Rev. Archer Thompson Gurney, who on March 10, 1846, is saluted as " my very kindest of critics "; and Edward Dowden, the second part of whose article on *Sordello* for *Fraser's Magazine* in the autumn of 1867 was rejected by J. A. Froude on the ground that " a poem which required an explanation is no poem at all." But by this time Browning had begun to get a hold on the younger intelligentsia. There is a significant passage in a letter to Isabella Blagden, August 19, 1865 :

There were always a few people who had a certain opinion of my poems, but nobody cared to speak what he thought, or the things printed twenty-five years ago would not have waited so long for a good word—but at last a new set of men arrive who don't mind the conventionalities of ignoring one and seeing everything in another : Chapman says, " The orders come from Oxford and Cambridge," and all my new cultivators are young men : more than that, I observe that some of my old friends don't like at all the irruption of *outsiders* who rescue me from their sober and private approval and take those words out of their mouths " which they always meant to say," and never *did*. When there gets to be a general feeling of this kind, that there must be *something* in the works of an author, the reviewers are obliged to notice him, such notice as it is. . . . As I began, so I shall end, taking my own course, pleasing myself or aiming at doing so, and thereby, I hope, pleasing God.

This academic approval of his work was officially recognized by the conferring on him in June, 1867, of the rare distinction of an Oxford M.A. by diploma. This was followed by his election to an honorary Fellowship at Balliol, and by the abortive movement, of which he gives an account to Miss Blagden, to make him the successor to Matthew Arnold in the Oxford Chair of Poetry.

For a wider recognition of his genius the poet had to wait till the founding of The Browning Society by F. J. Furnivall in 1881. Browning's letters to Furnivall and to other correspondents on the subject of the Society are in a vein of manly and dignified common sense. Thus on November 12, 1881, he writes to Miss E. Dickinson West (afterwards Mrs. Dowden) :

I will tell you how I feel about the Society. It was instituted without my knowledge, and when knowledge was, I do not think acquiescence had need of being asked for. I write poems that they may be read, and—fifty years now—people said they were unintelligible. If other people, in the fulness of days, reply " We understand them and will show that you may, if you will be at the pains," I should think it ungracious indeed to open my mouth for the first time on the matter with " Pray let the other people alone in their protested ignorance."

And somewhat more pungently to Edmund Yates, the editor of *The World* which had poked some fun at the Society :

The Browning Society, I need not say, as well as Browning himself, are fair game for criticism. I had no more to do with the founding of it than the babe unborn ; and, as Wilkes was no Wilkeite, I am quite other than a Browningite. But I cannot wish harm to a society of, with a few exceptions, names unknown to me, who are busied about my books so disinterestedly. The exaggerations probably come of the fifty-years'-long charge of unintelligibility against my books : such reactions are possible, though I never looked for the beginning of one so soon.

Oxford had its own Browning Society, or it may have been a branch of the parent body in London. I remember as a Balliol undergraduate in the eighteen-eighties being taken to a meeting of the Society in St. John's

College, where among those present were W. L. Courtney, then a New College don, and Rhoda Broughton, the novelist. The propagandist activities of Furnivall and his friends ; the publication of such studies in Browning's poetry as those of J. T. Nettleship, Arthur Symons, R. H. Hutton, Augustine Birrell, J. K. Fotheringham, and W. G. Kingsland, as well as the earlier papers of the Society during its dozen years of existence ; the success of the two admirably chosen volumes of selections from his shorter poems (1872 and 1880) ; and the revelation of his genius on a titanic scale in *The Ring and the Book*—all conspired to win for him in the closing phase of his career the recognition that had so long been denied. The crowning evidence of this was his burial, amid signs of national homage, in the Poets' Corner in Westminster Abbey on the last day of 1889.

Within the two following decades, from different angles and with varying methods of record or interpretation, a number of critics and chroniclers helped to consolidate Browning's poetic reputation. Edward Berdoe, Mrs. Orr, Stopford Brooke, G. K. Chesterton, Edmund Gosse, Henry James, William Sharp, W. Hall Griffin, Hugh Walker, F. G. Kenyon—the list might easily be extended. How far, by another turn of the wheel, his fame and influence have suffered a set-back owing to post-war iconoclasm is not easy to determine. The attitude of Mr. J. C. Powys, as revealed in his *Autobiography*, cannot be taken as typical. " Browning remains in fact the one single *great* author for whom I cherish a venomous and malignant hostility. My feeling is personal, *physical*. It is his virility that I find so objectionable." In any case it is questionable if the range of his poetic appeal to the present generation has been widened by the strange freak of fortune which has made his personality as the lover of Elizabeth Barrett familiar throughout two continents in the stage and screen versions of a triumphantly successful play. [1]

It may, therefore, be not amiss a century after its publication to reconsider the earliest of Browning's major works. The dedicatory inscription in *Paracelsus* is dated March 15, 1835. It thus followed *Pauline* after an interval of little more than a year and a half. Undeterred by the chilly reception of his first effort he made no attempt in this far more ambitious venture to conciliate the reading public of his day. Its subject and method were equally remote from the conventions of the period.

The central figure, Paracelsus, was unknown to the majority of Englishmen, or, if known at all, merely as a fantastic necromancer. He was one of the early Renaissance scholars on the Continent round whose personalities a mass of legends had quickly gathered. Albertus Magnus, Agrippa and Trithemius were members of the group, of which Doctor John Faustus and Paracelsus were the most prominent figures. Faustus had the good fortune to be singled out as the mouthpiece of Marlowe's aspirations after the infinite of knowledge, power, and loveliness two centuries before Gœthe gave him world-renown. Paracelsus (as Philippus Aureolus Bombastus ab Hohenheim, born in 1493, was familiarly known) was thus left to become in the popular imagination the typical

[1] See p. 147.

conjurer and practiser of the black art. Ben Jonson in
Volpone and Fletcher in *The Fair Maid of the Inn*, make
allusion to his " long sword," whose wondrous pro-
perties Samuel Butler describes in *Hudibras* :

> Bombastus kept a devil's bird
> Shut in the pummel of his sword ;
> That taught him all the cunning pranks
> Of past and future mountebanks.

Browning had probably obtained a worthier idea of
the wandering scholar from his father, who, we are told,
" was completely versed in mediæval legend, and seemed
to have known Paracelsus, Festus, and even Talmudic
personages personally." But it was a young French
royalist, Amédée de Ripert-Monclar, who first suggested
to Browning that he should make the Renaissance
scholar's career the subject of a poem, and it is to Ripert-
Monclar that the work was inscribed " by his affectionate
friend, R.B." The young poet proceeded to read up
the available authorities on the mystic's life and work,
and spared no pains, as Mr. Thurman Wood reminds
us in his Introduction to the *Letters*, " in collecting
quaint old prints of Paracelsus and fitting them in proper
sequence in his manuscript to represent the alchemist as
he developed, even more Olympian yet even more
strongly marked with the stamp of his time." He
became convinced, as the notes appended to the poem
show, that Paracelsus had been a true reformer of
medical science, who introduced the use of mercury and
laudanum, and whose personality needed re-interpreta-
tion to the world. For this purpose he adopted an
unconventional method which he explained in a signifi-

cant preface unfortunately (as I think) omitted in later editions of the work :

It is an attempt probably more novel than happy to reverse the method usually adopted by writers, whose aim it is to set forth any phenomenon of the mind or the passions by the operation of persons or events ; . . . instead of having recourse to an external machine of incidents to create and evolve the crisis I desire to produce, I have ventured to display somewhat minutely the mood itself in its rise and progress, and have suffered the agency by which it is influenced and determined, to be generally discernible in its effects alone, and subordinate throughout, if not altogether excluded.

Here we have Browning's first and fullest exposition of what was to be his distinctive method. He diffidently proclaims his aspiration to become the special poetic interpreter of the inner life. What brilliant results this method was to produce later is known to every reader of *Men and Women* and *Dramatis Personæ*. Yet the youthful poet had some justification of his mistrust of it for his immediate subject. It is peculiarly adapted to lay bare the secrets of the soul in some momentous crisis, or to flash a searchlight into the subconscious depths of personality. But it is not equally fitted to unfold the stages of a long and eventful career. For this a less subjective mode of interpretation is needed. The absence of an " external machinery of incidents " results at times in vagueness and obscurity.

It is, therefore, not surprising that *Paracelsus* fared little better with the " British public " than *Pauline*. Yet it did not go without appreciation from some discriminating readers. Forster (as Browning reminded

Furnivall on August 29, 1881) first reviewed it in the
Examiner, September 6, 1835, and also wrote a paper
on it in the *New Monthly Magazine*—in the same month
(March, 1836) that another by J. Heraud appeared in
Fraser. It is doubtful whether Forster did his young
friend a service when he declared " without the slightest
hesitation we name Mr. Robert Browning at once with
Shelley, Coleridge and Wordsworth." W. Johnson
Fox followed his already mentioned article on *Pauline*
by one on *Paracelsus* in *The Monthly Repository*,
November, 1835. It was at Johnson Fox's house on
November 27, 1835, that Browning first met the actor,
W. C. Macready, for whom he was to write *Strafford*,
produced at Covent Garden on May 1, 1837. Soon
after their first meeting Macready notes in his *Diary*,
November 27, 1835 : " Read *Paracelsus*, a work of
great daring, starred with poetry of thought, feeling,
and diction, but occasionally obscure ; the writer can
scarcely fail to be a leading spirit of his time." How
far, after the lapse of a century, can we endorse
Macready's judgement and recognize him as a true
prophet ?

As a preliminary to an attempted answer, it may be
useful to recall the outlines of the work. It is divided
into five parts dealing with widely separated episodes in
the life of Paracelsus. In Part I (1512) he is leaving
Würzburg, where he has sat at the feet of Trithemius
and is discussing his future plans with his friends Festus
and Michal, his young wife. His aspiration is " to
know," and he asserts that Truth is to be found not by
a slow inductive process but by a mystic liberation of
the inner light of the intellect from its fleshly trammels.

Festus energetically combats this doctrine and both he and Michal protest yet more earnestly against their friend's further declaration that he aims at knowledge only and that he abjures the claims of human love. In Part II (1521), after nine years of wandering, Paracelsus is found at Constantinople confessing the failure of his aims. His chance meeting with the poet, Aprile, who has likewise failed, through neglecting knowledge and pursuing love only, convinces him that the union of both is necessary for true attainment. In Part III (1526) he is a renowned Professor at Basil. But, as he confesses to Festus, who visits the University, he is still dissatisfied with his achievements viewed in the light of his early hopes. In Part IV (1528), in an interview with Festus at Colmar in Alsatia, he recounts the incidents that have led to his expulsion from his Chair. He attempts to mask his degradation by forced and reckless hilarity. In Part V (1541), a dozen years afterwards, he is dying in a cell in the hospital of St. Sebastian at Salzburg. Festus is again at his side, and to him in a last rally of his intellectual power he delivers his final judgement on life.

We thus gain an insight into the mind and temper of Paracelsus at successive crises. But the intervals are left in almost total shadow. Thus the confessions of Paracelsus throw a very nebulous light on the highly important period between Parts I and II, during which his confident hopes are so disastrously foiled. Similarly we learn next to nothing about the events of the fateful years between Parts IV and V which transform the reckless despondent exile from Basil into the sage whose mellow wisdom searches into the very depths of things.

The title which has been suggested, " The Epic of the Healer," is thus far from happy, for the epic elements of action and incident are almost entirely lacking. Nor can *Paracelsus*, though it introduces four " persons " and is cast in dialogue form, claim to be a drama. It has, indeed, as I seek to show later, more interest as a study of contrasted characters than appears at first sight. And here and there we have the swift, arresting verbal interchange which is the playwright's distinctive instrument. But at no time was Browning, in spite of his dramatic powers, to master the secret of dramatic technique. The series of long monologues in *Paracelsus* indicates what was to be a permanent weakness in his craftsmanship as a writer of plays.

What, then, are the qualities of this early hybrid work of the young poet which give it lasting fascination ? In the first place its sheer metrical beauty. It is doubtful whether even in the speeches of Caponsacchi and Pompilia in *The Ring and the Book* Browning ever again drew from blank verse such lovely music as in the finest passages of *Paracelsus*. The rhythm retains the sweetness of its predecessor *Pauline*, but it has gained immeasurably in freedom, elasticity, and fulness of melody. The secret of its charm, so far as it is at all analysable, lies in the skilful variations of the cæsura, in the introduction at intervals of lines with double-endings, in a delicate adjustment of the vowel-sounds, and a masterly use of alliteration. Matching the beauty of the verse and subtly interwoven with it is the beauty of the imagery. A striking feature of recent literary scholarship led by Professor Caroline Spurgeon has been the investigation of the imagery of Shakespeare and other Elizabethans.

133

In any similar investigation of Victorian poetry *Para-celsus* ought to take a leading place. The " fundamental brainwork " does not in it, as often in Browning's later poems, stand out bare and gaunt, but is swathed in fold after fold of lovely drapery. Whenever the discussion threatens to become too abstract, some apt simile or glowing analogy sheds warmth and colour over the dialogue. Thus when Paracelsus asserts in Part V that he will never accept from men their " officious praise " for his services, he compares himself to a knight who chances to free a desert people from their dragon foe ; and who, when the swarthy race would fain choose him for their king, points to the East whither his steps are bound. Or take the pregnant symbol with which Paracelsus heartens his friends when he is starting on his lonely quest :

> Are there not, Festus, are there not, dear Michal,
> Two points in the adventure of the diver—
> One, when a beggar, he prepares to plunge,
> One, when a prince, he rises with his pearl ?
> Festus, I plunge !

Or take again, in contrast, the vivid mythological simili-tudes to the sage's defeated hopes in Part V :

> We get so near—so very, very near !
> 'Tis an old tale : Jove strikes the Titans down,
> Not when they set about their mountain-piling
> But when another rock would crown the work.
> And Phaeton—doubtless his first radiant plunge—
> Astonished mortals, though the gods were calm,
> And Jove prepared his thunder : all old tales !

We think of Browning as an interpreter of men and

women rather than of nature. Yet in *Paracelsus* are
to be found some of the most original nature-similes and
analogies in modern poetry. Thus Aureole, as his
friends lovingly address him, justifies to them his confidence in the instinct that impels him upon his mission
by the proud appeal :

> Ask the geier-eagle why she stoops at once
> Into the vast and unexplored abyss ;
> What full-grown power informs her from the first.
> Why she not marvels, strenuously beating
> The silent boundless regions of the sky !

And was Wordsworth ever more tenderly inspired by the
" meanest flower " to thoughts too deep for tears than is
Browning in the lines where men's faint aspirings and
dim struggles for truth, " upward tending all, though
weak," are likened to

> Plants in mines which never saw the sun,
> But dream of him and guess where he may be,
> And do their best to climb and get to him ?

Almost Miltonic, on the other hand, in its colossal sweep
is the simile wherein the dying sage mirrors the lesson
of Aprile's fate and his own :

> Let men
> Regard me, and the poet dead long ago
> Who loved too rashly ; and shape forth a third
> And better-tempered spirit, warned by both :
> As from the over-radiant star too mad
> To drink the life-springs, beamless thence itself—
> And the dark orb which borders the abyss,
> Ingulfed in icy night—might have its course
> A temperate and equidistant world.

Thus by way of this simile we may pass from the versification and imagery of the poem to its " persons " and its criticism of life. Of the " perfect pair—each born for the other," Festus and Michal, the latter appears only in Part I and her words are few. She believes in Aureole as " God's commissary," but her woman's instinct warns her of ill fate in store, " You will find all you seek and perish so." Years afterwards in Basil Paracelsus cherishes the image of her face that

> Still wears that quiet and peculiar light
> Like the dim circlet floating round a pearl.

She is but a miniature yet not unworthy of the hand that was hereafter to draw Colombe and Pompilia.

It requires careful study of the poem to appreciate to the full the part played by Festus [1] as a foil to Paracelsus. He is the limited but loyal-hearted average man, reverencing profoundly his friend's genius, but mistrustful of his far-reaching, unconventional aims, till his doubts are overborne by the latter's eloquence and self-confidence. His naïvely expressed awe in Part III of " the wondrous Paracelsus, the idol of the schools and courts " ; and his inability to realize that a professorship at Basil and a crowded class-room can possibly spell failure—these are pungent strokes of self-revelation. But this commonplace student, *borné* and almost poor-spirited in his humility, gains a strange dignity in the final scene where he watches alone at the couch of his dying

---

[1] It was, however, unfortunate that Browning chose this name for the friend of Paracelsus. It is a variant of Faustus, but there is no relation between Browning's figure and Dr. John Faustus.

friend, and retains unshaken his conviction of his greatness :

> I am for noble Aureole, God !
> I am upon his side, come weal or woe.
> His portion shall be mine. He has done well.
> I would have sinned, had I been strong enough,
> As he has sinned. Reward him or I waive
> Reward.

I doubt if in 1835 Browning had read Marlowe's *Doctor Faustus*, less accessible then than now ; but Festus is akin to the students in that play who do not waver in their affectionate loyalty to the Wittenberg doctor even when the hour approaches of his awful doom.

In Aprile, whom Paracelsus encounters by chance in Constantinople, he finds a more subtle and illuminating contrast to himself. Mrs. Orr relates that after Count de Ripert-Monclar had suggested to Browning, as has been seen, the theme of his poem, he " on second thoughts pronounced it unsuitable because it gave no room for the introduction of love." Was it in part to meet this objection that the poet created Aprile, whose sole aim is " to love infinitely and be loved " ? The love that he embodies is not, however, amorous passion. It is the artistic impulse in its fullest form, seeking to realize itself progressively through the chisel, the pencil, the spoken word, and music—but doomed to impotence because divorced from the knowledge which alone can translate impulse into achievement. Aprile, the first of Browning's " lost leaders," is the type of those over-sensitive natures that abandoning productive effort are content with a dreamy emotional languor—æsthetic voluptuaries denying their fellow-men " one ray " of their " so hoarded luxury of light." It had been Aprile's ambition to interpret to others all the loveliness of the universe, but he had disdained the requisite methods. He had

> Grown mad to grasp
> At once the prize long patient toil should claim.

He had spurned " the tools so rude " to execute his purpose ; he had rebelled against the limitations that are as necessary to artistic as to moral achievement. Seduced into prostrate adoration by the siren forms of beauty thronging through the chambers of his brain he had become not their master but their slave. It is a subtle refutation of the idea, probably more widely held in 1835 than in 1935, that the poetic life is an indolent sensuous rapture. Aprile had failed to realize till too late that the true artist must be an ascetic, steeling himself against the spells of a myriad beckoning forms of loveliness, and sternly set

> To single out one, though the rest
> Should vanish, and give that one, entire
> In beauty, to the world.

To his fevered vision Paracelsus is the " master, poet, who hast done all this," and he hails him as his lord and king, only to be met with tears and with the confession :

> I too have sought to know as thou to love—
> Excluding love as thou refusedst knowledge.
> Still thou hast beauty and I power . . .
> . . . We must never part.
> Are we not halves of one dissevered world,

Whom this strange chance unites once more ?   Part ?
    never !
Till thou the lover, know ; and I, the knower,
Love—until both are saved.

This will always be one of the classic passages in
Browning's poetry, a proclamation of the essential inter-
dependence of the artistic and the scientific spirit.   But
it must be admitted that it conflicts with the claim that
he makes in the opening words of the Note that he
appended to *Paracelsus*, " the liberties I have taken with
my subject are very trifling."   So far from Paracelsus
ever having excluded love, he writes : " To become like
God we must become attached to God, and the power
that attracts us is love.   Love to God will be kindled in
our hearts by an ardent love for humanity ; and a love
for humanity will be caused by a love to God."

Moreover, the rigid separation of love and knowledge
involves a process of abstraction foreign to the sixteenth
century.   Renaissance thought dealt with life in the
concrete.   It grasped eagerly at new experiences, new
facts in their manifold and rich complexity, but it did
not pursue an isolated ideal of knowledge, sundered
from the other factors of life.   Bacon, it is true, while
taking all knowledge to be his province, scorned love
because it did much mischief, and commended the
saying, " It is impossible to love and be wise."   But
Bacon was alluding to the effects of amorous passion (as
he conceived them) on the serious affairs and actions of
life ; he was not thinking of love as an abstract faculty.
Indeed the distinguishing feature of his philosophy—
the source alike of its strength and its weakness—is its
emotional ardour in what he calls " the love-making or

wooing of truth." Thus Browning's Paracelsus, in his
repudiation of love, as he sets forth on his quest of
knowledge, is no true child of the Renaissance. He
belongs rather to the nineteenth century and embodies
a phase of its scientific spirit. Charles Darwin's famous
confession in his autobiography that in his later years
his mind had been a mere machine for grinding out
facts, and that he had lost all power of enjoying Shakespeare's plays, proves that Browning was curiously
prophetic in his conception of " the wolfish hunger after
knowledge " becoming the tyrannous master-motive of
a life.

It is in Parts III and IV of the poem that we get
nearest to the historical Paracelsus, and catch vivid
glimpses of Renaissance University life. We see the
crowded class in the lecture-room at Basil hanging on
the lips of the new teacher ; and we hear his audacious
denunciation of the traditional authorities in science and
philosophy, Galen, Rhasis, Avicenna, and Averröes, as
blocks. We learn that through his discoveries

> Men in racking pain may purchase dreams
> Of what delights them most, soaring at once
> Into a sea of bliss.

We see the jewel dangling from his neck, his fee for a
cure, the description of which is Browning's first masterpiece of ironical humour. We catch glimpses of the
scholar's shelves supporting " a pile of patents, licenses,
diplomas, titles " from all countries ; and we have report
of the great historical figures, Luther, Erasmus, Œcolampadius, and Frobenius, with whom Paracelsus had relations more or less direct. The story of his expulsion

from his Chair is full of life, and carries us back into the heart of the warfare between the champions of the new learning and the old.

And there is an arresting echo of these academic years in the episode of the dying sage's last lecture in Part V when, with a final rally of his powers, he rises from his couch, and with the help of Festus, arrays himself in gown and chain and grasps his sword, Azoth, in his hand. But in the lecture itself it is again the voice of Browning himself that we hear. It is true that the historical Paracelsus, as Dr. Berdoe has pointed out, spoke of the human body as composed of " primeval stuff," and declared that " matter is, so to say, coagulated vapour, and is connected with spirit by an intermediate principle which it receives from spirit." But it is an immense stride from such cloudy speculation to the articulated scheme of existence which Paracelsus, as the poet's spokesman, proceeds to unfold. He anticipates in some of its fundamental aspects Darwin's theory of evolution. Nearly half a century later, on October 11, 1881, Browning wrote to Furnivall from Venice assuring him that " all that seems proved in Darwin's scheme was a conception familiar to me from the beginning : see in *Paracelsus* the progressive development from senseless matter to organized, until man's appearance." He is referring to the passage which tells how " God tastes an infinite joy in infinite ways " : in the centre-fire heaving underneath the earth ; in the coming up of young volcanoes ; in the spring-time energies of grass and trees, of insects and birds ; in the loves of savage creatures in wood and plain. It is characteristic of the youthful Browning to find the presence of the divine

not in beauty but in vitality and power. Then at last
man appears :

> The consummation of this scheme
> Of being, the completion of this sphere
> Of life : whose attributes had here and there
> Been scattered o'er the visible world before,
> Asking to be combined, dim fragments meant
> To be united in some wondrous whole,
> Imperfect qualities throughout creation,
> Suggesting some one creature yet to make.

Thus man is linked indissolubly with " life's minute
beginnings," and God dwells in all. For from the first
Browning rejected the implication of materialism which
was for so many later to be a stumbling-block in the
acceptance of the evolutionary doctrine. As he wrote
to Furnivall in the letter where he refers him to
Paracelsus, " Go back and back, as you please, at the
back . . . you find . . . creative intelligence, acting as
matter but not resulting from it. Once set the balls
rolling, and ball may hit ball and send any number in
any direction over the table ; but I believe in the cue
pushed by a hand." And Browning further saw with
really prophetic insight that the doctrine of evolution,
rightly interpreted, levels not down but up. With the
appearance of man,

> A supplementary reflux of light
> Illustrates all the inferior grades, explains
> Each step-back in the circle.

Faculties and functions that had been exhibited by
lower organisms in rudimentary form are found perfected in him, and are then realized to have been potenti-

ally human from the first. Even inanimate nature is transformed, personalized, by his arrival :

> Man, once descried, imprints for ever
> His presence on all lifeless things : the winds
> Are henceforth voices, wailing or a shout,
> A querulous mutter or a quick gay laugh,
> Never a senseless gust now man is born.

But the end is not yet. As man is the consummation of one scheme of being, so he is the beginning of another :

> Prognostics told
> Man's near approach ; so in man's self arise
> August anticipations, symbols, types
> Of a dim splendour ever on before
> In that eternal circle life pursues.

Here the poet of 1835 will scarcely find a responsive echo a century later. The idea of man perfecting himself and becoming the herald of what Tennyson was to call in *In Memoriam* " the crowning race," and of an ascending progress as an " eternal circle," has grown faint. For the present our gaze is averted from visions of a future " dim splendour," and we are preoccupied with man as he is—with the manifold and pressing problems of how to preserve the civilization that he has built up through the ages and that is now paradoxically threatened by his own latest achievements. Like Paracelsus himself we stoop

> Into a dark tremendous sea of cloud.

May we echo his confident cry, " I shall emerge one day ! " As he dies in the hospital of St. Sebastian

Festus pronounces his epitaph, " And this was Paracelsus ! " Not indeed, as has been seen, the historical
Renaissance figure but a subtle and vital re-creation by
the youthful poet, not unworthy, in its Victorian way,
to be set beside Marlowe's Elizabethan re-creation of
Doctor Faustus. There could be no higher tribute.

VII

ELIZABETH BARRETT BROWNING : IN HER VERSE AND HER PROSE

THE reputation of Elizabeth Barrett Browning, like that of her husband, has gone through striking vicissitudes, though not in a similar sequence. To him after long neglect and obscurity fame came late and full, though in these last days there has been something of a reaction. To her it came early and in ever-increasing measure till it reached its peak with the publication of *Aurora Leigh* in 1856 and its overwhelming success. Thereupon followed a swift and continuous decline in her poetic fame which has, however, been arrested and is being replaced by a more balanced judgement. And a freak of fortune has lent of late an additional spice to the study of her most intimate verse. For a forged " first edition " of *Sonnets from the Portuguese* has become the " leading case " in the revelation of an almost incredible tale of bibliographical forgery.

During the reaction against Elizabeth's poetic reputation it was, however, becoming evident that, as with Byron, she had a second claim to immortality, as a letter-writer ; and that from her invalid chamber in London there had flowed an astonishing epistolary

stream, which continued after her marriage and throughout her residence in Italy. Her letters to R. H. Horne,
written between 1839 and 1846, were published in two
volumes in 1877. The two volumes of her letters to
various correspondents from 1832 to 1861, edited by
F. G. (now Sir Frederic) Kenyon, followed in 1897.
*The Letters of Robert Browning and Elizabeth Barrett
Barrett*, written during their courtship from January,
1845, to September, 1846, were given to the world by
their son, Robert Wiedeman Browning, in two volumes
in 1899. These three collections were made use of by
Mr. Percy Lubbock in *Elizabeth Barrett Browning in
her Letters* (1906); by Mr. Osbert Burdett in *The
Brownings* (1928); and by Mr. Dormer Creston in
Andromeda in Wimpole Street (1929). Then, thirty
years after the publication of the love-letters, there
appeared a further volume of Elizabeth's letters to her
sister, Henrietta (Mrs. Surtees Cook) edited by Leonard
Huxley. They ranged over 1846–59, all but the last
two years of the Brownings' married life. Then un-
expectedly in April, 1935, twenty-two unpublished
letters of Elizabeth and Robert Browning appeared in
a New York auction sale. They were said to have been
discovered by " a member of Mrs. Browning's family,"
and included thirteen from her pen, between October,
1846, and March, 1857. They were edited in 1936 by
Mr. William Rose Benét.

Even Clarissa did not ply a more constant pen than
Elizabeth. In the New York sale collection there are
two vivid pictures of her epistolary ardour by her husband, writing to her sisters. He speaks on May 6, 1847,
of " those long letters wherein I see her put her very

heart and soul when I watch the little rapid fingers working." And on April 2, 1848

a great letter from Ba [1]; whole sheets overflowing such as I used to see her perpetrating; while I could not find the heart to stop the quick little fingers, or do more than interpose at intervals, with " *Now*, Ba—What did you promise me ? There's your face getting red and redder," and the like ! All to no use ! " Just to the end of this page "—" only a word here—something I forgot and must say "—and so at last the letter was piled up story on story like a Tower of Babel.

Thus for a full understanding of her the letters must be read side by side with the poems. Yet they have recently, at second hand, placed her in a somewhat misleading perspective. Mr. Besier's play, *The Barretts of Wimpole Street* (and its later film version) inevitably took the letters as its basis, and allowing for the difference between biographical and dramatic truth the presentation of the family was in the main justified. But the fact that Elizabeth's father, Edward Moulton Barrett, occupied the centre of the stage, and was so powerfully impersonated, gave a distorted impression to thousands of his eldest daughter. Elizabeth, as revealed in her letters, was a more virile, and, in the highest sense, sagacious personality than was suggested on the stage by the recumbent and for the most part passive figure in the sick-room ; or, it may be added, by her deceptively feminine portraits.

Even in the matter of her familiar maiden name, Elizabeth Barrett Barrett was to show characteristic indepen-

[1] Elizabeth's pet name, used by her family and by Browning.

dence. Her father was originally Edward Barrett Moulton, but he assumed the additional surname of Barrett on succeeding to his grandfather's slave-plantations in Jamaica. It is necessary to bear this in mind if we are to realize the significance of a passage at the close of a letter to Robert Browning, with postmark December 20, 1845.

My true initials are E.B.M.B.—my long name, as opposed to my short one being Elizabeth Barrett Moulton Barrett! —there's a full length to take away one's breath !—Christian name . . . Elizabeth Barrett:—surname, Moulton Barrett. So long it is, that to make it portable I fell into the habit of doubling it up and packing it closely . . . and of forgetting that I was a *Moulton*, altogether. One might as well write the alphabet as all four initials. Yet our family name is *Moulton Barrett*, and my brothers reproach me sometimes for sacrificing the governorship of an old town in Norfolk. . . . Nevertheless it is true that I would give ten towns in Norfolk (if I had them) to own some purer lineage than that of the blood of the slave. Cursed we are from generation to generation.

It was the sense of the family connection with slavery, though this is one of her few direct allusions to it, that quickened her sympathy with all who were oppressed on either side of the Atlantic and found voice in such poems as *The Runaway Slave* and *The Cry of the Children*. There was another, different, way in which she was influenced by her early associations. She was born at Coxhoe Hall, her uncle's home, about five miles from Durham on March 6, 1806. But in 1809 her father bought the estate of Hope End, near Malvern, and here she lived till 1832.

"Do you know," she wrote to R. H. Horne in October, 1843, "the Malvern Hills? The hills of Piers Plowman's Visions? They seem to me my native hills." It was the Malvern neighbourhood that helped to stir in her an interest in Middle English poetry, rare at that time in either sex. Thus she commenced in 1842 a "Survey of the English Poets" with Langland of "Piers Plowman" and the Malvern Hills. When R. H. Horne edited The Poems of Geoffrey Chaucer Modernised in 1841, she contributed Queen Anelida and False Arcite. And in December, 1843, in discussing a metrical principle with H. S. Boyd she asserted that the tenacity of her judgement arose "from the deeper study of the old master-poets—English poets—those of the Elizabeth and James ages, before the corruption of French rhythms stole in with Waller and Denham, and was acclimatized into a national inodorousness by Dryden and Pope."

So she wrote in 1843, but that as a girl she had been for a time moulded by Pope's influence is plain from the title and the versification of an Essay on Mind written when she was seventeen or eighteen, and published when she was twenty in 1826. Though she could later declare that it "was long repented of as worthy of all repentance," and though it is an unduly ambitious, half-philosophical, half-historical, attempt in more than 1,200 lines to interpret the workings of the Mind, it is a remarkable piece of work for an adolescent. The range of reading behind the poem, however superficial this may have been, is surprisingly wide, and the discipline of the couplet was valuable to a poetic aspirant, to whom facility was always to be a temptation.

Are not these lines a clever imitation of Pope in The

Essay on Man, yet with a touch of the young writer's own individuality?

> Thou thing of light! that warm'st the breasts of men,
> Breath'st from the lips, and tremblest from the pen,
> Thou, form'd at once t'astonish, fire, beguile—
> With Bacon reason, and with Shakespeare smile!
> Thou subtle cause, ethereal essence, say,
> Why dust rules dust, and clay surpasses clay:
> Why a like mass of atoms should combine
> To form a Tully, and a Catiline?
> Or why, with flesh perchance of equal weight
> One cheers a prize-fight, and one frees a state.

There was an independent outlook in a girl who could thus characterize the historian of *The Decline and Fall*:

> Let Gibbon's name be trac'd, in sorrow, here—
> Too great to spurn, too little to revere!
> Who followed Reason, yet forgot her laws,
> And found all causes but the "great first cause."
>
> *   *   *   *   *
>
> In vain for us the polish'd periods flow,
> The fancy kindles, and the pages glow;
> When one bright hour, and startling transport past,
> The musing soul must turn—to sigh at last.

And the following lines disprove, as I think, Sir Henry Jones's statement in *The Cambridge History of English Literature*, Vol. XIII (1916), that Elizabeth was "quite unqualified to imitate [Pope's] terse neatness":

> When Horace chats his neighbour's faults away,
> The sportive measures, like his muse, are gay:
> For once Good humour Satire's by-way took,
> And all his soul is laughing in his book!

It was, however, Greek rather than Latin literature that cast its spell on the young student of Hope End. As she wrote later to Horne:

The love of Pope's Homer threw me into Pope on one side and into Greek on the other, and into Latin as a help to Greek ... I ... read Greek as hard under the trees as some of your Oxonians in the Bodleian; gathered visions from Plato and the dramatists and ate and drank Greek and made my head ache with it.

It was Pope's Homer that had stimulated her to write, at the age ·of fourteen, her epic in four books, *The Battle of Marathon*, in which Miltiades, Aristides, and Themistocles take the place of Achilles, Ajax and Hector. Even in this juvenile effort the prose preface is as remarkable as the verse that follows, and through the conventional phrasing we hear the authentic voice of Elizabeth Barrett at any age in the declaration that " The noblest of the productions of man, that which inspires the enthusiasm of virtue, the energy of truth, is Poetry: Poetry elevates the mind to Heaven, kindles within it immortal fires, and bids it throb with feelings exalting to its nature."

Her studies of Greek began in company with her eldest brother, Edward, under a tutor, but they were greatly stimulated by the blind scholar, Hugh Stuart Boyd, a neighbour at this time at Great Malvern, and afterwards one of her chief correspondents. And it was to be a lifelong interest. On March 5, 1842, she writes to him:

I had two volumes of Euripides with me in Devonshire, and have read him as well as Æschylus and Sophocles—that is from them—both before and since I went there. You know I have gone through every line of the three tragedians long ago, in the way of regular consecutive reading. You know also that I had at different times read different dialogues of Plato, but when three years ago . . . I became possessed of a complete edition of his works, edited by Bekker, why then I began with the first volume and went through the whole of his writings, both those I knew and those I did not know, one after another.

It was Boyd's gift of some wine of Cyprus that prompted the poem published in 1844 recalling the golden hours of their Greek reading :

> O, our Æschylus, the thunderous,
>   How he drove the bolted breath
> Through the clouds, to wedge it ponderous
>   In the gnarled oak beneath !
> O, our Sophocles, the royal,
>   Who was born to monarch's place,
> And who made the whole world loyal,
>   Less by kingly power than grace.
>
> Our Euripides, the human,
>   With his dropping of warm tears
> And his touches of things common
>   Till they rose to touch the spheres !
> Our Theocritus, our Bion,
>   And our Pindar's shining goals !—
> These were cup-bearers undying,
>   Of the wine that's meant for souls.

As critical appreciations of Sophocles or Euripides the lines may not entirely pass muster, but they are aflame with a Renaissance passion for the classics. So we could imagine Lady Jane Grey writing to Roger Ascham.

And it was in the same spirit that she attempted a translation of the *Prometheus Bound*, published in 1833, and replaced by a second version in her volume of 1850.

But Elizabeth for all her learning was at no time a blue-stocking. She never took sides with the ancients against the moderns. She read her contemporaries as eagerly as she did the classics. Among her early verses is an elegy on Byron :

> Britannia's Poet ! Graecia's hero, sleeps.

Has there ever been a more finely phrased and conclusive tribute to Wordsworth than in a letter to H. S. Boyd on December 31, 1843 : " The wings of his genius are wide enough to cast a shadow over its feet " ? And so she could declare, " I *will* be a blind admirer of Wordsworth's." But friendship did not delude her into mistaking pinchbeck for the real article. When Miss Mitford's reputation as a writer of poetic drama was at its peak, Elizabeth frankly stated her opinion that " she stands higher as the authoress of *Our Village* than of *Rienzi*, and writes prose better than poetry, and transcends rather in Dutch minuteness and high finishing than in Italian ideality and passion."

But in a letter of December 14, 1832, to her lifelong friend Mrs. Martin, for once she shows less than her usual critical discernment : " Bulwer has quite delighted me. He has all the dramatic talent which Scott has, and all the passion which Scott has not, and he appears to me to be besides a far profounder discriminator of character." But how many women in England at that day, or indeed in ours, could combine a love of Dumas with a whole-hearted devotion to Balzac? As she wrote in 1845 :

Never was a child who cared more for a " story " than I do ; never even did I myself, as a child, care more for it than I do. My love of fiction began with my breath, and will end with it ; and goes on increasing. On my tombstone may be written " *Ci-gît* the greatest novel reader in the world." . . . Are you shocked at me ? Perhaps so. And you see I make no excuses as an invalid might. Invalid or not, I should have a romance in a drawer, if not behind a pillow, and I might as well be true and say so.

This letter reminds us that she was brought up in that evangelical atmosphere to which a romance was shocking and had to be hidden away. There is no more striking scene in *The Barretts of Wimpole Street* than that in which her father after one of his most tyrannical outbursts calls for a Bible and reads aloud a passage in her presence. This is no merely dramatic invention, for Elizabeth writing to Robert Browning on October 11, 1845, emphasizes to him " the significance of the omission of those evening or rather night visits of Papa's —for they came sometimes at eleven, and sometimes at twelve—I will tell you that he used to sit and talk in them, and then *always* kneel and pray with me and for me."

From different angles the young poetess sought to bring into relation her evangelical beliefs and her humanist culture. In *The Seraphim*, the poem that gives its title to the volume of 1838, she sought to give a poetic interpretation to the Crucifixion in the terms of the *Prometheus Vinctus*. There is nothing in the verse

itself as striking as the remarkable sentence in her
Preface in which she explains how she came to write
the poem :

I thought that, had Æschylus lived after the incarnation and
crucifixion of our Lord Jesus Christ, he might have turned,
if not in moral and intellectual yet in poetic faith, from the solitude of Caucasus to the deeper desertness of that crowded
Jerusalem where none had any pity ; from the " faded white
flower " of the Titanic brow, to the withered grass of a
Heart trampled on by its own beloved ; from the glorying
of him who gloried that he could not die, to the sublimer
meekness of the Taster of death for every man ; from the
taunt stung into being by the torment, to His more awful
silence, when the agony stood dumb before the love !

She shows originality in her conception of the two
Seraphs, Ador and Zerah, the mouthpieces of her
" dramatic lyric," as entrusted with the Saviour, whose
agony they watch and describe. " One holiness differs
from another holiness in glory. To recoil from evil,
is according to the stature of an angel ; to subdue it,
is according to the infinitude of a God." But alike the
subject and the Æschylean scheme were beyond the
young writer's powers. There are here and there
striking lines as in Zerah's description of the two cruci-
fied thieves, but the treatment is too diffuse and Elizabeth is less successful with the varied lyrical measures
than with the couplets of *The Essay on Mind.*
" The model of Greek tragedy," as she herself tells
us, was again before her in *The Drama of Exile* which
headed her volume of 1844. Six years had passed since
the composition of *The Seraphim* and her powers had

matured. I, for one, cannot echo the harsh condemnation of Sir Henry Jones in *The Cambridge History of English Literature*, who dismisses it as an " interesting allegory." To begin with, it is not an allegory, a Morality, but a modern Miracle play, introducing Biblical characters, human and superhuman. Lucifer, fallen from heaven, and Adam and Eve, driven from Paradise, are the exiles. The beginning does not promise well, when Lucifer thus addresses his companion fallen angels :

> Rejoice in the clefts of Gehenna
> My exiled, my host !
> Earth has exiles as hopeless as when a
> Heaven's empire was lost.

Such a rollicking measure ill befits the lips of an archangel, though fallen, and to rhyme " Gehenna " with " when a " is not the sort of crime of which he should be guilty. The choruses, with their short lines and their frequent double rhymes, have too jingling an effect, and the work, as a whole, is too long drawn out. But its merits have been insufficiently recognized. The opening blank-verse dialogue between Lucifer and Gabriel is not without dramatic force and striking imagery, as when Lucifer cries :

> And good Gabriel,
> (Ye like that word in heaven, I *too* have strength)
> Strength to behold Him and not worship Him,
> Strength to fall from and not cry on Him,
> Strength to be in the Universe, and yet
> Neither God nor his servant

or when Gabriel answers :

> Through heaven and earth
> God's will moves freely, and I follow it,
> As colour follows light.   He overflows
> The firmamental walls with deity,
> Therefore with love.

And there is tender insight in the picture of Adam, after
the expulsion from Eden, thanking God,

> That rather thou hast cast me out with *her*
> Than left me lone of her in Paradise,
> With angel looks and angel sounds around
> To show the absence of her eyes and voice.

>   *   *   *
>
> *Eve.*   Where is loss ?
> Am I in Eden ?   Can another speak
> Mine own love's tongue ?
> *Adam.*   Because with *her* I stand
> Upright as far as can be in this fall.

In the closing part of the poem the figure of Christ
appears.   In her preface to the 1844 edition of her poems
and in a letter to her relative John Kenyon (March 25,
1843) concerning *The Dead Pan*, which appeared in
the volume, Elizabeth makes an admirable defence of
the introduction of divine figures and names into poetry.
" Did the poets," she asks, " of our best British days
shrink from speaking out Divine names when the
occasion came ?   Chaucer, with all his jubilee of spirit
and resounding laughter, had the name of Jesus Christ
and God as frequently to familiarity on his lips as a
child had his father's name."

But with regard to *The Dead Pan*, justly one of her

most popular poems, the charge to-day would be very
different. It was intended as a reply to Schiller's *Die
Götter Griechlands*, and was based on the legend that at
the time of the Crucifixion, a cry was heard on the
waters, " Great Pan is Dead."

Elizabeth paints in succession each of the chief classic
deities robbed of his or her godhead.

> Jove, that right hand is unloaded
> Whence the thunder did prevail,
> While in idiocy of godhead
> Thou art staring the stars pale !
> And thine eagle, blind and old,
> Roughs his feathers in the cold,
> > Pan, Pan is dead
>
> Bacchus, Bacchus ! on the panther
> He swoons, bound with his own vines !
> And his Mænads slowly saunter
> Head aside, among the pines,
> While they murmur dreamingly
> " Evohe ! ah—evohe !—
> > Ah, Pan is dead "
>
> Aphrodite ! dead and driven—
> As thy native foam thou art ;
> With the cestus long done heaving
> On the white calm of thine heart !
> *Ai Adonis !* at that shriek
> Not a tear runs down her cheek—
> > Pan, Pan is dead.

No one could have written such stanzas, even though
in the spirit of romanticism, who had not drunk deep

at the classic fountains, and it is a shock to us to-day
that they should lead up to the outburst:

> O ye vain false Gods of Hellas,
>   Ye are silent evermore.
> And I dash down this old chalice
> Whence libations ran of yore.
> See, the wine crawls in the dust,
> Wormlike—as your glories must,
>   Since Pan is dead.
>
> Earth outgrows the mythic fancies
>   Sung beside her in her youth,
> And those debonair romances
> Sound but dull beside the truth.
> Phœbus' chariot-course is run,
> Look up, poets, to the sun !
>   Pan, Pan is dead.

It is strange that this eager student of Æschylus and
Plato should not, even before the days of the interest
in comparative religion, have realized something of the
common ground between Greek and Hebrew inspiration.
Her instinct in childhood had been happier when, " as
to the gods and goddesses I believed in them all quite
seriously, and reconciled them to Christianity, which I
believed in too after a fashion, as some greater philo-
sophers have done." But the whole conception of
" development " or " evolution " was as foreign to her
as it was instinctive in the author of *Paracelsus*. In a
letter to Mrs. Martin of January, 1845, she tells how
Mrs. Jameson " tried vainly to convince me that the
Vestiges of Creation, which I take to be one of the most
melancholy books in the world, is the most comforting

... I persisted in a ' determinate counsel' not to be
a fully developed monkey if I could help it." That is
all she has to say of the epoch-making work of Robert
Chambers, which anticipated the evolutionary doctrine
of Darwin's *Origin of Species* in 1859.[1] Science for her
was chiefly represented by the spiritualistic phenomena
which later absorbed so much of her interest.

Another question concerned not with the thought,
but the form of *The Dead Pan* and other poems in the
volumes of 1838 and 1844 may be here considered. In
announcing the latter to H. S. Boyd she writes on
August 1, " You will find me a little lax perhaps in
metre—a freedom which is the result not of carelessness,
but of *conviction* and indeed of much patient study of
the great Fathers of English poetry—not meaning Mr.
Pope." Similarly she writes to R. H. Horne : " If I
fail ultimately before the public . . . it will not be
because I have shrunk from the amount of labour, where
labour could do anything. I have *worked* at poetry ;
it has not been with me reverie, but art."

Thus Elizabeth, anticipating the practisers of various
forms of free verse to-day, was a metrical experimenter,
who had studied versification in various ages and lan-
guages, and who was seeking to broaden the basis of
English prosody. It was in itself a laudable endeavour,
and when we understand her point of view, we can
appreciate her attempts to acclimatize Italian double-
rhymes or Greek strophic forms. Mr. Humbert Wolfe
who deliberately rhymes words with similar consonants
but different vowels, could scarcely quarrel with her for

[1] For Tennyson's very different attitude to this book, see
p. 207.

such a rhyme as " Hellas " and " Chalice " or, on the other hand, with such assonances as " islands " and " silence," " Sion " and " dying." But she seems to be getting out of bounds with " angels " and " candles " ; and where she comes to grief is in such artificial, even if technically correct, double rhymes as " Gehenna," and " when a," and " oak-wood," and " thunderstroke would." She had a wealth of poetic equipment— thought, imagination, feeling, technical knowledge, but she lacked the faultlessly sensitive ear, the nice judge- ment, the instinct for proportion that are their necessary complement for the highest artistic achievement. She did not realize the deadening effect of monotony. There is all the difference between the burden of a ballad, and the wearisome repetition at the end of each stanza of " Pan, Pan is dead," or " He giveth his beloved sleep," or "Sweetest eyes were ever seen" in *Catarina to Camoens* or " Toll Slowly " in the *Rhyme of the Duchess May*. The *Rhyme of the Duchess*, apart from the refrain, goes with something of a swing, and the noble bride of Sir Guy of Linteged who leaps to death with him on horse- back from his castle, is sympathetically drawn. But Elizabeth's attempts at mediævalism smack of Wardour Street.

Nor was she happier in a " ballad poem " of contem- porary life, *Lady Geraldine's Courtship* dealing with the love of a high-born maiden for a peasant poet for whom she rejects an earl of " high, straight forehead, nose of eagle, cold blue eyes." But for the weaknesses of the poem the publisher must share the responsibility. As she writes to H. S. Boyd, when Mr. Moxon found that the first volume of the poems of 1844 consisted of only 208 pages, and the second of 280, he wanted

> To tear away several poems from the end of the second and tie them on to the end of the first. I could not and would not hear of this because I had set my mind on having *Dead Pan* to conclude with. So there was nothing for it but to finish a ballad poem called *Lady Geraldine's Courtship* which was lying by me, and I did so by writing i.e. composing *one hundred and fifty lines last Saturday*. I seemed to be in a dream all day. Long lines too—with fifteen syllables in each : I see you shake your head all this way off.

And we too, a longer way off, in turn shake our heads. Not thus, to satisfy the mathematical caprices of publishers, are true poems written.

Elizabeth's authentic sources of inspiration were either lofty ideas and associations, even if they were in part beyond her range, arising out of her reading, or her intense and passionate sympathy with suffering and oppression. It is to this we owe such distinctive poems as *Cowper's Grave* (1838), and *The Cry of the Children*, first published in *Blackwood's Magazine*, August, 1843. It has a historical importance as commemorating for our warning and humiliation, the darkest episode in England's social history, the cruel exploitation of children in mines and factories that arose out of the Industrial Revolution. And in sheer poetic merit it ranks among Elizabeth's highest achievements.

It is hard to understand why she took so meekly Boyd's critical " castigation " of its rhythm. " The first stanza came into my head in a hurricane, and I was obliged to make the other stanzas like it—*that* is the whole mystery of the iniquity." Never were Elizabeth's elaborate stanzas and double rhymes more aptly employed than in echoing the endless whirr of the machinery with its constant accompaniment of children's tears :

Let them feel that this cold metallic motion
    Is not all the life God fashions or reveals :
Let them prove their living souls against the notion
    That they live in you, or under you, O wheels !
Still all day, the iron wheels go onward,
    Grinding life down from its mark.
And the children's souls, which God is calling sunward,
    Spin on blindly in the dark.

Thus for a quarter of a century, from 1820 to 1844, Elizabeth Barrett's mind and art had been concentrated upon heroic types of resistance to despotic power, Prometheus and Miltiades ; upon exiles from the bliss of Heaven or of Paradise, Lucifer, Adam and Eve ; of the helpless victims of the factory and the plantation. Is it fanciful to think that she was thereby steeled for the part which she was now to play in the extraordinary drama of her own life ? The Barrett family had moved in the latter part of 1832 to Sidmouth in Devon ; thence in the summer of 1835 to London, first at 74 Gloucester Place, and afterwards from early in 1838 at 50 Wimpole Street, which became their permanent home.

The Capital did not appeal to Elizabeth. " Was there anybody in the world," she writes to Mrs. Martin, December 7, 1836, " who ever loved London for itself ? " And again on August 6, 1837 : " It is almost surprising how we continue to be as dull in London as in Devonshire, perhaps more so, for the sight of a multitude induces a sense of seclusion which one has not without it." Again to Miss Commeline, August 19, 1837: " As to society in London, I assure you that none of us have much, and that as for me, you would wonder at seeing how possible it is to live as secludedly in the midst of a multitude as in the centre of solitude."

Her seclusion was all the greater because of the persistent ill-health which dogged her after her arrival in London, and which compelled her to spend three years, from the autumn of 1838 to September, 1841, at Torquay. But that lovely place had been made hateful to her by her favourite brother Edward's death by drowning in Babbacombe Bay on July 11, 1840. Henceforward her one desire was to get back to London and her books. Even as late as October, 1843, she could write to Mrs. Martin : " I do believe that I should be *mad* at this moment, if I had not forced back—dammed out— the current of rushing recollections by work, work, work."

But soon after the publication of the 1844 volumes another interest than work was to enter her life. Her first mention of " Mr. Browning the poet " is in a letter to H. S. Boyd on April 2, 1842, and on April 28, 1843, she wrote to Cornelius Mathews with reference to a criticism of Browning's *A Blot on the 'Scutcheon* :

I do assure you I never saw him in my life—do not know him even by correspondence—and yet whether through fellow-feeling for eleusinian mysteries, or whether through the more generous motive of appreciation of his powers, I am very sensitive to the thousand and one stripes with which the assembly of critics doth expound its vocation over him, and the *Athenæum* for instance made me quite cross and misanthropical last week.   The truth is—and the world should know the truth—it is easier to find a more faultless writer than a poet of equal genius.

In *Lady Geraldine's Courtship* she included a tribute to him ; among the verses read by the poet to the lady was

From Browning some "Pomegranate, which if cut deep down
the middle,
Shows a heart within blood-tinctured, of a veined humanity."

It may have been this allusion which nerved Browning, at the prompting of her cousin and his friend, John Kenyon, to write to her on January 10, 1845.   He goes straight to the point : " I love your verses with all my heart, dear Miss Barrett.—I do, as I say, love these books with all my heart—and I love you too—Yours ever faithfully, Robert Browning."   And his " obliged and faithful Elizabeth B. Barrett " answers in similar strain : " I thank you, dear Mr. Browning, from the bottom of my heart.   You meant to give me pleasure by your letter, and even if this object had not been answered, I ought still to thank you.   But it is thoroughly answered.   Such a letter from such a hand ! "   How from this beginning the correspondence grew for twenty months ever more frequent and intimate ; how Browning became a visitor to the invalid's room ; how sympathy and admiration were rapidly transformed to love—is known to all.   The loves of the poets are, in essentials, as the loves of lesser mortals, and it was the character of a " third-party," and a strange combination of circumstances that gave a well-nigh tragic significance to an idyll.

It was to her father that Elizabeth had dedicated, in terms of the deepest affection, not only her youthful *Battle of Marathon*, but her Poems of 1844. Since the premature death of his wife at Hope End in September, 1828, his eldest child had the foremost place in his affections. But as everyone now knows, he was more an antique Roman than an Englishman in his over-whelming sense of *patria potestas*. This is set forth, in a passage of penetrating analysis, in a letter of Elizabeth's to Browning, with postmark, August 25, 1845.

What you do *not* see, what you *cannot* see, is the deep tender affection behind and below all those patriarchal ideas of governing grown-up children " in the way they must go ! " and there never was (under the strata) a truer affection in a father's heart . . . no, nor a worthier heart in itself . . . a heart loyaller and purer, and more compelling in gratitude and reverence, than his, as I see it ! The evil is in the system —and he simply takes it to be his duty, to rule . . . like the Kings of Christendom by divine right. But he loves us through and through—and *I* for one, love *him*.

These words are all the more remarkable because they were written after the first serious rift had come between father and daughter.

Her doctors had told her that to escape the English winter was a necessity for her, and ordered her to go to Italy. Her father put a veto upon the plan. He declared angrily, as she writes on July 28, 1845, that " obstinacy and dry toast have brought me to my present condition, and that if I pleased to have porter and beef-steaks instead, I should be as well as ever I was, in a month."

Elizabeth was determined to take her only chance of a permanent recovery. She writes to Mrs. Martin in October :

If you were to see me you would be astonished to see the work of the past summer ; but all these improvements will ebb away with the sun—while I am assured of permanent good, if I leave England. The struggle with me has been a very painful one ; I cannot enter on the how and the wherefore at this moment. I had expected more help than I have found, and am left to myself, and thrown so on my own sense of duty as to feel it right for the sake of future years to make an effort to stand by myself as best I can. At the same time I will not tell you that at the last hour something may not happen to keep me at home.

And so it proved. On the eve of what should have been the date of her departure, October 17, her brother George sought to intercede with her father. The result appears in a letter to Browning next day :

I do not go to Italy . . . it has ended as I feared. What passed between George and Papa there is no need of telling : only the latter said that I might go if I pleased but that going it would be under his heaviest displeasure. George, in great indignation, pressed the question fully, but all was vain— and I am left in this position . . . to go, if I please with his displeasure over me (which after what you have said and after what Mr. Kenyon has said, and after what my own conscience and deepest moral convictions say aloud, I would unhesitatingly do at this hour !) and necessarily run the risk of exposing my sister and brother to that same displeasure—from which risk I shrink and fall back and feel that to incur it is impossible.

167

And then she adds in pregnant words that reveal the depth and not the tumult of her soul :

The bitterest "fact" of all is, that I had believed Papa to have loved me more than he obviously does : but I never regret knowledge . . . I mean I never would unknow anything . . . even were it the taste of the apples by the Dead Sea . . . and this must be accepted like the rest.

With the abandonment of the Italian visit Browning thought it time to press his suit. But Elizabeth warned him that there would be no " getting over " her father ; " you might as well think to sweep off a third of the Stars of Heaven with the motion of your eyelashes." None the less she again reveals her undaunted will :

Though I have been a submissive daughter . . . yet I have reserved for myself *always* that right over my own affections which is the most strictly personal of all things, and which involves principles and consequences of infinite importance and scope.

Was she echoing Shylock's words about Jessica when she wrote towards the end of January, 1846, " For *him* . . . he would rather see me dead at his feet than yield the point : and he will say so, and mean it and persist in the meaning." And yet she can pity him more than herself.

After all, he is the victim. He isolates himself—and now and then he feels it . . . the cold dead silence all round, which is the effect of an incredible system. If he were not stronger than most men, he could not bear it as he does.

In the midst of all this tragic tension she could be (to adopt Gordon Craig's double designation of his actress-mother) " Nellie " as well " as E.T." She could advise Browning to put his feet into hot water at night, to prevent morning headaches, " mustard mixed with the water, remember," and she could reproach him for being

hard on the mending of stockings and the rest of it . . . all the great work done in the world is done just by the people who know how to trifle, do you not think so ? When a man makes a principle of " never losing a moment " he is a lost man. Great men are eager to find an hour, and not avoid losing a moment.

She had promised Browning that if she got through the winter she would become engaged to him. It was an exceptionally mild one, and she became better instead of worse. By June 6, 1846, she could begin a letter to him. " This is the first word I have written out of my room these five years, I think . . . I am writing in the back drawing-room, half out of the window for air, driven out of my own territory by the angel of the sun this morning." Afterwards she was able to get out of doors, first driving, and then walking. Alarmed by the prospect of a temporary removal of the family into the country, on September 12 she slipped out with her maid, Wilson, to Marylebone Church, and was married to Browning, and went back home. As she protested later in a letter to her sisters, " There was no elopement in the case, but simply a private marriage." A week later, with Wilson and " Flush, my dog," in attendance, she crossed the Channel with her husband to Paris, where they found a friend in Mrs. Jameson. With her and her niece they journeyed by stages to Pisa, where they were to settle for the winter.

Hitherto the earliest known letter written by Elizabeth during this strange honeymoon, was one dated from Moulins, October 2, 1846, to Miss Mitford, giving an account of its earliest days. " I shut my eyes sometimes and fancy it all a dream of my guardian angel."

But the 1936 volume begins with another longer letter, also dated October 2, posted from Avignon, to her sisters,[1] written in an even more intimate strain, revealing her agony when she received her " death warrant " at Orleans.

Robert brought me in a great packet of letters . . . and I held them in my hands, not able to open one, and growing paler and colder every moment. . . . They were very hard letters, those from dearest Papa and dearest George—to the first I had to bow my head. . . . But from George, I thought it hard, I confess, that he should have written to me so with a sword. To write to me as if I did not love you all. . . . It was hard that he should use his love for me to break my heart with such a letter.

This letter now takes its place as a moving prelude to the well-known " dignified *apologia* for the action that she had taken," as Mr. Lubbock calls the long letters to Mrs. Martin written from Pisa apparently on October 20. Once again Elizabeth lays bare her feeling for her father :

My dear father is a very peculiar person. He is naturally stern, and has exaggerated notions of authority, but these things go with high and noble qualities : and as for feeling,

[1] This letter is almost eight weeks earlier than the first letter to Henrietta from Pisa on November 24, 1846, in the collection edited by Leonard Huxley.

the water is under the rock and I had faith.   Yes, and have it.
. . .   Always he has had the greatest power over my heart,
because I am one of those weak women who reverence strong
men.   By a word he might have bound me to him hand and
foot. . . .   I have loved him so and love him.

But Elizabeth does not describe herself truly as a weak
woman.   Her emotional nature flowed over, in her
poems and in her letters, into what seem to us to-day
sentimental extravagances.   And in her attitude towards
her father, to the memory of her brother Edward, and
later to Louis Napoleon, there was something of the
unbalanced fanaticism hereditary in the Barrett family.
But, as has already appeared, her life and her art were
rooted in an unshakeable belief in the freedom of the
soul, and in a crisis she showed herself to be true steel.

We can no longer associate with the honeymoon
period in Pisa Browning's first acquaintance with the
Sonnets from the Portuguese.   In 1894 Edmund Gosse
in an introduction to a reprint of the *Sonnets* told, on
the authority of a statement made by Browning eight
years before his death to a friend, a circumstantial story
how " one day early in 1847, their breakfast being over,"
Mrs. Browning " pushed a packet of papers " into her
husband's coat-pocket, telling him " to read that and to
tear it up if he did not like it " ; that Browning found
them to be " the finest sonnets written in any language
since Shakespeare's," and persuaded his wife to have them
printed, through Miss Mitford's agency, at Reading, in
an octavo volume of 47 pages, dated 1847.   This story,
repeated by others with some variations of detail, has
been till recently generally accepted.   But it has now

been discredited by the investigations of Messrs. John Carter and Graham Pollard.[1]

They have drawn attention to a passage in a letter written by Browning to Leigh Hunt from Bagni di Lucca, dated October 6, 1857, which was not published in full till 1933 among the letters edited by Mr. Thurman L. Hood[2]:

> I should like also to tell you that I never suspected the existence of those *Sonnets from the Portuguese* till three years after they were written : they were shown to me at this very place eight years ago, in consequence of some word of mine, just as they had been suppressed thro' some mistaken word : it was I who would not bear that sacrifice and thought of the subterfuge of a name.

Thus Browning himself certifies that he first saw the *Sonnets*, not at Pisa but at Bagni di Lucca ; that the date was 1849, three years after their composition in 1846 ; and that it was he who urged their publication under a deceptive title. There is no reference to the Reading edition of 1847, which manifestly could not be fitted into the sequence of this account. A gloss upon the enigmatic reference to " some mistaken word " is provided in characteristically breezy fashion by F. J. Furnivall who had his information from Browning himself [3]:

> Mrs. Browning's *Sonnets* to her husband. She wrote these in London. One day she timidly hinted to Browning that she'd tried to express her feelings about him. He answered that he didn't think people should wear their hearts on their

---

[1] *An Enquiry into the Nature of certain Nineteenth-century Pamphlets* (London : Constable ; New York : Charles Scribner's Sons), 1934.   [2] See above, p. 122.

[3] *Corrections, etc.* (For *Sharp's Life of Browning*, 1890), p. 3. Quoted by Carter and Pollard, *op. cit.*, pp. 11–12.

sleeves for daws to peck at, or something of the kind. This shut her up. When abroad she was one day late in putting on her bonnet to walk with him. He called to her. Spying about, he saw a tiny roll of paper on her looking-glass or table, pounst on it and said, " What's this ? " unrolling it the while. " Only something I wrote about you, and you frightened me from showing it to you," said she. And in her next edition the *Sonnets from the Portuguese* were printed.

The last sentence shows that Furnivall, an enthusiastic bibliographer, knew nothing of an 1847 edition. He represents Browning as finding the manuscript instead of being given it by his wife, as in Gosse's account. Messrs. Carter and Pollard accept Furnivall's version " as being more true to life," but Browning himself uses the words, " they were shown to me." However this may be, and however highly the *Sonnets from the Portuguese* are to be ranked, it is a relief to find nothing in Browning's own words corresponding to the utterance attributed to him by Gosse, " I dared not reserve to myself the finest sonnets written in any language since Shakespeare's." Setting aside the question of a comparative valuation with Milton's or Wordsworth's sonnets, any comparison of the *Sonnets from the Portuguese* with those of Shakespeare is misleading. They differ in form, in subject, and in spirit. In the Shakespearian cycle the English, as contrasted with the Petrarchan, type of sonnet reaches its apotheosis of rhythmical beauty. And through its tale of triangular love sweeps the tumultuous tide of Renaissance passion, with the poet swayed between his two loves " of comfort and despair." The *Sonnets from the Portuguese* enshrine the Wordsworthian ideal,

173

> The depth, and not the tumult, of the soul,
> A fervent, not ungovernable, love.

They are the self-revelation of a woman redeemed by the intensity of her feeling from death to life. The beginning of the transfiguration is unveiled in one of what may be called the key-sonnets of the series (VII) :

> The face of all the world is changed, I think,
> Since first I heard the footsteps of thy soul
> Move still, oh, still, beside me, as they stole
> Betwixt me and the dreadful outer brink
> Of obvious death, where I, who thought to sink,
> Was caught up into love, and taught the whole
> Of life in a new rhythm.

And it reaches its climax in another key-sonnet (XLIII) :

> How do I love thee ? Let me count the ways.
> I love thee to the depth and breadth and height
> My soul can reach, when feeling out of sight
> For the ends of Being and ideal Grace.
> I love thee to the level of every day's
> Most quiet need by sun and candlelight
>
>   *   *   *
>
>   I love thee with the breath,
> Smiles, tears, of all my life !—and, if God choose,
> I shall but love thee better after death.

Between these points emotion sometimes runs at an almost equal level of intensity ; at others it lingers round some incident of the courtship, the giving of a lock of hair ; the kiss on fingers, forehead, lips ; spoken or written words. Thus, as Mr. Osbert Burdett has said, the *Sonnets* " have the immediacy of her letters with the beauty of her best verse." [1]

[1] *The Brownings*, p. 218.

Never indeed did Elizabeth's prosodic knowledge and fondness for metrical experiment serve her better than in her choice of a medium for her love-poems. Since the Elizabethan period only two English poets of high rank, Milton and Wordsworth, had made any extensive use of the intricate rhyme-scheme of the Petrarchan sonnet. And their sonnets had been mainly on political themes, never on love. It was a true instinct that led the English poetess to restore the Italian model to its original and consecrated use. And it is a commonplace of criticism that the limitations of the form put a wholesome curb on the diffuseness which marred much of Elizabeth's verse. But has sufficient note been taken of how severe was the metrical discipline to which she subjected herself? With more rigid consistency than either Milton or Wordsworth she clung throughout the forty-four sonnets of the series to the rhyme-scheme, ABBA,ABBA,CDCDCD—notoriously more difficult to handle in English than in Italian. And with respect to the rhymes themselves she, who elsewhere had allowed herself much licence, here satisfied a completely purist standard. Where her technique, though she could have pleaded some precedents, may be criticized, is in the frequency with which she allows an unbroken overflow of sense and rhythm from the close of the octave into the beginning of the sestet. But in the essential mastery that she showed over what was to her an unfamiliar and exotic metrical form she reached the height of her poetic achievement.

The 1936 volume includes a letter from Elizabeth to Henrietta, enclosed in a note from Browning, dated from Pisa, March 26, 1847, which reveals the fact apparently hitherto unknown, that Elizabeth had a miscarriage, without, however, any evil results.[1] In the next month they moved to Florence, first to quarters in the Via delle belle Donne, and in the autumn to Casa Guidi which became their permanent headquarters. It was here that their happiness was crowned on March 9, 1849, by the birth of a son, christened Robert Wiedeman Barrett. And the realization of this happiness intensified Elizabeth's sympathy with Henrietta who was meeting the same fanatical opposition as she had done to an engagement with Captain Surtees Cook. Elizabeth's letters of advice to her sister, first published in the 1936 volume, are equally courageous and sagacious till Henrietta in April, 1850, followed her example, and Elizabeth could write " A letter from Henrietta and her husband glowing with happiness, it makes *me* happy." Arabel was now the only sister left in Wimpole Street, and it was the longing to see her again that was the strongest motive with Elizabeth in returning to London for a visit in the summer of 1851. She and her husband travelled by way of Venice (where she was " between heaven and earth "), Milan, Lucerne and Paris, and reached London towards the end of July, where they had rooms in Devonshire Street. They were visited by celebrities, including Fanny Kemble, Rogers and Barry Cornwall, and they spent an evening with Carlyle, " one of the great sights in England, to my mind." She found her beloved sisters " as ever, perfect to me," and there was a reconciliation with George.

[1] This letter is evidently " the last short one, with bad news too in it," to which Elizabeth refers at the beginning of her letter in March 31, 1847. The reference has hitherto not been understood.

But the last hope of another reconciliation was dashed for ever. There is nothing more common in fact and in fiction than the later softening of a father's heart towards a child who has married against his will. So it is natural that Elizabeth clung to such a hope, even though she had received no answer to a letter that she had written to Mr. Barrett announcing the birth of her son. Now, as she wrote to Mrs. Martin in September, she made a final venture :

It seemed to me right . . . to apprise my father of my being in England. I could not leave my land without the possibility of his seeing me once, of his consenting to see my child once. So I wrote and Robert wrote. . . . In reply he had a very violent and unsparing letter, with all the letters I had written to Papa through these five years *sent back unopened, the seals unbroken.* What went most to my heart was that some of the seals were black with black-edged envelopes ; so that he might have thought my child or husband dead, yet never cared to solve the doubt by breaking the seal. . . . So there's the end.

The end, it may be added, came in another sense on April 17, 1857, with the sudden death of her father, unrelentingly adamant to the last. How the iron had entered into Elizabeth's soul is plain from her words to Mrs. Martin, " I believe *hope* had died in me long ago of reconciliation in this world."

Nine months, from the end of September, 1851, to the end of June, 1852, were spent in Paris where the chief excitement was making the acquaintance of George Sand. A second visit of four months to London followed, when Landor, Charles Kingsley, and Ruskin were among their circle. By November, 1852, they were back in Florence, " in the old nest, still warm, of Casa Guidi." It was during this winter that Elizabeth began to show that intense interest in spiritualistic phenomena towards which her husband's attitude was frankly sceptical. And whatever may be thought of her views, she is again found taking a stand for the principle of free inquiry, " Profane or not," she wrote to Isa Blagden in March 1853, " I am resolved on getting as near to a solution of the Spirit question as I can, and I don't believe in the least risk of profanity, seeing that whatever is must be permitted ; and that the contempla-tion of whatever is, must be permitted also, where the intentions are pure and reverent." And when in December they were able to carry out a long-formed plan of spending a winter in Rome, her spiritualistic faith found surprising expression :

Twice I have been present at table experiments, and each time I was deeply impressed—impressed, there's the word for it ! The panting and shivering of that dead dumb wood, the human emotion conveyed through it—by what ? had to me a greater significance than the St. Peter's of this Rome.

We are thus prepared for another remarkable confession in a letter to Miss Mitford, on May 10, 1854, " I don't pretend to have a rag of sentiment about Rome," from which they returned a few weeks later to Florence. A period of residence at Casa Guidi till July, 1855, was followed by visits to London, Paris, London again, and the Isle of Wight, where John Kenyon was dying. In October, 1856, they returned to Casa Guidi which Elizabeth was never henceforth to leave for long periods.

Since Henrietta's marriage Elizabeth had kept up an

ardent correspondence with her. Much of it was vivacious chat on family matters, her own Penini, the Cook boy and girl, friends old and new. The theme of spiritualism also often recurs, and the cryptic figure of David Dunglass Hume appears. "He's the most interesting person to me in England out of Somersetshire (where Henrietta lived), and 50 Wimpole Street." To Browning it was a case of " humbugging," to be pilloried in *Mr. Sludge the Medium.* Political events also have their place in the letters to her sister, and to these in their relation to her poetry we may now turn.

It was with the beginning of the Brownings' residence in Florence that the problem of liberty had begun to present itself to Elizabeth in a new phase. From the early days at Hope End in its historic and traditional aspects it had inspired much of her verse. In Wimpole Street she had to confront it in its most sinister domestic form. At Casa Guidi she was drawn to it irresistibly from a political angle. As Mr. Percy Lubbock has pointed out, she seems to have been curiously unsusceptible to Italy's " brilliant and continuous past." Her vision was of the future and she hailed with passionate sympathy what promised in 1848 to be the beginning of a movement in Florence for liberation from despotic rule of " a beautiful and unfortunate country." In *Casa Guidi Windows* she gives what she calls " a simple story of personal impressions," as a witness. Part I of the poem was written contemporaneously with the events that it describes. The movement for enfranchise-ment was typified in a child's song :

> I heard last night a little child go singing
> 'Neath Casa Guidi windows by the church,

O bella libertà, O bella! . . .
A little child, too, who not long had been
   By mother's finger steadied on his feet,
And still *O bella libertà* he sang.

The great day of the movement in Florence was when
the people marched to the Pitti palace to thank the
reforming Grand Duke Leopold for allowing them to
" use their civic force, to guard their civic homes."
There is a vivid picture of the three hours' procession,
the banners, the bursts of martial strains, the " vivas," of
which there is an equally striking description in a letter
to Henrietta on September 13, 1847. But there was
doubt in the onlooker's heart :

                    Are ye freer
   For what was felt that day ?   A chariot-wheel
May spin fast, yet the chariot never roll.
        . . . men, upon the whole,
Are what they can be—nations, what they would.

Will therefore to be strong, thou Italy !
Will to be noble !

Alas for this exhortation ! Casa Guidi Windows saw
another sight, described in Part II of the poem, written
three years later, when the Duke, alarmed at the progress
of the reforming movement, had fled and the citizens
cried, not " Live the Duke," but " Live the People. "

How down they pulled the Duke's arms everywhere !
How up they set new café-signs, to show
   Where patriots might sip ices in pure air—
(The fresh paint smelling somewhat!)   To and fro
   How marched the civic guard, and stopped to stare

When boys broke windows in a civic glow !
　How rebel songs were sung to loyal tunes,
　And bishops cursed in ecclesiastic metres.

And then yet another sight from the windows when the
Duke came back to restore absolutism, escorted by

　　Austria's thousand : sword and bayonet,
　　　Horse, foot, artillery—cannons rolling on.

And in sadly changed mood Elizabeth turns back to the
thought of the singing child :

　　Alas for songs and hearts ! O Tuscany,
　　　O Dante's Florence, is the type too plain ?
　　Did'st thou, too, only sing of liberty
　　　As little children take up a high strain
　　With unintentioned voices, and break off
　　　To sleep upon their mothers' knees again ?

The disillusionment here voiced had found earlier and
more unrestrained expression in a letter.

　The saddest thing is the impossibility (which I, for one,
feel) to sympathize, to go along with the *people* to whom and
to whose cause all my natural sympathies yearn. The word
" Liberty " ceases to make me thrill as at something great
and unmistakable, as, for instance, the other great words
" Truth " and " Justice " do. The salt has lost its savour,
the meaning has escaped from the term : we know nothing
of what people will *do* when they aspire to Liberty. The
holiness of liberty is desecrated by the sign of the ass's hoof.

But in the autumn of 1851, the year in which *Casa
Guidi Windows* was published, she recaptured, as she
thought, on her visit to Paris, the ideal that had eluded

her in Florence. Louis Napoleon, the Prince-President, seemed to her to embody the loftiest principles of French Republicanism. Even the *coup d'état* of December 2nd and his proclamation as Emperor did not disillusion her. "The government," she wrote on December 10, "was in a deadlock—what was to be done? . . . In throwing back the sovereignty from a 'representative assembly' which had virtually ceased to represent, into the hands of the people, I think Louis Napoleon did well. The talk about 'military despotism' is absolute nonsense." Similarly, a few days later she warned Henrietta, "*Don't believe the Times.* To talk about 'carnage' is quite absurd." Like Wordsworth sixty years before [1] she threw herself passionately on the side of France as the champion of democracy, in defiance of the prevailing sentiment in England. "Mr. Cobden and the Peace Society," she wrote to Miss Mitford in February, 1853, "are pleasing me infinitely just now in making head against the immorality (that's the word) of the English press. The tone taken up towards France is immoral in the highest degree, and the invasion cry would be idiotic if it were not something worse."

Her ardent belief in Louis Napoleon as a liberator seemed to be fully vindicated when in April, 1859, he declared war on Austria in support of Piedmont. "To Mrs. Browning," as Mr. Percy Lubbock has said, "when she saw her hero stretching out his hand to lift her adored Italy into freedom, it seemed as if her last and best dream had come true." The victories at Magenta and Solferino swiftly followed, and it was in a mood of exultation that Elizabeth wrote her pæan, *Napoleon III in Italy.*

[1] See above, pp. 64–5.

Now, shall we say
  Our Italy lives indeed ?
*   *   *

Ay, if it were not for the tears in our eyes,
These tears of a sudden passionate joy,
  Should we see her arise
From the place where the wicked are overthrown,
Italy, Italy—loosed at length
  From the tyrant's thrall.
Pale and calm in her strength ?
*   *   *

Shout for France and Savoy !
  Shout for the helper and doer,
Shout for the good sword's ring,
  Shout for the thought still truer.
*   *   *

  Shout for the head of Cavour ;
And shout for the heart of a King
That's great with a nation's joy !
  Shout for France and Savoy !

The treaty of Villafranca, by which Nice and Savoy
were ceded to France, shattered her dream of a liberated
and united Italy. But unlike the more realistically-
minded Wordsworth she would not accept the teachings
of experience. In *A Tale of Villafranca* she is seen
clinging fanatically to her faith in her hero, frustrated
in his noble aims by wickedness in high places :

  A great man (who was crowned one day)
    Imagined a great Deed.
*   *   *

  Then sovereigns, statesmen, north and south,
    Rose up in wrath and fear,
  And cried, protesting by one mouth,
    What monster have we here ?

183

A great Deed at this hour of day ?
A great just Deed—and not for pay ?
    Absurd,—or insincere.

              *   *   *

But HE stood sad before the Sun
    (The peoples felt their fate).
" The world is many—I am one ;
    My great Deed was too great.
God's fruit of justice ripens slow :
Men's souls are narrow, let them grow ;
    My brothers, we must wait."

Napoleon III in Italy and *A Tale of Villafranca* were
published with other cognate verses in *Poems Before
Congress* (1860). The unity of Italy was to be achieved
by other means than by the sword of France, and with
paradoxical results in our own day that would have been
a fiery test of Elizabeth's devotion. But *Poems before
Congress* will always have a historical interest, and the
ringing challenge of the prose Preface anticipates much
that is finest in the ideals of The League of Nations.

Non-intervention in the affairs of neighbouring states is
a high political virtue ; but non-intervention does not mean
passing by on the other side when your neighbour falls
among thieves—or Phariseeism would recover it from
Christianity. Freedom itself is virtue, as well as privilege ;
but freedom of the seas does not mean piracy, nor freedom
of the land, brigandage ; nor freedom of the senate, freedom
to cudgel a dissident member ; nor freedom of the press,
freedom to calumniate and lie. So if patriotism be a virtue
indeed, it cannot mean an exclusive devotion to our country's
interests. . . . If the man who does not look beyond this
natural life is of a somewhat narrow order what must be the man
who does not look beyond his own frontier or his own sea ?

Her passionate absorption in the rapidly changing facets of the 1859 campaign had sapped her dwindling strength; and the death of Cavour, " that great soul," on June 6, 1861, helped to hasten her own end on June 29.

Florence was her appropriate last resting-place. It was five years since she had last visited England, and it was there, in the latter part of 1856, that *Aurora Leigh* had been published, with the dedication to John Kenyon in which she called it " the most mature of my works, and the one into which my highest convictions upon Life and Art have entered." As early as February 27, 1845, she had confided to Browning that she was intending to write " a sort of novel-poem." She was, however, " waiting for a story, and I won't take one, because I want to make one, and I like to make my own stories, because I can take liberties with them in the treatment." Did she nevertheless find hints, as John H. Ingram has suggested, for her story in *Jane Eyre*, which appeared in 1847, and which in 1849 she was comparing favourably for its " spontaneousness and earnestness " with *Shirley*? Aurora, like Jane, tells the story of her life from childhood to marriage. Each is an orphan brought up by an aunt to whom the memory of her mother is hateful; each, after misunderstandings and separation, is married to a man who has lost his sight during the burning of his home. But, of course, Elizabeth also exercised her own invention in what may be called the sub-plot of Romney Leigh's doctrinaire project of marrying the seamstress, Marian Earle, thwarted by the jealousy of the Society widow, Lady Waldemar; and the melodramatic sequel wherein Marian is lured into a house of ill-fame, becomes the mother of an illegitimate child, and is rescued on the Paris quays by Aurora.

In the 1845 letter to Browning, Elizabeth had spoken of her intended novel-poem as " completely modern," and as meeting face to face and without mask " the Humanity of the age." Through the long period during which she was engaged upon it she kept this aim in view. It finds notable utterance in Book V of *Aurora Leigh*:

> Nay, if there's room for poets in this world
> A little overgrown (I think there is),
> Their sole work is to represent the age,
> Their age, not Charlemagne's—this live, throbbing age,
> That brawls, cheats, maddens, calculates, aspires,
> And spends more passion, more heroic heat,
> Betwixt the mirrors of its drawing-rooms
> Than Roland with his knights at Roncesvalles.
> To flinch from modern varnish, coat or flounce,
> Cry out for togas and the picturesque
> Is fatal—foolish too. . . .
>   Never flinch,
> But still, unscrupulously epic, catch
> Upon the burning lava of a song
> The full-veined, heaving, double-breasted Age.

And it cannot be gainsaid that, judged by the verdict of her own generation, the poetess achieved her ambition. *Aurora Leigh* struck home as swiftly and surely in 1856 as did *The Everlasting Mercy* in 1911 and *The Testament of Beauty* in 1929. Walter Savage Landor, whom the Brownings befriended in his old age in Florence, declared : " I had no idea that anyone in this age was capable of so much poetry. I am half drunk with it." Nor was it merely a brilliant flash in the pan.

Fourteen editions were called for in twenty years.   And in a broad sense the work remains a faithful image of its period.   As a discriminating critic wrote in *The Times Literary Supplement*, July 2, 1931 :

Aurora Leigh, with her passionate interest in social questions, her conflict as artist and woman, her longing for knowledge and freedom, is the true daughter of her age.   Romney, too, is no less certainly a mid-Victorian gentleman of high ideals who has thought deeply about the social question and has founded, unfortunately, a phalanstery in Shropshire.

But Elizabeth had not the born novelist's aptitude for interesting us in the fortunes of her personages.   And the problems of class and sex and art in which Aurora and Romney are so continuously immersed have so shifted their values since the mid-nineteenth century that much of the argumentation in the poem has now the effect of beating the air.   Where its appeal is still living is in the passages where Elizabeth is not self-consciously expounding her " highest convictions," but is speaking with the spontaneity and freshness that mark her best letters.   Thus she distils the very essence of " Victorianism " in its stuffiest aspects into the description in Book I of Aurora's prim maiden aunt and her scheme of education for the girl, including

> The royal genealogies
> Of Oviedo, the internal laws •
> Of the Burmese empire, by how many feet
> Mount Chimborazo outsoars Teneriffe,
> . . . because she liked
> A general insight into useful facts.

Aurora indeed was to be the " model of a child " ;

already pilloried by Wordsworth in Book V of *The Prelude*, who

> Can string you names of districts, cities, towns,
> The whole world over.

And thus, with accomplishments and tongues, she was to become, in her aunt's eyes, a " womanly " woman :

> And English women, she thanked God and sighed
> (Some people always sigh in thanking God),
> Were models to the universe.

English scenery, like English womanhood, was viewed by Aurora with censorious eyes. Though she learnt in time to love it, at first it struck her as a pale contrast with her native Italy.

> Not a grand nature. Not my chestnut-woods
> Of Vallambrosa, cleaving by the spurs
> Of the precipices
>   *   *   *
>   On English ground
> You understand the letter,—ere the fall
> How Adam lived in a garden. All the fields
> Are tied up fast with hedges, nosegay-like
>   *   *   *
>   A nature tamed
> And grown domestic like a barn-door fowl.

When after her aunt's death she turns to a literary career in London we can hear through the lips of Aurora the accents of Elizabeth. Her plea for modernity in the epic, or in any form of narrative verse, has been in part quoted. Equally significant is the declaration that follows :

                    I will write no plays,
Because the drama, less sublime in this,
Makes lower appeals, submits more menially,
Adopts the standard of the public taste
To chalk its height on, wears a dog-chain round
Its regal neck, and learns to carry and fetch
The fashions of the day to please the day,
Fawns close on pit and boxes.

Such is the characteristic attitude of an English intellectual towards the drama in the depressed period between
Kean's Shakespearian revivals and T. W. Robertson's
naturalistic revolution.[1] But in a further passage we
see the influence of the author of *Paracelsus*, with its
Preface deprecating " recourse to an external machine
of incidents." [2]   The buskin, the mask, and the mouthpiece have disappeared from the theatre :

    The growing drama has outgrown such toys
    Of simulated stature, face, and speech,
    It also peradventure may outgrow
    The simulation of the painted scene,
    Boards, actors, prompters, gaslight and costumes,
    And take for a worthier stage the soul itself,
    Its shifting fancies and celestial lights,
    With all its grand orchestral silences,
    To keep the pauses of the rhythmic sounds.

And if Aurora in this highbrow temper wrote no plays,
she merely condescended to prose in the form of anonymous hackwork.

                    I apprehended this—
    In England no one lives by verse that lives ;

[1] See below, pp. 251-2, and 266-9.   [2] See above, p. 130.

And, apprehending, I resolved by prose
To make a space to sphere my living verse.
I wrote for encyclopædias, magazines,
And weekly papers, holding up my name,
To keep it from the mud.

Here again Aurora voices the sentiments of her creator. Hence springs a paradox. Elizabeth wishing, as she emphasizes, to deal realistically with the problems of her own age chose as her medium blank verse—a metre which she had hitherto employed (except in translations from Greek) only in *A Drama of Exile.* Now she made the challenging venture of using it for a versified novel of 11,000 lines. In spite of her interest in prosody she does not seem to have realized that blank verse, though superficially the easiest, is in essence the most exacting, of poetic instruments. If it is indeed to be " verse that lives " it must bear the authentic stamp of distinctive and spontaneous rhythm. This is a test that *Aurora Leigh,* in spite of many felicities of thought and diction, cannot, as a whole, endure.

How astonished, even scandalized, Elizabeth would have been to hear that her *magnum opus* might have had a better chance of immortality had it been written in prose ! She undervalued prose as an instrument of literary art. Perhaps it was because, in the classic phrase, she wrote prose without knowing it. It is only by degrees that her full activity in this medium has been realized. The Prefaces to her poems, even in her youthful days, are of remarkable quality. And with the successive publication of collections of her letters her place in the epistolary gallery has become more established and defined. The letters, judged as literature, have their defects. The topics follow one another pell-mell, their emotionalism is at times cloying, the *mot juste* is too often lacking. But what compensations there are in their range of subjects and moods, in their spontaneity and sincerity, in their acute criticism of books and men, above all in the classic dignity with which they invest Elizabeth's irrevocable choice between father and lover, confinement and freedom, death and life, in the crisis of her fate. What if such qualities had found an imaginative outlet in a prose *Aurora Leigh* ?

But if her most ambitious poetic testament has lost the greater part of its contemporary appeal, and if her ballads and lyrics are often too sentimental and artificial for the taste of to-day, yet her place in verse is assured. Her longer early poems have qualities that have not always been appreciated. The *Cry of the Children* and *Cowper's Grave* have lost nothing of their poignancy, nor *Wine of Cyprus* and *The Dead Pan* of their magnetically romantic classicism. The *Sonnets from the Portuguese* enshrine one of the most arresting episodes in the age-long chronicle of the loves of the poets. Nor is the dynamic force of Elizabeth's personality, thrown into stronger relief by her physical frailty, to be measured solely by her own output of verse and prose. It was at her feet in life that her husband laid his " fifty poems finished " of *Men and Women*, with the exquisite epilogue of " One Word More " ; it was to her after her death that he addressed the invocation in *The Ring and The Book*, " O lyric love, half angel and half bird " ; it was to reunion with her that he looked forward when " the black minute's at end " in *Prospice*.

VIII

ARTHUR HENRY HALLAM
AND *IN MEMORIAM*

THE fifteenth of September, 1933, was the hundredth anniversary of the sudden death in Vienna of Arthur Henry Hallam. That tragic event can never be forgotten so long as Tennyson's *In Memoriam* is read. To most of us to-day Arthur Hallam is little more than the subject of the great Victorian elegy, much as Edward King's memory survives only in *Lycidas*. But to all his contemporaries, not to Tennyson alone, Hallam appeared as a spirit of the rarest sort and his death was as the shadow of a great eclipse. Arthur was the elder son of Henry Hallam, the historian of the Middle Ages, and of his wife Julia Maria, daughter of Sir Abraham Elton. He was born on February 1, 1811, in Bedford Place, London. From the anonymous memoir prefixed by his father to the privately printed edition of his *Remains in Verse and Prose* (1834)[1] we learn that Arthur began to show his exceptional powers from his earliest days. At seven he had learned to read French with facility. At nine he was sent to a preparatory school at Putney, and within twelve months he was tolerably proficient in Latin.

[1] This was afterwards published by John Murray in 1862.

After some months of foreign travel with his parents, who had moved to 67 Wimpole Street, he entered Eton, in the Rev. E. C. Hawtrey's house, in 1822 and remained there till 1827. The Eton curriculum was predominantly classical, and, according to his father, Arthur became a " good though not perhaps a first-rate scholar " in the two ancient tongues. But he read also widely in English literature, especially the Elizabethan dramatists and the poets of his own day. These included his predecessor at Eton, Shelley, over whom the waters closed in the Bay of Spezzia in the same year as Arthur entered the school. His earliest effort in verse, on a story connected with the Lakes of Killarney, appeared in *The Eton Miscellany* in 1827.

But it was as a debater on religious and philosophical subjects that he made his chief mark at school. Among his contemporaries was W. E. Gladstone, who noted in his Diary, May 14, 1826: " Stiff arguments with Hallam as usual on Sundays, about Articles, Creeds, &c." They both belonged not only to the famous Eton " Society," known as " Pop," but to an inner circle which met in a private apartment to discuss such questions as whether " mathematics or metaphysics are more beneficial as a discipline of the mind." This drew a caustic comment from Arthur's more pedestrian-minded father, " Your debate on ' mat.' and ' met.' truly ridiculous." But Gladstone, though their paths after Eton lay apart, retained to the end of his long life the most vivid memory of what his schoolfellow was and promised to be. As was noted by the anonymous contributor of an article to *The Times* of September 15, 1933, the statesman in his ninetieth year wrote of Hallam that he "possessed the greatest genius he had ever known"; that it was "a rare privilege and a high election to have enjoyed his friendship," and that " he resembled a passing emanation from some other, and less darkly chequered, world." In *The Bulletin of the John Rylands Library, Manchester*, January, 1934, Dr. M. Zamick has printed ten unpublished letters of Arthur Hallam written by him from Eton to a senior school-fellow, William Windham Farr, who had proceeded to St. John's College, Cambridge.

Before going up to Cambridge, Arthur spent eight months in Italy, including Florence, Rome and the Tyrol. During this period the art and poetry of the southern peninsula became a passion with him, and he composed half a dozen sonnets in Italian which Anthony Panizzi, who was to become Chief Librarian of the British Museum, declared to be the best ever written by an Englishman. Was he comparing them with those of Milton, composed when he was almost twice Hallam's age during his visit to Italy nearly two centuries before?

When Arthur came into residence at Trinity College in October, 1828, he was to find the Cambridge mathematical curriculum as little to his taste as Milton had found "the grammatick flats and shallows" of his undergraduate days. "I have no aversion to study," he wrote, "but my ideas of what is essential do not precisely square with those of the dons at Cambridge." Thus even more than at Eton it was outside the prescribed academic routine that he displayed his powers. He was one of an exceptionally brilliant undergraduate set which included Charles and Alfred Tennyson, Frederick Denison Maurice, R. C. Trench (afterwards

Archbishop of Dublin), James Spedding, Charles Merivale, and Richard Monckton Milnes, afterwards Lord
Houghton and father of the Marquess of Crewe. In
his paper on Lord Houghton in the Royal Society of
Literature volume, *The Eighteen-Seventies*, Lord Crewe
recalls how he had heard his father say that Hallam stood
easily first of them all. They were members of a
College debating society, The Apostles, which Tennyson has described in famous lines in canto lxxxvii of
In Memoriam, where Arthur is " the master-bowman " :

> Where once we held debate, a band
>   Of youthful friends, on mind and art,
>   And labour, and the changing mart,
> And all the framework of the land ;
>
> When one would aim an arrow fair,
>   But send it slackly from the string ;
>   And one would pierce an outer ring,
> And one an inner, here and there ;
>
> And last the master-bowman, he,
>   Would cleave the mark. A willing ear
>   We lent him. Who, but hung to hear
> The rapt oration flowing free ?

In 1829 Arthur visited the home of the Tennysons,
Somersby Rectory in Lincolnshire. He had planned
to include some of his verse in a joint volume with
Alfred, but partly under pressure from his father, and
partly from modesty he did not do so. Tennyson's
own collection appeared in 1830 as *Poems, Chiefly
Lyrical*, and Hallam's sheaf of verse was printed privately
in the same year. As Tennyson's volume was pub-

lished by Effingham Wilson, in London, Arthur apparently undertook to furnish copies to Somersby, and at the same time sent to Alfred's mother a copy of his own work privately printed by Littlewood & Co. For he writes to her :

As I have at last the pleasure of sending to Alfred his long-expected book, I take this opportunity of begging that you will accept from me a copy of some poems which I originally intended to have published in the same volume. To this joint publication, as a sort of seal of our friendship, I had long looked forward with a delight which I believe was in no way selfish. But there are reasons which have obliged me to change my intention, and withdraw my own share of work from the Press. One of these was the growing conviction of the exceeding crudeness of style which characterized all my earlier attempts.

It would seem that the copy of his verses which Arthur sent to his friend's mother has disappeared. For apparently there are only two copies now extant, one in Mr. T. J. Wise's Ashley Library in Hampstead with the inscription, " W. Donne from the Author, May 26, 1830 " ; and another, inscribed by the author to " his sincere friend, R. C. Trench," in the possession of the contributor of *The Times* article noticed above. It is, however, not quite clear whether this copy is not additional to the two copies known to Mr. Wise.

In the same year, 1830, the two friends were to engage in an enterprise of a different kind from the frustrated joint publication. Inspired, I imagine, by Byron's example in Greece, they set out for the Pyrenees to help with money the insurgent Torrijos, who was leader of a rebellion against the restored despotism of King Ferdinand. "A wild bustling time we had of it," writes Hallam, but fortunately they did not prolong their stay with the conspirators, who in the following year met their fate at Malaga. The adventure left its mark on Tennyson's portrayal of mountain scenery in *Œnone*. I have not found traces of its influence on Hallam's verse, but the exciting episode made him more restive than ever under academic routine. After their return he writes to Alfred on October 4, 1830, to tell him that his father " does not seem quite to comprehend that, after helping to revolutionize kingdoms, one is still less inclined than before to trouble one's head about scholarships, degrees, and such gear." He proceeds to comment on the general European situation such as, *mutatis mutandis*, a clever young undergraduate would do to-day : " Spanish affairs, you will see by the papers, go on slowly : not therefore, I trust, less surely . . . What think you of Belgium ? . . . The chances of a general war in Europe are great. . . . 'Twas a very pretty little revolution in Saxony, and a respectable one at Brunswick."

It was love, not war or revolution, that was to be a new inspiration to Hallam's verse. As soon as he had visited Somersby he became strongly attached to Emily, Alfred's second sister. She had the dark hair and eyes of the Tennysons, " the colouring of Italy or the south of France " and " a profile like that on a coin." After a year they became privately engaged and in the summer of 1832 their betrothal was made public. " I am now at Somersby," Arthur wrote to Trench, " not only as the friend of Alfred Tennyson but as the lover of his

sister. An attachment on my part of nearly two years'
standing and a mutual engagement of one year are, I
fervently hope, only the commencement of a union
which circumstances may not impair, and the grave
itself may not conclude."

" A union which circumstances may not impair "—
the words were only too soon to have a tragic irony !
But the depth of his feeling for Emily was to give a
new note to his hitherto chiefly meditative verse. It
is heard in the stanzas " to the loved one " written in
absence from her in January, 1831 :

> Sometimes I dream thee leaning o'er
>   The harp I used to love so well.
> Again I tremble and adore
>   The soul of its delicious swell.

> Again the very air is dim
>   With eddies of harmonious might,
> And all my brain and senses swim
>   In a keen madness of delight.

It is the same scene that is pictured in a stanza of canto
lxxxix of *In Memoriam* :

> Or in the all-golden afternoon
>   A guest, or happy sister, sung,
>   Or here she brought the harp and flung
> A ballad to the brightening moon !

The " happy sister " with the harp in both these quotations is surely Emily, and it is therefore somewhat
puzzling to find the second Lord Tennyson in his
Memoir of his father speaking of Mary, the eldest sister,
as playing the harp and accompanying those who sang.

Again and again, especially in his sonnets inspired by Italian example, Arthur returns to the impression made on him by Emily's music:

> Still here—thou hast not faded from my sight,
>   Nor all the music round thee from mine ear;
>   Still grace flows from thee to the brightening year,
> And all the birds laugh out in wealthier light.
>
> Still am I free to close my happy eyes,
>   And paint upon the gloom thy mimic form,
>   That soft white neck, that cheek in beauty warm,
> And brow half hidden where your ringlet lies.

If Emily could enchant Arthur with her music, he could lead her, by teaching her Italian, into another sphere of enchantment—the world of Dante, Petrarch, Tasso and Ariosto, who were the favourite reading at Somersby when Hallam was there. The record of this remains in another stanza of canto lxxxix of *In Memoriam*:

> O bliss, when all in circle drawn
>   About him, heart and ear were fed
>   To hear him, as he lay and read
> The Tuscan poets on the lawn.

A revealing commentary on these lines is to be found in one of Arthur's sonnets to Emily:

> Lady, I bid thee to a sunny dome
>   Ringing with echoes of Italian song;
>   Henceforth to thee these magic halls belong,
> And all the pleasant place is like a home.

199

Hark, on the right with full piano tone
  Old Dante's voice encircles all the air :
  Hark yet again, like flute-notes mingling rare,
Comes the keen sweetness of Petrarca's moan.

Pass then the lintel freely : without fear
  Feed on the music : I do better know thee
  Than to suspect the pleasure thou dost owe me
Will wrong thy gentle spirit, or make less dear

That element whence thou must draw thy life,
An English maiden and an English wife.

It is significant of the somewhat apprehensive attitude towards Italian thought and letters a century ago that even such an enthusiast for them as Hallam should think it right to end on the reassuring national note of the last lines. This sonnet is a favourable example of his poetry which is throughout of biographical interest and which has a considerable measure of grace and charm. But when we remember what had been achieved twenty to fifteen years before by the youthful Shelley and Keats, and what was to be accomplished in the next few years by the youthful Tennyson and Browning, it must be allowed that in Hallam's poetry we do not find a sufficient explanation of the unique spell that he cast over his contemporaries. We come nearer to a solution when we turn to his prose *Remains*, in which his studies of the " Tuscan poets " form an important section. They include his oration on " The Influence of Italian Works of Imagination on the same class of composition in England," delivered in Trinity College Chapel on December 16, 1831. For a young man, of about twenty years, such a comparative study of modern European literatures was an unusual feat. But the chief merit of the oration, as I think, was not so much its attempt at analysing the influence of Dante and Petrarch, Tasso and Ariosto on Chaucer, Spenser and Milton, as its interpretation of the chief characteristics of the earlier Italian literature itself. Here Hallam displays his remarkable generalizing power, which would need copious extracts for its full illustration. But he sums up by asserting that the two directive principles of this literature are " a full and joyous reception of former [i.e. classical] knowledge" and "a deep and intimate impression of forms of Christianity. The combined operation of the two is seen in their love-poetry. . . . Its base is undoubtedly the Troubadour poetry, but upon this they have reared a splendid edifice of Platonism and surmounted it by the banner of the Cross."

It was Hallam's keen insight into Dante's genius that led him to publish in 1832 his *Remarks on Professor Rossetti's " Disquisizioni sullo Spirito Antipapale."* Gabriele Rossetti, the father of a family of genius, was a political refugee, who had been made Professor of Italian at King's College, London. In his *Disquisizioni* he had interpreted Dante's exquisite early work, the *Vita Nuova,* in the terms of an anti-Papal allegory. Hallam rallies him in words that might be applied today to those who discover hidden meanings in the plainest passages of Shakespeare.

A man must be careful indeed in whose words and actions Signor Rossetti would not discover something to help out his argument. If two persons at opposite ends of the world do but chance to light on the same mode of expression, our learned professor calls out, like honest Verges [1] " Fore God, they are both of a tale."

Then he proceeds in more serious vein :

Certainly until Signor Rossetti suggested the idea, we never dreamed of looking for Ghibelline enigmas in a narrative apparently so remote from politics. Nor did it occur to us to seek even for moral meanings, that might throw a forced and doubtful light on these obscurities. Whatever uncertain shape might, for a few moments, be assumed by the Beatrice of the *Commedia*, imparadised in overflowing effluences of light and music, and enjoying the immediate vision of the Most High, here at least in the mild humility and modest nobleness of the living and loving creature, to whom the sonnets and canzones were addressed, we did believe that we were safe from allegory. Something indeed there was of vagueness and unreliability in the picture we beheld ; but it never disturbed our faith : for we believed it to arise from the reverential feeling which seemed to possess the poet's imagination, and led him to concentrate all his loftiest sentiments and pure ideas of perfection in the object of his youthful passion, consecrated long since and idealized to his heart by the sanctities of the overshadowing tomb.

I have quoted this passage not only for its sane and persuasive content but as an example of the special quality of Hallam's prose style. To my ear at any rate the rhythmic movement of these sentences anticipates the rising and falling cadences in the earlier volumes of Ruskin's *Modern Painters*.

Though literature in Italian attracted Hallam more

[1] Here Hallam made a slip in substituting Verges for Dogberry.

than in its ancestral Latin, his college prize essay on *The Philosophical Writings of Cicero* is a notable performance. Here again he is at his best in passages of generalization —in his contrast of the Greek and the Roman genius, in his distinction between eloquence and oratory, in his balancing of the respective merits and defects of the Epicurean and the Stoic schools. When he passes to Cicero himself, he presents him as contemplating the universe under the forms of order and administration : all created beings, according to him, form an immense commonwealth. The Roman statesman and jurist dwells on " the indelible sanctity of human law and its foundations, not in blind concurrence, but in the universal analysis of an Eternal Mind." And this argument from design, as it may broadly be called, had gained immeasurably in force, as Hallam points out, since Cicero's day. " Beautiful as the fitness of things appeared in the eyes of Cicero, how insignificant was the spectacle when compared to the face of nature, as we behold it, illuminated on every side and reflected in a thousand mirrors of science. What then was the study of the mortal frame ? What the condition of experimental physics ? What the knowledge of the two infinites " to be revealed by the microscope and the telescope ?

This striking passage, with its references to " a thousand mirrors of science," and to " experimental physics " is of particular significance. It shows that Arthur had not only a passion for philosophical speculation, but that he shared his friend Alfred's keen interest in the progress of scientific discovery, which was to leave so deep a mark on *In Memoriam.*

It was a fortunate chance, as it proved, that Hallam did not have a share in Tennyson's 1830 volume, *Poems, Chiefly Lyrical*. For in that case he would not have left us the most notable legacy of his critical power in a modern field. This was his review of *Poems, Chiefly Lyrical* which appeared in *The Englishman's Magazine*, August, 1831, and which was entitled *On some of the Characteristics of Modern Poetry and on the Lyrical Poems of Alfred Tennyson*. It begins with a penetrating discussion of Wordsworth's poetic reformation, and of the respective qualities of the genius of Shelley and Keats, whom he classes with the " Cockney School," of which Leigh Hunt was the harbinger. Hallam defends that school, but he thinks that Tennyson may incur some of its unpopularity, and he therefore proceeds to set forth what he considers the new poet's distinctive excellences.

First, his luxuriance of imagination and at the same time his control over it. Secondly, his power of embodying himself in ideal characters, or rather works of character . . . Thirdly, his vivid, picturesque delineation of objects, and the peculiar skill with which he holds all of them fused . . . in a medium of strong emotion. Fourthly, the variety of his lyrical measures, and exquisite modulation of harmonious words and cadences to the swell and fall of the feelings expressed. Fifthly, the elevated habits of thought, *implied* in these compositions, and imparting a mellow soberness of tone.

In all the circumstances of his relation with Tennyson probably Hallam could not be a completely impartial critic. The third and fourth of the excellences that he indicated are those which readers of to-day would be most likely to endorse, even if they do not countersign his enthusiastic eulogies of *Recollections of the Arabian Nights* and of *Oriana*. But he was essentially right in discerning in this volume of lyrics a new poetic voice to which loftier arbiters of literary taste were for the time deaf. The publication towards the close of 1832 of *Poems by Alfred Tennyson* more than vindicated his friend's poetic insight. But Arthur had meanwhile left Cambridge and had been entered at the Inner Temple, and had begun his legal training in the office of a conveyancer in Lincoln's Inn Fields. He found " the dusty purlieus of the law " more congenial than might have been expected from his other interests, but as a relaxation he accompanied his father in August, 1833, on a continental journey to Germany and Austria. A wet day brought on an intermittent fever, to which he had been subject, and in Vienna a rush of blood to the head on September 15 was immediately fatal. His father had been out for a walk and came back to find him apparently asleep on the sofa. Made anxious by Arthur's stillness and silence, he drew near to ascertain why he had not moved or spoken, and found that all was over. " God's finger touched him and he slept."

His body was brought back by sea, and was buried in the family vault of the Eltons, his mother's family, in Clevedon Church, Somerset, on January 3, 1834. It was the slow homeward voyage of the ship that first stirred Tennyson's imagination to transmute his overwhelming grief into song. For, as we learn from his son's *Memoir*, there were found in a manuscript book containing *The Two Voices* the earliest written five cantos of *In Memoriam*, of which the first in order, on a stray leaf, is the invocation beginning :

> Fair ship, that from the Italian shore,
>   Sailest the placid ocean-plains
>   With my lost Arthur's loved remains,
> Spread thy full wings, and waft him o'er.

It was the paradox of fortune that the man who was the cynosure of all contemporary eyes should be cut off by " the blind fury " and owe his immortality not to his own genius, but to that of his friend.   Yet Henry Hallam was justified by more than paternal feeling when in 1834 he collected Arthur's productions in verse and prose.   It is true that we cannot say of him in his own words about Shelley and Keats that he was one of the men " who were born poets, lived poets, and went poets to their untimely graves."   Indeed, according to his father, after leaving Cambridge he " ceased in a great measure to write poetry and expressed to more than one friend an intention to give it up."   However this may have been, it is mainly in his prose that we recognize something of the quality that won for him in so short a time such unique recognition.   His critical work is marked by a breadth of view, an independence of tone, and a rhythm in its stately periods that are astonishing in one who was an undergraduate or little more. But for the malice of fate Arthur Hallam would, as far as we can tell, have joined the critical galaxy of Coleridge, Hazlitt and Lamb.   But then we should have lost *In Memoriam.*

Yet the elegy itself might have suffered the untimely fate of its subject.   The cantos, as Tennyson has related, were written in almost haphazard way, "at many different places and as the phases of our intercourse came to my memory and suggested them. I did not write them with any view of weaving them into a whole, or for publication, until I found that I had written so many." They were completed in "a long butcher-ledger-like book" which Tennyson, in February, 1850, left behind in a London lodging, in a closet where he used to keep some of his provisions, and which some weeks afterwards was rescued by Coventry Patmore. Anonymous publication followed in the same year.

The spasmodic method of composition over a period of some fifteen years goes far to explain the difference between *In Memoriam* and such elegies as *Astrophel*, *Lycidas* or *Adonais* expressing their writers' mood at the moment of bereavement. *In Memoriam* is a poetic diary of grief, recording how it is intensified or relieved by the recurrence of anniversaries or by visits to places associated with memories of Arthur. But had it been no more than this Tennyson's elegy would not have gone home so deeply to the heart and mind of Victorian England. As early as 1833 (a year before Browning's *Paracelsus*) Tennyson's muse had skirted the field of biology in *The Two Voices*. In 1844 he was eagerly inquiring for a copy of *Vestiges of the Natural History of Creation* in which Robert Chambers anticipated some of Darwin's views on development in the *Origin of Species* (1859). In his letter about Chambers's book Tennyson wrote, "It seems to contain many speculations with which I have been familiar for years and on which I have written more than one poem." He is probably referring here to cantos liv–lvi of *In Memoriam*,

for his son has stated that the sections of the elegy dealing with evolution had been read by the poet's friends
some years before the publication of *Vestiges of Creation*.

It was in these and similar cantos that Tennyson gave
his poem far more than a personal significance. He
confronted the issues raised by an un-Wordsworthian
Nature " red in tooth and claw," careless not only of
the single life, but of the type. He faced the ultimate
question whether " Man, her last work, who seem'd so
fair,"

> Who loved, who suffer'd countless ills,
> Who battled for the True, the Just

should suffer the same annihilation as the lower types,
should

> Be blown about the desert dust,
> Or seal'd within the iron hills.

It was by his attempted spiritual solution of these
problems, by his final affirmation of faith in

> That God, which ever lives and loves,
> One God, one law, one element,
> And one far-off divine event,
> To which the whole creation moves,

that he brought comfort and consolation, especially
when the evolution controversy was at its height, to so
many in his own generation. Like the youthful Browning he was prophetic in his anticipation that no solution
in terms of materialism could be satisfactory. And he
showed an admirable faculty of translating scientific
phraseology into lucid and melodious verse.

But scientific inquiry and speculation have largely shifted their ground in the twentieth century. The geologist and the biologist have yielded place in the forefront of popular interest to the physicist and the astronomer. There are new riddles of the cosmos to which we have to seek clues beyond Tennyson's ken. Hence the abiding interest and value of *In Memoriam* will probably after all be mainly found in what may be broadly called its personal aspects. To Arthur Hallam himself, the young Marcellus of his time, we may come closer in his own garnered relics of verse and prose than in the transfigured lineaments of his friend's elegy. But idealization apart, he was a type of the English society of the eighteen-thirties and later at its highest moral and intellectual level. And in Tennyson's clear-cut cameos the life of that society is for ever preserved, set against the lovely background of Cambridge college courts and the trees and flowers of the Somersby Rectory garden, while the verse echoes the flow of the tidal rivers near Clevedon or the peal of the wild bells of Waltham Abbey ringing on New Year's Eve to the winter sky.

IX

TENNYSON AND THE ARTHURIAN LEGEND

"THE Reaction against Tennyson," which is the subject of an illuminating study by Professor A. C. Bradley in an English Association pamphlet, has culminated in the prevalent depreciation of his most ambitious and, for long, most popular work, *Idylls of the King*. Even the most advanced anti-Victorian critic, unless paradoxically careless of any reputation for poetic taste or insight, could not deny the exquisite verbal felicity of many of the shorter poems. And however lightly he rated *The Princess* or *Maud* as a whole, they contained songs and lyrical passages " that envy could not but call fair." *In Memoriam* might be discounted as a speculative and religious poem, but, as I have sought to show in the preceding section, it was impossible to question its enduring interest as a personal record, and as an idealized delineation of aspects of Victorian culture and social life.

Idylls of the King lay more open to a frontal attack partly because weapons for the purpose could be sought in Malory's *Morte d'Arthur*, the source of the chief episodes in the poem. Yet many of the attempts to use the prose romance to discredit the *Idylls* have been based upon a misunderstanding, and have missed the really vulnerable point in Tennyson's reinterpretation of the Arthurian story. Malory was a fine artist, but in selecting and adapting from his " French books " he did not trouble overmuch about consistency. There are two contradictory elements in *Morte d'Arthur*. On the one hand, the downfall of the Table Round is represented as due to an early sin of Arthur, who in his youth had betrayed Bellicent, not knowing she was his own half-sister. The issue of this lawless passion was *Modred*, the traitor knight, who brought the king to his doom. This version of the story is the subject of the interesting Elizabethan play, *The Misfortunes of Arthur*, and it has been contended that Tennyson should have followed similar lines, and shown us Arthur as the victim of Nemesis.

Such a treatment would not only have been alien from the Victorian poet's temper and outlook, but it would have been false to the dominant element in *Morte d'Arthur* itself, where the king is pictured as the flower of knights and men, and where at the close his tomb bears the inscription, *Rex quondam, rexque futurus*. Thus Tennyson would have been justified by Malory's example in representing Arthur as the perfect knight and ruler. But he was not content with this. From the time of his earliest study of the story, he began, as his son has told us in his *Memoir*, to allegorize it, though he wavered as to the form of his interpretation. In a memorandum drawn up in the 'thirties of last century, and presented in 1869 to James Knowles, Arthur appears as " Religious Faith," and the Round Table as " liberal institutions." But Knowles himself states that Tennyson said to him, " By King Arthur I always meant the soul, and by the Round Table the passions and capacities of a man. . . . There is no grander subject in the world than King Arthur."

Tennyson, however, found it impossible to give a strictly allegorical interpretation to the story. His method (as has been often pointed out) is more akin to the parable, wherein the characters are not personifications of some single quality, but where the story as a whole has a secondary moral or spiritual meaning. He makes this clear in his Epilogue addressed to Queen Victoria :

> Accept this old imperfect tale,
> New-old, and shadowing Sense at war with Soul,
> Ideal manhood closed in real man,
> Rather than that gray king, whose name, a ghost,
> Streams like a cloud, man-shaped, from mountain peak,
> And cleaves to cairn and cromlech still; or him
> Of Geoffrey's book, or him of Malleor's.

It is the endeavour to turn the great romance to edifying uses that has been, apart from changes in poetic taste, the stumbling-block to a younger generation more deeply versed than Tennyson's contemporaries in medieval literature, and impatient of the intrusion of ethics into art. And I would not deny that Tennyson's scheme necessitates an illegitimate transvaluation of parts of the Arthurian story, and leads to some insoluble entanglements. But even here there are episodes of sheer romantic beauty. And the general conception of Arthur as an embodiment of the spiritual principle in the world leavening human society and lifting it above the beast is not only lawful, but is of the very essence of Tennyson's genius. It therefore produces, when his genius is working at white heat, poetry that is not Victorian in any sense, good or bad, but in its degree as timeless as that of Spenser or Milton. And as *Paradise Lost* and *The Faerie Queene*, both of which have a didactic purpose, present new angles of interest to every succeeding age, so Tennyson's distinctive interpretation of the medieval romance may be found after the world-upheaval of the war to have a significance which it lacked for a generation which had not known, nor even dreamt of, such a cataclysm.

One of Tennyson's favourite images is that of the soul coming from the deep and returning to it. Hence the mystery of Arthur's origin is symbolised in the tale believed by Bellicent, that on the night of King Uther's death in Tintagil, Merlin on the shore had—

> Watch'd the great sea fall,
> Wave after wave, each mightier than the last,
> Till last, a ninth one, gathering half the deep
> And full of voices, slowly rose and plunged
> Roaring, and all the wave was in a flame:
> And down the wave and in the flame was borne
> A naked babe, and rode to Merlin's feet,
> Who stoopt and caught the babe, and cried, " The King !
> Here is an heir for Uther ! "

The authority of the spiritual ruler must be taken on faith, and it has that within it that overbears doubt and opposition :

> The savage yells
> Of Uther's peerage died, and Arthur sat
> Crowned on the dais, and his warriors cried,
> " Be thou the king, and we will work thy will,
> Who love thee."

Arthur's answer to the cry is to found his ideal society,
the fair Order of the Table Round, "a glorious company, the flower of men," whereon his own image is to
be impressed.   His words work with such power upon
his followers—

> That when they rose, knighted from kneeling, some
> Were pale as at the passing of a ghost,
> Some flush'd, and others dazed.

It is with the same mystical authority that he appears
in the vision of Leodogran, King of Cameliard.   Leodogran, dreaming, saw upon a peak haze-hidden—

> A phantom king,
> Now looming, and now lost,

who 'mid the smoke and fire of war—

> Sent out at times a voice ; and here or there
> Stood one who pointed toward the voice, the rest
> Slew on and burnt, crying, "No king of ours,
> No son of Uther, and no king of ours";
> Till with a wink his dream was changed, the haze
> Descended, and the solid earth became
> As nothing, but the King stood out in heaven,
> Crown'd.

And Leodogran, realizing with the eye of faith who and
what Arthur is, gives him his daughter Guinevere to
wife.   But Guinevere, swearing at the altar a deathless
love, "with drooping eyes," is to prove fatal not only
to the Table Round but to the scheme of the poem.   It
was possible for Tennyson to represent Arthur as the
soul or the spiritual principle in relation to the ideal
society of his knights.   But insuperable difficulty arises
when thus regarded he is brought into individual

human relationships, above all that of a husband. It is true that Spenser, whose Prince Arthur, as Magnificence, represents all the moral virtues, makes him the lover of the " Faerie Queene." But then she is herself a transcendental figure, and their union, had Spenser lived to complete his epic, would have been that of perfected humanity with glory in its noblest form. It is only thus that the love of the ideal Knight and King can find fitting interpretation. If we are to keep the Guinevere of medieval story, Arthur cannot be completely spiritualized.

But this can be only fully realized later in the poem. Meanwhile in the *Idylls* that immediately follow *The Coming of Arthur*, in *Gareth and Lynette*, *The Marriage of Geraint* and *Geraint and Enid*, the King and Queen are in the background, and the parabolic intention wears so thin that it well-nigh disappears. These *Idylls* are of the versified novelette type, and they are very loosely knit to the main theme. But in *Gareth and Lynette* there is one significant episode, in the description of Camelot, the shadowy city of palaces, which, as Gareth and his companions approach it, flashes with its spires and turrets through the mists and then again disappears, so that they cry, " Here is a city of enchanters," and—

> There is no such city anywhere,
> But all a vision.

And when Merlin meets them at the gate, he gives a riddling key to the mystery :

> For truly as thou sayest, a Fairy King
> And Fairy Queens have built the city, son . . .
> And, as thou sayest, it is enchanted, son,

215

> For there is nothing in it as it seems
> Saving the King; tho' some there be that hold
> The King a shadow, and the city real.

Camelot, as Tennyson himself said, is " symbolic of the gradual growth of human beliefs and institutions and of the spiritual development of man." It is therefore—

> Never built at all,
> And therefore built for ever.

And as always, when he is developing this *leit-motif* of the poem, the verse suddenly thrills with a subtler cadence that marks off the episode from the *Idyll* as a whole. The figure of Gareth has a virginal charm, but the story of his adventures has not much poetic significance, and so far as it has a definitely allegorical intention, as in the contests with Morning Star, Noon-Sun, Evening Star, and Night or Death, it is an excrescence on the general symbolism of the Idylls.

Tennyson shows more of the art of the story-teller in verse in *The Marriage of Geraint*, where he found his materials in the *Mabinogion*, not in *Morte d'Arthur*. The tale of Cinderella and Prince Charming in all its variants has an eternal attraction. Enid of the faded silk, doing blithely the menial service in her father's ruined hall, is one of the most exquisite of Cinderellas, and none of them has been heralded into the presence of the Prince to lovelier music. The lines have still their thrush-like sweetness and purity :

> And while he waited in the castle court,
> The voice of Enid, Yniol's daughter, rang
> Clear thro' the open casement of the hall,

> Singing; and as the sweet voice of a bird,
> Heard by the lander in a lonely isle,
> Moves him to think what kind of bird it is
> That sings so delicately clear, and make
> Conjecture of the plumage and the form;
> So the sweet voice of Enid moved Geraint.

And the journey of Enid, at Geraint's wish, to court in the faded silk, instead of the gorgeous gown in which her mother had clothed her, is in the true romantic vein. But the stupid tests to which Geraint later puts his wife's loyalty and obedience leave us cold. The pattern of the wife who meekly endures all tribulation at her husband's hands has been drawn once for all by Chaucer, after Petrarch and Boccaccio, in the Clerk's *Tale of Griseldis*, and anyone else attempts it at his peril. But even were the narrative of Enid's trials more pedestrian than it is, it would be redeemed by the seraphic sweetness of the lines that tell of the reconciliation of the twain:

> And never yet, since high in Paradise
> O'er the four rivers the first roses blew,
> Came purer pleasure unto mortal kind
> Than lived thro' her, who in that perilous hour
> Put hand to hand beneath her husband's heart
> And felt him hers again: she did not weep,
> But o'er her meek eyes came a happy mist
> Like that which kept the heart of Eden green
> Before the useful trouble of the rain.

How exquisite here is not only the cadence of the verse, but the suggestion of a love as pure and perfect as that of our first parents before the Fall.

With *Balin and Balan* we come closer again to the central theme of the war of Sense against Soul. We see the beginning of the break-up of the spiritual society of the Round Table. In the *Memoir* of the poet by his son we are told that this *Idyll*, of which an earlier version by Tennyson is printed, was written because he felt that some further introduction to *Merlin and Vivien* was necessary. I do not know whether he had been moved at all by the criticism of R. H. Hutton that the atmosphere of *Merlin and Vivien* was too dark and lurid for its position in the epical series. But so far as Vivien is concerned, I wish that the addition had not been made. The " damsel-errant," as she appears in *Balin and Balan*, making mock of her boyish squire, " Sir Chick," maddening Balin with her lies and proclaiming the return of the old sun-worship, is more crudely drawn than the wily Vivien whom we see lying at Merlin's feet before an oak in the wild woods of Broceliande. She is here no mere damsel-errant, but another Lilith or Lamia, the woman-snake with the horrible beauty of the serpent, its cunning, its malignant hiss, its envenomed bite. She has fascination in the real meaning of the word, and she seeks to capture the great Enchanter with an enchantment more potent than his own. Merlin is the type of the sceptical intellect which can discern the true spiritual king and enlist in his service, and therein perform mighty works, but which is not spiritual itself, and is thus exposed to the snares of Sense. The duel between the two is worthy of its magnificent elemental setting of wild woods and gathering storm, for it is vital to the future of the spiritual society. And as always when he is dealing with this central theme, Tennyson's art catches fire. If we read again the *Idyll* from Vivien's opening manœuvre—

And lissome Vivien, holding by his heel,
Writhed towards him, slided up his knee and sat,
Behind his ankle twined her hollow feet
Together, curved an arm about his neck,
Clung like a snake ;

to the close when (in one of the poet's most original
similes)—

The pale blood of the wizard at her touch
Took gayer colours, like an opal warmed,

and he told her all the charm and slept ; and—

In one moment she put forth the charm
Of woven paces and of waving hands,
And in the hollow oak he lay as dead,
And lost to life and use and name and fame—

we shall find that Tennyson has here shown a dramatic
power for which to-day he does not receive due credit.
But it is a power that extends only to symbolic types,
as both Vivien and Merlin are, and not to complex
personalities. That is partly why Tennyson fails with
Lancelot, who is, taken all in all, a lay figure. But it is
not the whole reason.

Noi leggevamo un giorno per diletto
Di Lancilotto, come amor lo strinse . . .
Quando leggemmo il disiato riso
Esser baciato da cotanto amante,
Questi, che mai da me non fia diviso,
La bocca mi baciò tutto tremante :
Galeotto fu il libro e chi lo scrisse :
Quel giorno più non vi leggemmo avante.

Dante was an austere enough moralist, and it is from
the second circle of the Inferno that Francesca is speaking.

But he knew what medieval love was, and Tennyson did not. It is in the gingerly handling of the passion of Lancelot and Guinevere that he lays himself most open to the charge of " Victorianism." It is a vain thing to draw out leviathan with an hook, to turn the romance of these grand amorists to moral edification. It is not thus that these immortal stories enlighten and inspire, as of a truth they do. Nor is it by the love of the maid of Astolat that we would see Lancelot redeemed, when we remember that in Malory it is Elaine who bears Galahad as son to Lancelot. Yet no one could wish that Tennyson had not written his *Idyll*. The lily maid, as uncompanioned of women as Miranda, living her lonely life of fantasy, till it flames into sudden and destroying love, is an exquisite creation. And she is loveliest of all in death, when she passes at last as she had wished—

> Beyond the poplar and far up the flood,
> Until I find the palace of the King.

This is one of the high places of romance, where Tennyson had ventured with eager, youthful step in *The Lady of Shalott*, and where he now walks again with statelier pace :

> So those two brethren from the chariot took
> And on the black decks laid her in her bed,
> Set in her hand a lily, o'er her hung
> The silken case with braided blazonings,
> And kiss'd her quiet brows, and saying to her,
> " Sister, farewell for ever," and again
> " Farewell, sweet sister," parted all in tears.
> Then rose the dumb old servitor, and the dead,

Oar'd by the dumb, went upward with the flood—
In her right hand the lily, in her left
The letter—all her bright hair streaming down—
And all the coverlid was cloth of gold
Drawn to her waist, and she herself in white
All but her face, and that clear-featured face,
Was lovely, for she did not seem as dead,
But fast asleep, and lay as tho' she smiled.

In *The Holy Grail*, too, Tennyson was treading again
on ground long familiar to him. His early lyric, *Sir
Galahad*, in its lustrous beauty and spiritual intensity
had anticipated the work of the pre-Raphaelites. He
might well have seemed the predestined re-interpreter
of the San Graal story to a generation awakening anew
to its significance. But, unfortunately, in *The Holy
Grail* he twisted the symbolism of the legend. The
quest for the Grail is no longer the search for absolute
union with Christ. It means the renunciation of
ordinary ties and duties for the sake of spiritual excitement. A society already decadent through indulgence
in sensual excess rushes feverishly into the opposite
extreme of an overstrained asceticism, and thereafter
recoils into yet lower depths.

Such is in essence Tennyson's application of the Grail
story, as it is voiced by King Arthur himself:

And spake I not too truly, O my knights?
Was I too dark a prophet when I said
To those who went upon the Holy Quest,
That most of them would follow wandering fires,
Lost in the quagmire?—lost to me and gone,
And left me gazing at a barren board,
And a lean Order—scare return'd a tithe.

Thus while Wagner in *Parsifal* was drawing from Wolfram von Eschenbach's High German version of the legend renewed sacramental significance, Tennyson was emptying Malory's narrative of the Quest of much of its spiritual content. Yet this shifting of values is not consistently carried out. The figure of Galahad enthralled his imagination as in his youthful days. With the virgin-knight the " Holy Thing " moves night and day uncovered, and in the strength of it he rides " shattering all evil customs everywhere." And the narrative art of the *Idylls* reaches its climax of luminous beauty in Sir Percivale's recital of Galahad's passing " in silver-shining armour starry-clear " over the great sea while " o'er his head the holy vessel hung " to the spiritual city.

But even of Galahad himself, Arthur speaks with a note of yearning, which is discordant with the spirit of the Grail story :

> And one hath had the vision face to face
> And now his chair desires him here in vain,
> However they may crown him otherwhere.

As for the other knights they have followed wandering fires. They have deserted, in the quest for signs and wonders, the service of their true King, who is seeking to leaven the world about him here and now, and who irradiates it with his own spirituality :

> Until this earth he walks on seems not earth,
> This light that strikes his eyeball is not light,
> This air that smites his forehead is not air
> But vision.

If the Grail story has suffered violence at Tennyson's hands, his own ideal finds noble utterance here.

In *The Last Tournament* another of the great medieval stories goes through a transvaluation. Tristram and Isolt are originally as high figures of romance as Lancelot and Guinevere, and fate has an even more overmastering part in the tale of their tragic love. We all know how the story has come again to glorious life in the greatest of love-operas. But Tennyson's aim was again as different from Wagner's as in their treatment of the Grail theme. He did not want to magnetize us with the glamour and pity of the old-world tale. He took Tristram as the type of the Round Table in its decay, when even Arthur begins to fear—

> Lest this my realm, uprear'd,
> By noble deeds at one with noble vows,
> From flat confusion and brute violences,
> Reel back into the beast, and be no more?

And from this point of view, if we can bring ourselves to enter into it, Tennyson's Tristram, just because he is a type, is a more successful creation than his Lancelot. In him sense has completely triumphed over spirit, and finds its fitting hymn on his lips :

> New leaf, new life—the days of frost are o'er ;
> New life, new love, to suit the newer day :
> New loves are sweet as those that went before :
> Free love—free field—we love but while we may.

In the impassioned last dialogue with Isolt in the casemented room in Tintagil, when Tristram repudiates his fealty to the King, who once seemed to him " no man, but Michael trampling Satan," and who is now "a doubtful lord" seeking to bind men—

> By inviolable vows
> Which flesh and blood perforce would violate

—in that dialogue, broken by the avenging battleaxe of King Mark, we hear the death-knell of the Table Round.

With the flight of Guinevere, when her sin is discovered, comes the end. In Malory it is to her lover himself, in the convent at Almesbury, that she makes her confession of wrong done and avows her hope that she may yet be saved:

> Therefore, Sir Launcelot, wit thee well I am set in such a plight to get my soul's health; and yet, I trust, through God's grace, that after my death to have a sight of the blessed face of Christ, and at doomsday to sit on his right hand, for as sinful as ever I was are saints in heaven. Therefore, Sir Launcelot, I require thee and beseech thee heartily for all the love that ever was betwixt us, that thou never see me more in the visage; and I command thee on God's behalf that thou forsake my company . . . For as well as I have loved thee, mine heart will not serve me to see thee; for through thee and me is the flower of Kings and Knights destroyed.

There speaks the voice of the Middle Age. Its earthly and its heavenly passion—all is there. But with Tennyson's interpretation of the story it was necessary that Arthur himself should be brought face to face with Guinevere and unfold to her the ruin that her sin has wrought. And if we think of the King and Queen as types, he of the spiritual ideal, she of the voluptuous life of the senses, that has sapped and brought low the fair fabric of the Round Table, then all is consonant. Such an Arthur to such a Guinevere not only can but must use the mighty words that we all know :

> Well is it that no child is born of thee.
> The children born of thee are sword and fire,
> Red ruin and the breaking up of laws.

He must lay bare the sin that has spoilt the purpose of his life ; he must forgive her as eternal God forgives, must cry :

> Let no man dream but that I love thee still.

And by this love and forgiveness such a Guinevere must be uplifted and redeemed :

> I thought I could not breathe in that fine air,
> That pure severity of perfect light.
> I yearn'd for warmth and colour which I found
> In Lancelot—now I see thee what thou art,
> Thou art the highest and most human, too,
> Not Lancelot, nor another.

To question or deny the poetic splendour of this last dialogue between husband and wife is idle. But just because it is between husband and wife it has been fiercely assailed. And of a truth Tennyson here finds himself in the impasse to which, as I have said, he was predestined by his mystical conception of Arthur. To show a figure, so conceived, in the role of the blameless and accusing husband was to invite the charge so hotly made that the King has here become a prig and Pharisee. To those who choose to make it there is no answer except that the Arthur whom they impeach is not Tennyson's Arthur, and for this the poet must himself bear the responsibility. A keener sense of the incongruous would have saved him from exposing his ideal King in a situation round which cluster a thousand disturbing associations from the novel and the stage.

In *The Passing of Arthur* the King reassumes his true role of the hero of a spiritual epic. He rides forth to meet " death or he knows not what mysterious doom " in the last weird battle in the west. The battle is fought amid spectral gloom ; it is a confused mêlée :

> For friend and foe were shadows in the midst,
> And friend slew friend, not knowing whom he slew.

It is the twilight of the gods, wherein all spiritual values are obscured. And into the rhythm of the lines that picture the stricken field by the winter sea has crept the chill of a world in eclipse :

> Only the wan wave
> Brake in among dead faces, to and fro
> Swaying the helpless hands, and up and down
> Tumbling the hollow helmets of the fallen,
> And shivered brands that once had fought with Rome,
> And rolling far along the gloomy shores
> The voice of days of old and days to be.

From Arthur's lips as he gazes on the spectacle rises the cry of the despair that assails the highest, holiest nature in its dark hour :

> I know not what I am,
> Nor whence I am, nor whether I be King,
> Behold, I seem but King among the dead.

226

Yet even now to the eye of faith his true royalty lies open and bare :

> Then spake the bold Sir Bedivere, " My King,
> King everywhere, and so the dead have kings,
> There also will I worship thee as King."

And when Sir Bedivere belies in part these brave words by hesitating to throw away Excalibur, the last visible memorial of the glories of the Round Table, Arthur's spiritual authority still avails to overawe him into obedience.   Betrayed, defeated, sorely stricken, Arthur is yet, in the truest and most majestic sense, every inch a king.

" The vision of Leodogran's dream," as R. H. Hutton has said, " is literally fulfilled.   The cloud has rolled down upon the earth, and the King, a mighty phantom, stands out in heaven, but stands out crowned, for he has lost nothing in himself of the spiritual elements of his kingdom."   Such a life cannot end in death.   It came with signs and wonders and with them it passes away. We hear again the echoes of Merlin's riddling prophecy :

> From the great deep to the great deep he goes.

Whither he is borne on the dusky barge we cannot tell, but we know that there is no thought of failure in his heart.   " The old order changeth yielding place to new."   The fair and stately fabric of the Round Table has been shattered.   But the spirit which was regnant at its core, which irradiated its being with living light and fire, can take no hurt from " the waves and weathers " of Time, and tramples with victor-feet Death itself into the dust.

Thus Tennyson uses the Arthurian story to symbolize his own " Welt-Anschauung," that there is a spiritual principle in the universe, incessantly struggling with the material elements, liable to temporary defeat, but in essence unconquerable and immortal. When the author of the *Idylls* was in the heyday of his fame a Dorset-shire poet and novelist was slowly catching the ear of a smaller public with a strangely different interpretation of life. To Thomas Hardy man is the plaything of ironic powers :

> As flies to wanton boys are we to the Gods,
> They kill us for their sport.

When the President of the Immortals has finished his sport with Tess, and with the rest of us, there is no more to be said. By his consummate expression of this view of the world Hardy had become a classic in his lifetime. But to Tennyson this would have been a creed of despair. For him human society could only exist on a spiritual basis, with God renewing himself in many ways. He clothed this conception in the garb, half-medieval, half-modernized of the Arthurian story. Hence have sprung the flaws and inconsistencies which have provoked so violent a reaction against the poem that at first was so widely acclaimed. For all that is shallow or half-hearted in his handling of the great romance for his own purposes Tennyson has paid dearly. But Time is the most impartial of critics, and the generation that has lived through the Great War may be able to do more justice to the *Idylls* than that which preceded. Words-worth's sonnets have spoken with a new voice to those who have found in them not only a poetic record of the

Napoleonic struggle, but a majestic proclamation of those ever-living principles which were at issue once again in the World-War. For Wordsworth those principles were enshrined in the historic national liberties of England, Switzerland and Spain, assaulted by tyrannic military power. Tennyson viewed them in the legendary form of an ideal society reared for a time above the encircling welter of pagan savagery. In either case the poets were concerned with the war of Sense against Soul. And has not the world-conflict, and much that has followed in its train, revealed to shuddering humanity this elemental struggle in its most naked form beneath the laboriously built-up structure of civilization?

> The children born of thee are sword and fire,
> Red ruin, and the breaking up of laws.
>
>   *   *   *
>
>   The fear lest this my realm, uprear'd
> By noble deeds at one with noble vows,
> From flat confusion and brute violences,
> Reel back into the beast, and be no more.

Such familiar lines have gained immensely in significance since August 1914. They are the more poignant and arresting because they have originally no relation to historic facts. It is one of the tests of genius that its utterances are perpetually proving their value and aptness in unforeseen applications. *Idylls of the King* is not an organic whole; it is a medley, with a strangely fitful inspiration. But when this inspiration is at work on this central theme of the poem, it gives birth to verse that no change of literary fashion can affect, because, like all true art, it is incomparable and timeless.

X

MATTHEW ARNOLD IN HIS LYRIC VERSE

MATTHEW ARNOLD, born on December 24, 1822, was educated at Rugby of which his father, Dr. Thomas Arnold, became Headmaster in 1828. From Rugby he went up to Balliol College, Oxford, in October, 1841, with a scholarship, and won in 1843 the Newdigate with a prize poem on Cromwell. After his election to a fellowship at Oriel in 1845 the publication successively of three volumes of verse in 1849, 1852 and 1853 seemed to give promise of a constant poetic output. But his official duties as an Inspector of Schools, to which he was appointed in 1851, and his activity as an essayist on literary, religious, and social subjects, left him in later years little time for the exercise of his muse. Thus in comparison with the other major Victorian poets he has bequeathed a relatively small body of verse.

In my approach to it I have always felt it to be a piece of good fortune that my schooldays were spent, if not at Rugby, at the younger school, Clifton, which counted Rugby as its mother; and that I was an undergraduate within the same Balliol walls—or as much as the restoring builder had left of them—that had formerly sheltered Arnold and Clough. But such associations, though they may quicken appreciation, cannot create it. They certainly are not in themselves responsible for my conviction that Arnold's finest verse will be one of the most enduring memorials of the Victorian age, as a stately poetic manifesto of intellectual " resolution and independence."

Arnold was from his Rugby days brought into contact with the highest culture of his time, and found himself at the centre of many of its most stirring intellectual forces. Religious and political discussions were in the air around him ; classical, foreign, and English literature all lay open to him. These early influences have left their mark equally upon his verse and his prose, though they are all dominated by his own strong personality. The elder Arnold, while belonging to the liberal school in theology, had based his teaching upon firm and definite religious convictions ; from these convictions his son broke away, and throughout his life he was seeking to replace them by something which, like them, would nerve the will, and yield a peace like unto theirs. In this effort he failed, and his finest verse is thus the utterance of a baffled aspiration, a deep-seated despondency : it is one long variation, to use R. H. Hutton's words, " on a single theme, the divorce between the soul and the intellect, and the depth of spiritual yearning and regret which that divorce produces." But of the poetry of pessimism the mid-Victorian age yielded an over-abundant store, and did Arnold give us no more than this, he would not take the rank he does nor wield so peculiar an influence. The distinctive feature of his verse is that joined to the despondency and the yearning there is a tone of haughty, almost imperious self-control ;

there is an inner resistance to the counsels of despair.
We may account partly for this by the influence of the
Rugby teaching, with its earnest, strenuous temper, of
which he always felt the moral effect, long after he had
cut its religious ground-work from under his feet.
But it is still more due to certain elements in his own
personality, a fine egotism that thinks scorn of absolute
spiritual defeat, a consciousness of what has been aptly
called an " Olympian dignity and grace." And thus
he naturally turned to the two poets who have in some
measure the same characteristics, Goethe and Wordsworth. And scarcely inferior to the influence on him
of these two great moderns was that of the poets of
Greece, especially Homer and Sophocles. The repose,
the self-control, the chastened severity of Greek art
appealed to the kindred qualities of his own mind ; they
braced and strengthened them ; they tempered his
melancholy ; they were an anodyne to the fever of his
spirit. And thus the total impression left by his verse
is one, indeed, of despondency, but a despondency kept
at bay, powerless to ruffle an inner zone of calm.

From this point of view I am not speaking of Arnold's
narrative poems, *Sohrab and Rustum* and *Balder Dead*,
or of semi-dramatic poems, *The Sick King in Bokhara*,
Tristram and Iseult, and *Empedocles on Etna*, though
Empedocles contains some of his most masterly work.
It is in his lyric verse that tells of the tumult of the soul,
of spiritual fever and unrest, that we hear his most spontaneous cry. Sometimes it has in it the tone of un-
relieved despondency. Thus as he stands on Dover
Beach at night listening to the ceaseless wash of the
waves to and fro on the pebbles, " bringing the eternal

note of sadness," this is the thought suggested to his
mind :

> The sea of faith
> Was once too at the full, and round earth's shore
> Lay like the folds of a bright girdle furled ;
> But now I only hear
> Its melancholy, long, withdrawing roar,
> Retreating to the breath
> Of the night-wind down the vast edges drear
> And naked shingles of the world.

The fair shows of the world are only delusive, for it—

> Hath really neither joy, nor love, nor light,
> Nor certitude, nor peace, nor help for pain,
> And we are here as on a darkling plain
> Swept with confused alarms of struggle and fight,
> Where ignorant armies clash by night.

In the *Stanzas from the Grande Chartreuse* we hear
the same melancholy note.   In utter weariness of the
" haste, unrest, and disarray," the mingled hardness and
frivolity, of the modern world, the poet seeks shelter for
a time with the men from whom he is intellectually poles
asunder—the Carthusian monks in their cloister of the
Grande Chartreuse.

The austere and solemn rhythm of Arnold's verse is
in consonance with the austere and solemn rule of the
Alpine monastery :

> The silent courts, where night and day
> Into their stone-carved basins cold
> The splashing icy fountains play !
> The humid corridors behold
> Where, ghostlike in the deepening night
> Cowl'd forms brush by in gleaming white.

The chapel, where no organ's peal
Invests the stern and naked prayer—
With penitential cries they kneel
And wrestle; rising then, with bare
And white uplifted faces stand
Passing the Host from hand to hand;

Each takes, and then his visage wan
Is buried in his cowl once more.
The cells! the suffering Son of Man
Upon the wall—the knee-worn floor—
And where they sleep, that wooden bed
Which shall their coffin be, when dead.

When Arnold thus seeks shelter with the stern disciples of the ancient creed he is, in a sense, treading the
same path as the Pre-Raphaelites—Rossetti or Morris.
They found a refuge from the disorder and ugliness of
modern life in a revival of the Catholic tradition, though
they did not hold the creed upon which it rests, and
which gives it its vitality. But Arnold cannot be satisfied with such a compromise, such a make-belief. The
incongruity between himself and his surroundings in
the Monastery glares in upon him, and wrings from him
the cry almost of alarm, "And what am I, that I am
here?"

For rigorous teachers seized my youth,
And purged its faith, and trimm'd its fire,
Showed me the high, white star of Truth,
There bade me gaze, and there aspire.
Even now their whispers pierce the gloom:
"What dost thou in this living tomb?"

But it is not in the spirit of a deserter that he thus tarries for a moment in the camp of those whom he considers enemies of " the masters of the mind." His one point of contact with the Monks is that both they and he are out of harmony with the modern world. They recoil from its infidelity—an infidelity which he shares ; he mourns over the materialism, the hardness of which that infidelity is in large part the cause. Hence in stanzas of haunting sadness, all the sadder because of the complete absence of sentimentality, he craves asylum within the cloister-walls :

> Wandering between two worlds, one dead,
> The other powerless to be born,
> With nowhere yet to rest my head,
> Like these on earth, I wait forlorn.
> Their faith, my tears, the world deride,
> I come to shed them at their side.

> O hide me in your gloom profound
> Ye solemn seats of holy pain !
> Take me, cowl'd forms, and fence me round
> Till I possess my soul again ;
> Till free my thoughts before me roll,
> Not chafed by hourly false control.

To his despondent mood the ferment of the Revolutionary movement, " all the noise and outcry of the former men," seem to have been fruitless. What boots it that Byron unfolded to the gaze of Europe the pageant of his bleeding heart, that the breeze carried Shelley's lovely wail through the Italian trees ? Hearts are still restless ; " the eternal trifler," the world, still takes her frivolous course. He can only bide sadly the coming of a happier, more harmonious day:

> Years hence, perhaps, may dawn an age
> More fortunate, alas, than we,
> Which without hardness will be sage
> And gay without frivolity.
> Sons of the world, oh speed those years,
> But while we wait, allow our tears.

Similar in spirit to these *Stanzas* are the two poems, *Stanzas in Memory of the Author of Obermann*, and *Obermann Once More*. It has been said that it may be questioned whether anywhere within equal space there is to be found so much of the real Arnold as in these three poems.

Obermann is a collection of letters from Switzerland treating of Nature and the human soul, something after the fashion of *Amiel's Diary*, and its author, Etienne de Senancourt (1770–1846), was a curiously kindred spirit to Arnold. He had scanned well " the hopeless tangle " of the age, an age whose haste and unrest are graphically pictured in the well-known verses:

> We brought forth and reared in hours
> Of change, alarm, surprise—
> What shelter to grow ripe is ours,
> What leisure to grow wise?
>
> Like children bathing on the shore
> Buried a wave beneath,
> The second wave succeeds before
> We have had time to draw breath.

In the Alpine solitudes he had attained to calm, though " if any calm, a calm despair." His state of feeling is

pictured by Arnold in verses, which apply exactly to his
own poetry :

> A fever in these pages burns
>   Beneath the calm they feign,
> A wounded human spirit turns
>   Here, on its bed of pain.
>
> Yes, though the virgin mountain-air
>   Fresh through these pages blows,
> Though to these leaves the glaciers spare
>   The soul of their white snows ;
>
> Though here a mountain-murmur swells
>   Of many a dark-boughed pine ;
> Though, as you read, you hear the bells
>   Of the high-pasturing kine :
>
> Yet, through the hum of torrent lone
>   And brooding mountain bee,
> There sobs I know not what ground-tone
>   Of human agony.

This alternation between calm and despondency, till
we are at a loss to tell which is really the predominating
note, is exactly what is most distinctive of Arnold's own
intellectual attitude, and we are therefore not surprised
to find him, after he has taken a last farewell of this
" master of his wandering youth," returning many years
after to commune with him in spirit again. In *Obermann Once More* Senancourt takes Arnold back in
thought to the birth-time of Christianity and the down-
fall of the " hard pageantry of Roman civilization " at
the touch of the new religion. In lines of almost

passionate self-revelation the poet gives voice through
the lips of Senancourt to his yearning for the spiritual
ecstasy of those first years :

> O had I lived in that great day,
>   How had its glory new
> Fill'd earth and heaven, and caught away
>   My ravish'd spirit too.

> No cloister-floor of humid stone
>   Had been too cold for me.
> For me no Eastern desert lone
>   Had been too far to flee.

But, as his prose writings testify, Arnold believed that
that early Christian religious enthusiasm had no solid
basis in historic facts.

Humanity, he held, must throw over its supernatural
creeds, must labour henceforth unduped of fancy. The
inevitable results at first are disorganization of the social
order and widespread suffering. These are incidental
to an epoch of transition, when—

> The old is out of date,
> The new is not yet born.

But this state is not to be permanent :

> Men have such need of joy !
> But joy whose grounds are true :
> And joy that should all hearts employ
> As when the past was new.

Of the new era marked by—

> The common wave of thought and joy
> Lifting mankind again—

we get a vague and shadowy vista at the close of the poem.

The shadow of the fierce intellectual strife of the Victorian age hangs over *The Scholar-Gipsy* and *Thyrsis*. These two poems, from one point of view, are Arnold's tribute to Oxford, "the sweet city of the dreaming spires," whom he loved so dearly, and of whom in prose, too, he has written words never to be forgotten by her sons. Those to whom almost every line in these poems has an association of its own will always keep for them a peculiar corner in their affections, but judged simply on their own merits they are noble and stately structures of verse. *The Scholar-Gipsy* is founded on a passage in a book by Glanvil, a writer of Charles II's time. It tells :

> The story of that Oxford scholar poor
> Of shining parts and quick inventive brain
> Who, tired of knocking at preferment's door,
>   One summer-morn forsook
> His friends, and went to learn the gipsy-lore
> And roamed the world with that wild brotherhood,
> And came, as most men deemed, to little good,
> But came to Oxford and his friends no more.

But though to Oxford itself he came no more, the poet thinks of him as still haunting its neighbourhood. And Arnold's love of, and intimate familiarity with, the scenery surrounding the university city, gives to his descriptive verse here a richness and wealth of colouring unusual in his sculpturesque poetry :

> Thee at the ferry Oxford riders blithe
> Returning home on summer nights have met

Crossing the stripling Thames at Bab-lock-hithe,
Trailing in the cool streams thy fingers wet,
   As the punt's rope chops round,
And leaning backward in a pensive dream,
And fostering in thy lap a heap of flowers
Plucked in shy fields, and distant Wychwood bowers,
   And thine eyes resting on the moonlit stream.

But then the thought comes that such fancies are only
a dream. Two hundred years have flown since the
Scholar-Gipsy wandered forth, now he is gone from
earth, " long since and in some quiet churchyard laid."
And yet must this be so? May he not, in his restful
woodland life, possess an immortal lot? It is not the
lapse of years that kills, but " the sick fatigue, the lan-
guid doubt" of those " who hesitate and falter life
away." And in contrasting the wanderer's untroubled
existence with our own Arnold gives us a marvellously
true picture of himself and his special achievement :

We suffer, and amongst no one
Who most has suffered, takes dejectedly
His seat upon the intellectual throne,
   And all his store of sad experience he
      Lays bare of wretched days :
Tells us his misery's birth and growth and signs,
And how the dying spark of hope was fed,
And how the breast was soothed, and how the head,
   And all his hourly varied anodynes.

From the infection of this mental strife the Scholar-
Gipsy is bidden fly far. It is this that kills : once let
him come into contact with it and his

Glad perennial youth would fade,
Fade and grow old at last, and die like ours.

Thyrsis is his masterpiece in elegy in the stricter sense.
It lacks the deep, poignant note of grief that we find in
In Memoriam; it paints no such exquisite picture of
early Victorian life. But it is the lineal successor in
English poetry to *Lycidas*. Like Milton, Arnold, with
exquisite skill, blends the refinement, the restraint of
the Greek pastoral elegy with modern imagery and
meditation.

Clough had gone to his grave in his time, worn out
by mental struggle; he had not been strong enough to
wait the passing of the storm. And in magnificent
verses the poet compares him to the cuckoo, who, when
spring is ushered out with rain and wind, takes a hasty
leave and will not stay to see the greater glories of
summer :

So, some tempestuous morn in early June
When the year's primal burst of bloom is o'er,
Before the roses and the longest day—
When garden-walks and all the grassy floor
With blossom red and white of fallen May,
    And chestnut flowers are strewn,
So have I heard the cuckoo's parting cry,
From the wet field, through the vext garden-trees,
Come with the volleying rain, and tossing breeze :
" *The bloom is gone, and with the bloom go I.*"

Too quick despairer, wherefore wilt thou go ?
Soon will the high mid-summer pomps come on,
Soon will the musk carnations break and swell,
Soon shall we have gold-dusted snapdragon,
Sweet-William with his homely cottage-smell,
    And stocks in fragrant bloom :

Roses that down the alleys shine afar,
And open jasmine-muffled lattices,
And groups under the dreaming garden trees,
And the full moon, and the white evening star.

As superb delineations of English spring and summer
scenes it would be impossible to out-rival these
stanzas.

But as the poet, with an exquisite turn of thought,
laments, it is just because he is an English shepherd,
singing among English fields, that he cannot summon
back his friend from the underworld. A Sicilian shepherd, in like case, could cross the river Styx and appeal
to Pluto's bride, Proserpine, and flute his friend, like
Orpheus, from the dead :

O easy access to the hearer's grace
When Dorian shepherds sang to Proserpine !
For she herself had trod Sicilian fields,
She knew the Dorian water's gush divine,
She knew each lily white which Enna yields,
    Each rose with blushing face ;
She loved the Dorian pipe, the Dorian strain,
But ah, of our poor Thames she never heard !
Her foot the Cumnor cowslips never stirr'd,
And we should tease her with our plaint in vain.

But though Thyrsis is thus gone for ever, and may
not be recalled, we feel that as the poet lingers lovingly
among their old haunts his grief becomes milder :

I know what white, what purple fritillaries
The grassy harvest of the river-fields
Above by Ensham, down by Sandford, yields,
And what sedged brooks are Thames' tributaries.

And it seems only fitting that he should end with the determination not to despair while—

'Neath the soft canopy of English air—

he can see the slopes, the fields, the woods, dear to the Scholar-Gipsy and his own dead friend. " Such English-coloured verse," says Swinburne, " no poet has written since Shakespeare, who chooses his field-flowers and hedgerow blossoms with the same sure and loving hand, binds them in as sweet and simple an order."

It is Wordsworth who has most deeply influenced Arnold's descriptive poetry, but their method of treating Nature is nevertheless essentially different. With Wordsworth, as Hutton has said, " Nature is the occasion, but his own mind always the *object* of thought ; in the midst of outward beauties, and at their suggestion, he exercises the inward eye that is the bliss of solitude." But Arnold does not thus re-create Nature in his own consciousness ; he pictures her simply as she is ; he gives us a delicate transcript " painted in the clear, dewy water-colours of tranquil memory." Hence follows another difference between the two poets. Wordsworth infuses into his descriptions something of his own ardent and rapt personality. His heart leaps up when he beholds a rainbow in the sky ; in the jocund company of the daffodils he cannot but be gay, and even in thinking of them in memory, his

> heart with pleasure fills,
> And dances with the daffodils.

He rejoices when he hears the voice of the cuckoo,

bringing to him a tale of visionary hours. But in Arnold Nature never causes this exaltation of spirit; she does not stir his pulse or quicken the throbs of his heart; she merely lays a cooling hand upon his brow; she turns the mood that would be despondency into calm.

Thus his favourite objects of contemplation are those in which there is something subdued—mist rather than cloudless brightness, moonlight rather than sunlight, sounds of gentle melancholy rather than the roar of the tempest or cataract; the slow, imperceptible operations of growth and decay rather than sudden throes and convulsions. His love of moonlight is very noticeable, and it can hardly be a mere fancy which connects it with his habitual mood of mind. Moonlight in literature has several functions. It is widely associated with romance, because its glamour leaves the fancy less confined than the full daylight. But in Arnold's poems its function is not to deepen the sense of mystery; it is rather to tone down the colours to an eye weary of the world.

Even into the half-playful elegies on his dead pets— his dogs and his canary—the melancholy undertone creeps in. The short span of life allotted to Geist, the dachshund, and the spirit in which he met his fate suggests a homily to man. Four years were Geist's whole day:

> Yes, only four—and not the course
> Of all the centuries yet to come,
> And not the infinite resource
> Of Nature—with her countless sum
> Of figures, with her fulness vast
> Of new creation evermore,
> Can ever quite repeat the past,
> Or just thy little self restore.

Stern law of every mortal lot !
Which man, proud man, finds hard to bear,
And builds himself I know not what
Of second life, I know not where.

But thou when struck thine hour to go,
On us, who stood despondent by,
A meek last glance of love didst throw,
And humbly lay thee down to die.

Still more characteristic is the elegy on the canary,
poor Matthias, whose dainty trochaic rhythm has an
echo of the dead songster's trilling note :

Poor Matthias ! Found him lying
Fall'n beneath his perch and dying ?
Found him stiff, you say, though warm
All convulsed his little form ?
One more gasp—it is the end,
Dead and mute our tiny friend.

He has gone to join " Atossa sage," the cat who used
to sit for hours beside his cage :

Cruel, but composed and bland,
Dumb, inscrutable and grand ;
So Tiberius might have sat,
Had Tiberius been a cat.

And the pity of it is that no one divined Matthias's
approaching end :

Poor Matthias, couldst thou speak,
What a tale of thy last week !
Every morning did we pay
Stupid salutations gay,

Suited well to health, but how
Mocking, how incongruous now !
Cake we offer'd, sugar, seed,
Never doubtful of thy need ;
Troubling with our chatter vain
Ebb of life and mortal pain.

Between birds and men there is a great gulf fixed :

What they want, we cannot guess,
Fail to track their deep distress.

But this severance is, after all, only typical of the
isolation of man from his fellow men :

Birds we but repeat on you
What amongst ourselves we do.
What you feel, escapes our ken—
Know we more our fellow men ?
Human longings, human fears
Miss our eyes and miss our ears.
Brother man's despairing sign
Who may trust us to divine ?
Who assure us sundering powers
Stand not 'twixt his soul and ours ?

It is a significant return in this, almost his last poetic
utterance, to the melancholy *leit-motif* :

In the sea of life enisled
We mortal millions live alone.

Yet the isolation is not absolute. It is the function
of a few great men in every age, " heroes," as Carlyle
would have called them, to bridge over the severing sea
of individualism, to guide and guard their fellows.

Such a man in Arnold's eyes was his father, and in the touching lines written in Rugby Chapel we have the filial tribute from the philosopher-poet to the ruler of boys and of men, whose moral temper he reverenced and shared, though intellectually their paths had far diverged.

> Thou wouldst not *alone*
> Be saved, my father ! alone
> Conquer and come to thy goal,
> Leaving the rest in the wild.

It is the mission of such as he to recall the stragglers, refresh the weary among the host of humanity on its toilsome march :

> Beacons of hope ye appear,
> Languor is not in your heart,
> Weakness is not in your word,
> Weariness not in your brow.
> Ye alight in our van ! at your voice
> Panic, despair, fly away.

It was the lack of more of such heroic souls " tempered with fire " in the England of the eighteen-sixties —an England, as he thought, under the domination of the Philistines—that moved him in the lines on *Heine's Grave* to echo the German poet's denunciations :

> I chide with thee not, that thy sharp
> Upbraidings often assail'd
> England, my country—for we,
> Heavy and sad, for her sons,
> Long since, deep in our hearts

Echo the blame of her foes.
We, too, sigh that she flags;
We, too, say that she now
Scarce comprehending the voice
Of her greatest golden-mouthed sons
Of a former age any more—
Stupidly travels her round
Of mechanic business, and lets
Slowly die out of her life
Glory, and genius, and joy.
So thou arraign'st her, her foe,
So we arraign her, her sons,
Yes, we arraign her! but she,
The weary Titan, with deaf
Ears, and labour-dimm'd eyes,
Regarding neither to right
Nor left, goes passively by
Staggering on to her goal;
Bearing on shoulders immense
Atlantëan, the load,
Well nigh not to be borne,
Of the too vast orb of her fate.

It is questionable if the more quickly ear-catching Imperialist verse of the next generation contained so noble and permanently impressive an image of England as this of " the weary Titan." Here we have the conception of the White Man's Burden translated, so far as it affects England, into lofty and essentially poetic phrase. It would be impossible to picture more graphically the responsibilities of wide-world empire, or to arraign more effectually the temper in which they should not be met. This firm, undaunted spirit is of the very essence of the man. Like Shelley in his *Ode to the West Wind*, he may cry at times : " I fall upon the thorns of life ! I bleed." But he could never echo the lines that follow in the *Ode* :

> A heavy weight of years has chained and bowed
> One too like thee—tameless and swift and proud.

Arnold is at the end " tameless and proud," unchained, unbent by the heavy weight of years. His lot is cast in an iron time. He does not see the end of the struggle, but he fights and he endures. It is enough, as he tells us in *The Last Word*, if at the close he falls, arms in hand and with his face to the foe :

> They out-talked thee, hissed thee, tore thee ?
> Better men fared thus before thee,
> Fired their ringing shot and passed,
> Hotly charged and sank at last.

> Charge once more then and be dumb ;
> Let the victors, when they come,
> When the forts of folly fall,
> Find thy body by the wall.

I am not one of those who accept Arnold's view of life as adequate. But the power of poetry is not dependent upon the views that it sets forth. In hours when the edge of our intellect is blunted, our keenness of vision dimmed, our nerve unstrung, Arnold's poetry, so exquisite in finish, so restrained in tone, so keen and lucid in analysis, has a peculiar, a unique appeal. There is no other body of verse quite akin to it : it is the poetry of the *Götterdämmerung*, the twilight of the Gods.

XI

SIR ARTHUR PINERO: DRAMATIST AND
STAGE-CHRONICLER

I
N 1856 Mrs. Browning in *Aurora Leigh* anticipated
that the drama might outgrow

The simulation of the painted scene,
Boards, actors, prompters, gaslight and costume.

In the previous year, on May 24, 1855, there had been
born in the Old Kent Road, London, Arthur Wing
Pinero, who as a playwright was to do much to defeat
such a sombre prophecy, but who, as a student of
theatrical history, was to depict the depressed condition
of the English stage at the period when *Aurora Leigh*
was published. In a paper that he read to the Royal
Society of Literature on March 27, 1929, on "The Theatre
in the Seventies", [1] Pinero described the state to which
the theatre had fallen in the middle of the nineteenth
century :

It was a theatre, so far as the higher aims of the drama were
concerned, of faded, outworn tradition. Shakespeare was

[1] Printed in *The Eighteen Seventies : Essays by Fellows of
the Royal Society of Literature*, edited by Harley Granville-Barker
(Cambridge Univ. Press), 1929.

acted pretty regularly in a plodding, uninspired way ; but for modern poetic drama audiences were still asked to listen to the jog-trot rhetoric of James Sheridan Knowles and to the clap-trap of Edward Bulwer-Lytton. For the rest the staple fare at our playhouses consisted mainly of pirated versions of pieces of foreign origin and the works of Dion Boucicault, [H. J.] Byron and a few others of smaller talent.

From this condemnation Pinero partly excepted Tom Taylor who, " though an adapter," possessed the skill, which his fellow literary tinkers lacked, or did not care to exercise, to give his dramas a home-brewed flavour. His severest strictures were on " those domestic dramas which had no more semblance to life than in stature a flea has to an elephant."

Pinero then proceeded to tell again the story of the revolution in " domestic drama " effected by Thomas William Robertson whose career was the basis of his play, Trelawny of the Wells.[1] T. W. Robertson and his sister Madge (afterwards Dame Madge Kendal) were members of a theatrical family which had been connected with the Lincoln Circuit. He had been brought up amidst the stage-traditions of the preceding period, and had himself been forced by circumstances to adapt himself to them. Thus when he came up to London he tried his hand at every kind of work connected with the theatre, as actor, prompter, box-office keeper, adapter from the French, writer of original pieces. His first success was in 1863 with David Garrick, adapted from a French play and founded upon an imaginary episode in the life of the great actor.

Throughout his early vicissitudes Robertson had kept

[1] See below, pp. 266–70.

before him the ideal of a more natural and lifelike form of comedy, breaking with the conventions and artificial jargon of his day. In writing an original play, *Society*, he achieved his aim—with the result that the piece was refused by J. B. Buckstone, manager of the Haymarket, and by other managers. But the young actress, Marie Wilton (afterwards Lady Bancroft), had the courage to produce it on November 11, 1865, at the Prince of Wales Theatre, Tottenham Street. She had the full reward of her pluck and insight, for *Society* drew the town and Robertson's success was assured. As Kean half a century before had on a single night vindicated a more natural form of acting, so Robertson on a single night won recognition for a more natural form of playwriting. *Society* was followed by *Ours*, *Caste*, *Play*, *School* and *M.P.*, of which *Caste* and *School* were the most popular. But Robertson was not to enjoy for long the success of his dramatic innovation. He died at the early age of forty-two in February, 1871.

The year of Robertson's death saw the beginning of the rise to fame of a new actor, Henry Irving. He had joined the company at the Lyceum Theatre, then under the management of an American, H. L. Bateman. He electrified London by his performance of Matthias in *The Bells*, a version of the French melodrama, *Le Juif Polonais*. His moving impersonation of Charles I in the play by W. G. Wills followed, and, with his reputation thus established, he succeeded Bateman as manager of the Lyceum company. This event was to be of momentous importance for Pinero's career.

Pinero's father was a solicitor and after leaving school he had entered his office in Lincoln's Inn Fields. Such knowledge of the law as he there obtained he supplemented by attending evening classes at the Birkbeck Institute (as it was then called). But from the first his interests were mainly theatrical. He distinguished himself as an amateur actor, and at the age of nineteen became a professional, making his début at the Theatre Royal, Edinburgh, at a salary of a guinea a week. Soon after his arrival this theatre was burnt down, but he found another engagement in Liverpool. Thence he had the good fortune to pass into Irving's Lyceum Company, where he made his first appearance as Stanley in *King Richard the Second* on January 29, 1877. In his Royal Society of Literature paper Pinero thus speaks of Irving :

It must be confessed that his ambition was centred in himself. He aimed at being acknowledged as the greatest actor of the age, and to be hailed as the legitimate successor of Garrick and of Kean ; and he was content to achieve that aim, adding lustre to his calling in the process. But it was said of him, I think with truth, that such were his inherent gifts, his determination and his infinite patience, that there was no walk in life in which he could not have succeeded. He was the most dignified figure in any assembly, no matter how eminent.

Pinero here testifies to the ineffaceable impression left upon him by Irving's dominant personality. Yet to those of us who remember the Lyceum in its heyday this estimate of Irving's distinctive achievement is somewhat surprising. His rank as an actor has always been a matter of debate, and it is doubtful if from this point of view he is to be classed with Garrick and Kean. Where he added " lustre to his calling " was by his lofty conception of theatrical art in its varied aspects and his single-minded devotion to its service. He made of the Lyceum a true temple of the drama and inspired in the Victorian public a new realization of the importance of the stage in the national life. Irving's idealism could not but influence profoundly his young subordinate interested from the first in the history and scope of theatrical art.

Pinero after appearing in minor Shakespearian parts soon found that his own bent was not for acting but for play-writing. While still at the Lyceum he produced three little pieces which drew from Irving the prophecy that if he went on as he had begun he would be sure to make a good position as a dramatic author.

With *The Money-Spinner* performed, after a preliminary production in Manchester, at the St. James's Theatre on January 8, 1881, the prophecy began to be fulfilled. This two-act play takes its name from the chief character, a young wife who cheats at cards to pay off a sum stolen by her husband. Here from the very beginning of his career as a playwright Pinero was fortunate in his actors. The chief parts in *The Money-Spinner* were taken by Mr. and Mrs. Kendal and John Hare [1]; and it was the same trio, especially Mrs. Kendal, who helped to make the success of his next play, *The Squire*, based upon a strange marriage tangle.

But it was as a writer of farce that Pinero was first to show his originality, and to break as new ground in this field as T. W. Robertson had done in comedy. The

[1] My introduction to Pinero as a dramatist was when the play went on tour and I saw it performed in the Belfast Theatre Royal.

type of farce that had hitherto held the Victorian stage was based on incident or intrigue, such simple, if entertaining, fare as Morton's *Box and Cox* or the more highly seasoned adaptations from the French, like *Pink Dominoes*. In three pieces produced at the Court Theatre between 1885 and 1887, *The Magistrate*, *The Schoolmistress* and *Dandy Dick*, Pinero, as Mr. Hamilton Fyfe has truly said,[1] " brought back to life the farce of character, the farce based upon incongruity, the farce which shows us in the most light-hearted and entertaining fashion, possible people doing improbable things."

Thus in *Dandy Dick* the Dean of St. Marvell's, eager to raise money to preserve the Cathedral spire, and urged on by his sporting widowed sister, Georgiana Tidman, commissions his butler to put £50 for him on a horse, Dandy Dick. He plunges deeper by administering a bolus mash to the horse, and is arrested on suspicion of " trying to poison a starter on the eve of a race." After a period of confinement in the local lock-up he is released through the combined efforts of the constable's wife, formerly cook at the Deanery, Georgiana and Sir Tristram Marden, who are the joint owners of Dandy Dick. They rescue him from the cart in which the constable is driving him over to be tried in the magistrate's court. And Georgiana is so affected by Sir Tristram's exploit of pulling " the horse's nose-bag over my brother's head so that he shouldn't be recognized," that she rewards him with her hand.

It was Mrs. John Wood's impersonation of the sporting widow that had done most to ensure the success of *Dandy Dick*. Six years later, in 1893, Pinero pre-

[1] *Sir Arthur Pinero's Plays and Players*, p. 37.

sented in *The Amazons* another widow, Lady Castle-
jordan, whose three girls had been trained on similarly
mannish lines. Thrice she and her husband had been
disappointed in their hopes of a boy :

By that time Jack and I had agreed to regard anything that
was born to us as a boy, and treat it accordingly ; and for the
rest of his life my husband taught our three children—there
never was another—to ride, fish, shoot, swim, fence, fight,
wrestle, throw, run, jump, until they were as hardy as Indians,
and their muscles burst the sleeves of their jackets. And
when Jack went I continued their old training.

But the three " boys," after an entertaining series of
complications, prove themselves, in the words of Lady
Noeline, the eldest, to be " nothing but ordinary, weak,
affectionate, chicken-hearted young women," who find
their affinities respectively in a muscular, resourceful
cousin, Lord Litterly, an effete descendant of the Fitz-
brays, Lord Tweenwayes, and a preposterous but good-
natured French Count.

But in the half-dozen years between *Dandy Dick* and
The Amazons Pinero had shown that his dramatic powers
ranged far beyond the limits of farce. With *Sweet
Lavender*, produced at Terry's Theatre in the Strand
on March 21, 1888, he achieved a triumphant success
in the field of domestic sentimental drama. And here
it was an actor, not an actress, who gave the dramatist
outstanding support. Edward Terry was the ideal
embodiment of Dick Phenyl, the broken-down, tippling,
good-hearted barrister, the most deeply observed character that Pinero had yet drawn. What a self-revelation there is in his classic query—" If you don't take

drop weak whisky an' water after the labours of the day, when do you take drop weak whisky an' water ? " And when he is rebuked by his young friend, Clement Hale, who shares his rooms in the Temple, for breaking his promise to reform, Dick greets Clement with his favourite formula, " Blame, blame, blame ; but praise —oh dear, no ! " Clement, the adopted son of a rich banker, Wedderburn, has fallen in love with Lavender, the seventeen-year-old daughter of Mrs. Rolt, their housekeeper at the Temple. But Mrs. Rolt discovers that Wedderburn is an early lover of her own and the father of Lavender. She at once leaves the Temple, taking the girl with her. But the failure of Wedderburn's bank, and the reduction of Clement to poverty, give an opening to Lavender to come back. All ends with the prospect of marriage bells not only for Clement and Lavender, charmingly played by Rose Norreys, but for Clement's cousin, Minnie, and the agreeably importunate American, Horace Bream. When the play was produced in New York by Daniel Frohman,[1] he found it necessary after the first night, with Pinero's reluctant consent, to remove the slur of illegitimacy from Lavender. To those who know the New York stage to-day this sounds almost incredible, but it reminds us that behind the somewhat treacly sentiment of *Sweet Lavender* there lurked the uglier side of sexual relationships.

With *The Profligate*, produced at the newly built Garrick Theatre on April 24, 1889, a little more than

---

[1] Mr. Frohman is still active as a veteran of the theatre. I took part with him in the celebration of Shakespeare's birthday in Central Park, New York, in 1935.

a year after the appearance of *Sweet Lavender*, this uglier
sexual side came into the foreground, and Pinero began
the series of plays which, in a far more significant way
than his farces, marked a new departure in the Victorian
theatre. Robertson had pointed the way from artifice
to reality, but English drama still went in blinkers so
far as the serious treatment of the seamier elements in
life was concerned. Pinero signalized his new departure by inscribing on his play-bill some lines which
conclude as follows:

> You can't turn curds to milk again,
> Nor Now by wishing back to Then;
> And having tasted stolen honey,
> You can't buy innocence for money.

Dunstan Renshaw had "tasted stolen honey." He
had heartlessly betrayed Janet Preece in a career of
selfish profligacy. As he says himself, loving was to
him "like a tune a man hums for a day and can't recall
a week afterwards." As often happens with a roué of
his type he has been captivated before the play opens
by the innocent charms of a schoolgirl, Leslie Brudenell.
After a farewell carouse with some boon companions
he marries her at a registry office. But almost at the
same moment his seduction of Janet is accidentally
discovered by Hugh Murray, another lover of Leslie.
He hides the secret from the girl, but Renshaw knows
that his guilt may be revealed at any moment. "The
Past has overtaken me! I am in deadly fear. I
dread the visit of a stranger, or the sight of strange
handwriting, and in my sleep I dream that I am mutter-
ing into her ear the truth against myself." After their

marriage he has grown in earnest to love Leslie, and he is now tortured by the thought that she has recognized his real character. He determines, as the play was originally written, to seek a way out by suicide. But again managerial scruples stood in the way. Hare, the lessee of the Garrick, afraid of an unhappy ending, persuaded Pinero to bring about a reconciliation between the reformed profligate and his innocent bride. So at the last moment he dashes the glass of poison to the ground, while Leslie cries, " Dunstan, don't fear me, I will be your wife not your judge." If Renshaw had had a less completely sympathetic interpreter than Johnston Forbes-Robertson, whom I can still see kneeling on the stage at Leslie's feet, it would have been easier to rate at its true value his closing cry, " Wife ! Ah, God bless you. God bless you, and forgive me ! "

But a few months after the production of *The Profligate* an event occurred which made it impossible that there should ever again be such a concession to popular prejudice as the " happy ending " patched on to that play. On June 7, 1889, *The Doll's House* was performed at the Novelty Theatre. It was the first revelation of Ibsen to an English audience. In 1891 George Bernard Shaw published his *The Quintessence of Ibsenism*. Early in the same year J. T. Grein produced *Ghosts* at the Independent Theatre. *Rosmersholm* and *Hedda Gabler* followed. In spite of the indignant outcry led by Clement Scott of the *Daily Telegraph*, there was the revelation of a more severe and economic dramatic technique and of a more unflinching, realistic attitude to all the facts of life. Pinero's art had already been moving in both these directions, and the measure of the Ibsenite influence

on him, direct or indirect, may be gauged by the distance
that separates *The Profligate* from *The Second Mrs.
Tanqueray* produced at the St. James's Theatre, May 27,
1893. Perhaps only those of us who saw the play during
its first London run can realize the thrill that *The Second
Mrs. Tanqueray* gave to the theatrical world of forty
years ago. There was the daring novelty of the subject.
An Englishman of mature age and good position deliberately takes as his second wife a courtesan—a woman
whose name is Paula Ray but who, under different
aliases, has been the mistress successively of a number
of men. Aubrey Tanqueray's motives are mixed. His
daughter by his first marriage, Ellean, now being educated in a convent in Ireland, has refused to come
home, and he has a lonely prospect before him. But
his chief aim is to right a wrong, to redeem a woman to
whom the world has never given a chance. As he tells
his closest friend, Cayley Drummle, the typical man
about town :

To you, Cayley, all women who have been roughly treated
and who dare to survive by borrowing a little of our philosophy, are alike. You see in the crowd of the ill-used only one
pattern ; you can't detect the shades of goodness, intelligence,
even nobility there. . . . She has never met a man who has
treated her well. I intend to treat her well. That's all.
And in a few years, Cayley, if you've not quite forsaken me,
I'll prove to you that it's possible to rear a life of happiness,
of good repute on a miserable foundation.

How masterly is the opening Act where the whole
situation is unfolded in conversation over a dinner-table.
The receipt by Aubrey of Ellean's letter on the very

eve of his wedding announcing her sudden change of
mind and her immediate return home is indeed a somewhat forced coincidence. But thereafter all proceeds
with remorseless logic to the tragic close. In the Surrey
home to which Aubrey takes his wife, Ellean, though
she does not know her stepmother's history, and though
Paula attempts to win her affections, recoils instinctively
from her. The girl is taken to Paris for a visit by Mrs.
Cortelyon, a neighbour and old friend of Aubrey, who
has aroused Paula's anger by delaying to call on her.
Here Ellean has a proposal from Captain Hugh Ardale,
on leave from India where he has won the V.C. for his
bravery, and he accompanies the ladies home to get
Aubrey's sanction to the engagement. By chance he
meets Paula first—Paula with whom he had lived for a
time in London. Hitherto she has done little to justify
Aubrey's faith in her. She has been bored with the
countryside, jealous of his love for Ellean, rude to Mrs.
Cortelyon, defiant of his command that she should not
invite another former woman of the town and her sottish
titled husband. But now with disastrous consequences
to him and his and herself she is to vindicate his belief in
her. In spite of Hugh's entreaties she reveals to Aubrey
her former relations with him and he forbids the match
between Hugh and Ellean. The girl whose happiness
had just begun to draw her closer to Paula, realizes that
it is her stepmother who has come between her and Hugh,
and guesses the truth of the situation.

Ell. I have always known what you were.
P. Ah. Who told you?
Ell. Nobody but yourself. From the first moment I
saw you I knew you were altogether unlike the good woman

I'd left; directly I saw you I knew what my father had done. You've wondered why I've turned from you? There—that's the reason. Oh, but this is a horrible way for the truth to come home to every one.

Between Ellean and Paula there must be separation, but Aubrey does not yet despair:

We'll go out of this place and go abroad again and begin afresh. . . . We'll make our calculations solely for the future, talk about the future, think about the future.

P. I believe the future is only the past again, entered through another gate.

A. That's an awful belief.

P. To-night proves it. You must see now that do what we will, go where we will, you'll be continually reminded of what I was. . . . You'll do your best—oh, I know that—you're a good fellow. But circumstances will be too strong for you in the end, mark my words.

He forestalls the end by going out and taking poison. Even Hare could scarcely have asked for another ending. But he had already declined the play for the Garrick, and it had appeared, paradoxically enough, at the St. James's, the sacred home of high comedy. For such a part as that of Aubrey Tanqueray, George Alexander was more perfectly fitted than Forbes-Robertson, for whom it had been designed. And the magnetic personality of a hitherto almost unknown actress, Mrs. Patrick Campbell, made her the ideal representative of Paula. Yet it was almost by accident that the part of Paula had fallen to her. Pinero had first thought of Miss Olga Nethersole for it ; afterwards of Miss Janet Achurch who had acted Nora in *The Doll's House*; Alexander had

suggested Miss Winifred Emery. For various reasons
they had to be put aside, and the eyes of the author
and manager were inquiringly turned to Mrs. Patrick
Campbell, then playing in a melodrama at the Adelphi
for the brothers Gatti. It seemed highly doubtful, however, whether they would release her in time for a new
production at the St. James's, and Miss Elizabeth Robins
was engaged to play Paula. Then the Gattis unexpect-
edly set Mrs. Campbell free, and with splendid self-
abnegation Miss Robins surrendered to a younger
and less-known rival the opportunity of creating one of
the classic roles on the modern stage.

The impersonator of Cayley Drummle was also in
doubt till the last moment. Cyril Maude was wanted for
the part, but would he be free? So others were considered, including (as Mr. A. E. W. Mason has recently
told us)[1] Seymour Hicks, of whom Pinero remarked,
" Hicks is a bright young actor. Would he look too
much like a young man with a wig on?" But Hicks
was destined to follow very different theatrical lines leading eventually to a knighthood; and as with Mrs. Campbell, Cyril Maude, at the eleventh hour, was able to act
at the St. James's. Maude Millett as Ellean, Amy Roselle
as Mrs. Cortelyon and Ben Webster as Captain Ardale
completed what was to be an historic cast.

The Second Mrs. Tanqueray was played after its first
production 227 times in London, its run being broken
during a ten weeks' provincial tour when Alexander performed it with three other plays. Mr. Mason has dis-
closed that the takings for the play at the St. James's were
£36,688 13s., and during the tour £4,392 9s. 8d., while

[1] *Sir George Alexander and the St. James's Theatre.*

Alexander's net profit from it was £10,946 5s. 2d. We
have no similar record of Pinero's royalties from the
performances, but they must have made a handsome sum.

The triumph of *The Second Mrs. Tanqueray* opened
all theatrical doors to Pinero and it was at the Garrick
that, like *The Profligate* in 1889, the *Notorious Mrs.
Ebbsmith* was produced in March, 1895. Hare , the
shrewd, cynical Duke of St. Olpherts, and Forbes-Robertson as his nephew, the attractive weak epicure, Lucas
Cleeve, achieved two of their most successful impersonations. But in Agnes Ebbsmith Mrs. Patrick Campbell
could not repeat her unequivocal triumph as Paula. The
clear-cut psychology of Aubrey's second wife struck
home far more surely than that of the "notorious"
woman agitator who had nursed Lucas Cleeve back to
health, dreamt of a companionship between them for
high public ends, found herself in love with him, and
then discovered, as the Duke had warned her, that his
feeling for her was merely that " of a sensual man of the
world "—with the consequent collapse of her scheme of
life. But though the *Notorious Mrs. Ebbsmith* missed
a popular triumph, it gained critical applause.

This may be said also of *The Benefit of the Doubt*,
performed at the Comedy Theatre in October, 1895. It,
too, won the suffrages of the critics more than of the
theatre-going public, and for similar reasons. Theo
Fraser has sought diversion from the boredom of her
marriage with a dull Scotch laird by indiscreet conduct
with an old friend, Jack Allingham, and has been dragged
into the divorce court by his jealous wife, Olive. The
judgement is in her favour, but only " with the benefit
of the doubt." Her husband shows her that he is still

suspicious, and, to punish him, she takes flight to Jack's cottage. Here she has been preceded by Olive whom Jack arranges to overhear his interview with Theo, in proof of the innocence of their relations. But Theo, unbalanced by too much champagne, appeals to Jack to take her away with him to Paris, before falling down in a swoon when she sees Olive and knows that she has been a listener. And when later Fraser, now anxious for a reconciliation, tells her that she was not herself in her hysterical outburst, she retorts, " Who says I was not myself ? It *was* myself, the dregs of me that came to the top last night." Here Pinero in pre-Freudian days anticipates the doctrine of the sub-conscious, submerged self. In the end Theo's shrewd, efficient aunt, Mrs. Cloys, wife of the Bishop of St. Olpherts, finds a way out of the tangle by offering to take Theo under the episcopal wing and thus hush the voice of scandal. But it is a somewhat forced solution and neither Theo nor Olive stirs our sympathies. Yet the technical handling of the theme is masterly and in Mrs. Emptage, Theo's valetudinarian mother, and Sir Fletcher Portwood, M.P., her fussy, pompous and ineffectual uncle, Pinero drew two of his most brilliantly " humorous " personages, in the Jonsonian manner.

Unlike *The Benefit of the Doubt*, Pinero's next play, *The Princess and the Butterfly*, produced at the St. James's in March, 1897, appealed more to the public than to the critics. Its success was largely due to the acting of Miss Fay Davis in the part of Fay Zuliani, a high-spirited, temperamental girl, supposedly of Anglo-Italian parentage, and brought up under the care of her reputed uncle, Sir George Lamorant. He, the " butterfly " (a some-

what irrelevant nickname), is a middle-aged bachelor who
is on the point of settling down in wedlock with an old
friend, the widowed Princess Pannonia, now in her
fortieth year. But before a probationary month is ended
she finds herself returning the love of the youthful
diplomat, Edward Oriel, and Lamorant discovers that
Fay is not his niece, and that she has won his heart.
It is highly difficult to make artistically plausible such
unions between disparate ages, especially between a
matron and young man, as even Thackeray has found
in *Esmond*. And apart from this major *crux* there are
other features of the play—the " humour " of Levan
with his box of toys, the hen-pecking of St. Roche, and
the introduction of Mrs. Ware, a vulgarized Paula
Tanqueray—that are not in Pinero's happier vein.

After *The Princess and the Butterfly* Pinero turned aside
for a time from his inquisition into affairs of the heart,
grave or gay, and poignant personal issues, to indulge
his interest in stage-history, and to weave a " comedietta " round the career of T. W. Robertson, disguised
by changes of name and *locale* in *Trelawny of the Wells*,
produced at the Court Theatre on January 20, 1898.
Robertson appears as Tom Wrench, an actor of small
parts in the Bagnigge Wells theatre. Pinero here borrowed the name of a mineral spring in Islington, with
gardens which were a popular resort. The real " Wells "
playhouse was in the neighbouring district of Sadler's
Wells, where Samuel Phelps had made his reputation
as a Shakespearian actor, and which has now been
restored as a dramatic and operatic complement to the
Old Vic in Waterloo Road.

Tom occupies " the chamber nearest heaven," otherwise the garret, in Mrs. Mossop's theatrical lodgings, but when the play opens, he has just entered the first-floor sitting-room of two members of the company, Mr. and Mrs. Telfer, to have the frayed edges of his shirt cuffs and collar clipped by his landlady. Here he is found by Miss Imogen Parrott, formerly of the Wells company, now promoted to the West End Royal Olympic Theatre. She questions him in an off-hand way and in Tom's answers we hear the voice of Robertson in his early struggling days.

Imogen. What about your plays? Are you trying to write any plays just now?

Tom. Trying! I am doing more than trying to write plays. I am writing plays. I have written plays.

Imogen. Well?

Tom. My cupboard upstairs is choked with them.

Imogen. Won't anyone take a fancy?

Tom. Not a sufficiently violent fancy.

Imogen. You know the speeches were so short, and had such ordinary words in them, in the plays you used to read to me—no big opportunity for the leading lady, Wrench.

Tom. M'yes. I strive to make my people talk and behave like ordinary people, don't I?

Imogen. I suppose you do.

Tom. To fashion heroes out of actual, dull everyday men —the sort of men you see smoking cheroots in the club windows in St. James's Street and heroines from simple maidens in muslin frocks. Naturally, the managers won't stand that.

Imogen. Why, of course not.

Tom. If they did, the public wouldn't.

Imogen. Is it likely?

Tom. Is it likely? I wonder!

Imogen. Wonder what?

Tom. Whether they would.

Imogen. The public !

Tom. The public. Jenny, I wonder about it sometimes so hard that that little bedroom of mine becomes a banqueting hall.

They are interrupted by the entrance of other members of the Wells company—James Telfer, a tragedian of the old school, " elaborately dignified in bearing, but a little uncertain about his H's " ; Ferdinand Gadd, " a flashily-dressed young man of seven and twenty," the *jeune premier* ; Augustus Colpoys, unable to forget even off the stage that he is a low comedian ; Mrs. Telfer, " a tall massive lady of middle age—a faded tragedy queen," formerly Miss Violet Sylvester, and Avonia Bunn, " a tawdrily dressed young woman of about three and twenty, with the airs of a suburban soubrette."

The portrayal of these mid-Victorian stage types was singularly congenial to Pinero. They are gathering for a farewell " cold collation " to Miss Rose Trelawny— " Trelawny of the Wells "—who is leaving the company on her engagement to Mr. Arthur Gower, grandson of Sir William Gower, a judicial magnate. Nothing is happier in Pinero's lighter vein than Telfer's oration in honour of Miss Trelawny, with its references to the Queen, coupled with the name of the tragedy-queen, Miss Violet Sylvester, and to " our Immortal Bard, Shakespeare," followed by Arthur Gower's stammering reply. And in Miss Irene Vanbrugh and Gerald Du Maurier, both at the outset of their theatrical careers, the dramatist found perfect representatives of Rose and Telfer.

In the scene in the Gower household, where Rose is yawning away a period of probation before her marriage, the mannerisms and prudish conventions of the genteel society of Cavendish Square are accentuated to the pitch of burlesque. In violent contrast are the free-and-easy ways of Rose's old associates who are driven at midnight by stress of weather to take shelter under the Gower roof. But even here Tom Wrench is preoccupied with his plans for a new type of play and takes notes for this purpose :

This is the kind of chamber I want for the first act of my comedy. . . . I won't have doors stuck here, there, and everywhere ; no, nor windows in all sorts of impossible places. . . . Windows on the one side, doors on the other —just where they should be architecturally. And locks on the doors, *real locks*, to work, and handles—to turn ! Ha ! ha ! you wait, wait !

Pinero himself may not have known how closely he was echoing Robertson's very words. For his sister, Dame Madge Kendal, relates in her autobiography (1933):

When Tom planned this play [*Society*], he confided to my father that in the club scene—the Owl's Nest—he intended when the play was produced to have real hooks screwed into the walls of the room so that the actors could hang their real coats on them. . . . " I think, Tom," he said, " you'd better try something more romantic than hats and coats on pegs in which to interest the public." The scene made an instant success by its realism.

Tom Wrench's meditations and his companions' revelry are suddenly interrupted by the return of Sir William Gower, roused from his bed, and by his furious outburst against the " gipsies " who have violated the

sanctities of Cavendish Square. The sequel is Rose's
flight back to the Wells company, and the disappearance
of Arthur Gower who goes off (not very plausibly) to
join the staff of the theatre at Bristol, then one of the chief
local centres of the drama.

In the resolution of these complications Pinero makes
use of a great theatrical figure of an earlier day. Sir
William Gower, anxious for news of his nephew, pays
a visit to Rose, who cannot enlighten him. But his heart
is softened when he learns that her mother had acted
with the " splendid gipsy " of his own youth, Edmund
Kean, and that Rose still preserves the fillet which her
mother had worn as Cordelia in Kean's production of
Lear,[1] and the order, chain and sword which Kean himself
had worn as Richard III.[2] I have already quoted proof
of Pinero's particular interest in Kean,[3] and he doubtless
felt it an act of *pietas* thus to make him, with some
imaginative embroidery, a reconciling agent in this
" comedietta " of theatrical traditions.

It taxes our credulity, it must be confessed, when Sir
William goes so far in his conversion as to provide the
necessary capital for the production by Miss Imogen
Parrott of Tom Wrench's play, *Life*, at the Phœnix
Theatre, with Rose and Arthur Gower (making a surprise
entrance from Bristol) in the chief parts. So was figured
the staging of Robertson's *Society* by Marie Wilton at
the Prince of Wales's Theatre. And the successful
revival of *Trelawny of the Wells* at the Malvern Theatrical
Festival in 1935 showed that the comedietta had not

[1] See above, p. 108.
[2] See above, pp. 105–6.
[3] See above, pp. 120–1.

270

lost its fragrance nor power of re-creating the atmosphere
of a vanished theatrical age.

Miss Irene Vanbrugh had shown her quality as Rose
Trelawny. In April, 1899, Pinero was to put it to a
different and more exacting test when he chose her to
play the Bond Street manicurist, Sophy Fullgarney,
opposite to John Hare in *The Gay Lord Quex*. Sophy,
the daughter of a bailiff, is the foster-sister of Muriel
Eden, a society girl who has just become engaged under
family pressure to a roué nobleman nearly fifty years of
age, euphemistically known as " the gay " Lord Quex.
Sophy is determined, if she can, to prevent the marriage :
she spies upon Quex when he is having a midnight farewell with an old flame, the Duchess of Strood. In vain
Quex tries to buy the girl's silence. Then he tries a
more effective weapon. He and Sophy are locked alone
in the room. If she is found with a man of his reputation
at such an hour, her own character and her occupation
are gone for ever. For the moment she yields, and writes
a letter that puts her in his power. But with a sudden
revulsion of feeling she cries, " Why, it's like selling
Muriel, just to get myself out of this. I'm simply handing her over to you. I won't do it ! I won't." And
reckless of the consequences to herself she pulls the bell
to summon the household. Quex is so impressed by
her self-sacrificing action that he thrusts back the letter
into her hand and invents an excuse to satisfy the servants
who now appear. Across all the years that have flown
since 1899 I can still hear that duel of wits on the stage
of the Globe Theatre, and can still see Miss Vanbrugh
tugging at that bell-rope.

It might have been well had she been cast for the

heroine in Pinero's next Garrick play, *Iris*, produced two years later in September 1901. Her versatile powers and her sure grasp of character would have better fitted her for this exacting part than Miss Fay Davis whose youthful charm had made her a delightful Fay Zuliani, but who was here taxed beyond her special gifts.

As a piece of construction *Iris* is not in the first rank of Pinero's plays. The first and third Acts are awkwardly divided into three episodes marked by the falling of the curtain, and two years pass between the third and fourth Acts. But the portraiture of Iris Bellamy is a masterly achievement in relentless analysis of character. She is a young widow, very well left, who will forfeit her income if she remarries. She is a spoilt favourite of Fortune, who cannot face the harsher realities of life. So she lets herself drift between young Laurence Tremwith, whom she loves, but who can offer her only a log-hut in Canada, and the millionaire half-foreign Frederick Maldonado whose passion she cannot return. She will not marry either but bids Tremwith follow her as a lover, to Cadenabbia on Lake Como ; and then, when he has gone to Canada, and after a catastrophic turn in her fortunes, she lets herself step by step be pushed into the position of Maldonado's mistress. She idly fancies that Tremwith will overlook all this when she tells him the story on his return. She can scarcely believe her eyes when he goes out from her with merely a muttered "I am sorry." And she has a still ruder awakening when Maldonado, who has overheard their interview, rushes furiously at her and orders her out into the street at night. Her further fate is veiled. There is no purgative tragic self-sought doom as with Paula Tanqueray, but it is a more fitting close in the case of one who, as Mr. Fyfe has most aptly suggested, would have been placed by Dante among those who in their lives earned neither praise nor blame :

> Ouesti non hanno speranza di morte,
> E la lor cieca vita è tanto bassa
> Che invidiosi son d'ogni altra sorte.[1]

For nearly nine years the memorable association of Pinero and George Alexander at the St. James's Theatre had been broken. At the rehearsals of *The Princess and the Butterfly* there had been differences of opinion between author and manager which had rankled in Pinero's memory ; so when Alexander had written to him offering the autumn opening date in 1900 for a play at the St. James's, which had just been enlarged, Pinero declined the offer in a remarkably frank letter which has recently been printed by Mr. Mason [2] and part of which runs :

I know you take a pride in being an autocrat in your theatre ; it is a natural pride in a position which you have worthily won for yourself. But I have also won—or have chosen to usurp—a similarly autocratic position in all that relates to my work. . . . There is not room for two autocrats in one small kingdom ; and in every detail, however slight, that pertains to my work—though I avail myself gratefully of any assistance that is afforded me, I take to myself the right of dictation and veto.

It is almost as if we heard again the voice of Kean, " The throne is mine and I will maintain it." [3] It reminds us

---

[1] These have no hope of death, and their blind life so nearly changes that they are envious of every other fate.

[2] *Sir George Alexander and the St. James's Theatre*, pp. 122–3.

[3] See above, p. 119.

of how in the complex world of the theatre there are always three factors in collaboration and collision—the dramatist, the actor and the producer.   Pinero, with his high conception of the playwright's function, was determined not to let it slip into the subordinate place which some would assign to it to-day.

It is to Alexander's credit that he took the unexpected refusal in good part and offered to have Pinero back at the St. James's on his own terms.   But it was not till February, 1906, that they were again associated in *His House in Order*, with Irene Vanbrugh once more as Pinero's leading lady.   Filmer Jesson, M.P., is devoted to the memory of his highly methodical first wife.

When I ask [he explains] that my house shall be in order, I am asking not only that my luncheon, my dinner, shall be decently and punctually served ; not only that this inkstand, this paper-knife may be found in the same places ; but that every wheel of the mechanism of my private affairs, however minute, may be duly oiled and preserved from grit.

In the hopes of her developing the same qualities as Annabel, Jesson has now married his little son Derek's governess, Nina, played by Irene Vanbrugh.   But as he explains to his brother Hilary, a diplomatist on leave, played by Alexander, the experiment has proved a failure, To keep his house in order he has had to call in Annabel's sister, Geraldine, who tyrannizes over and crushes Nina. But a skilfully contrived set of circumstances puts Nina suddenly in possession of a packet of letters written by another guest in the house, Colonel Maurewarde, which show that he had been the lover of the supposed paragon, Annabel, and that Derek is their son.   Here is a weapon

with which Nina can take revenge on Geraldine for all
the misery she has inflicted on her. In vain Hilary
pleads with her to destroy the letters. But at last he
makes an idealistic appeal :

Nina, there are some people walking the earth who are
wearing a halo. It's invisible to you and me. . . . They
are the people who have made sacrifices, who have been
tempted and who have conquered. . . . They are the people
who have *renounced.* Nina, be among those who wear the
halo. Burn Maurewarde's letters, my dear—or give them to
me and forget you've ever read them.

" I'll forget them," she answers as she hands him the
letters. Hilary lets Maurewarde know that the letters
have been found and bids him clear out. After a vain
attempt to persuade Filmer to get rid of Geraldine on
other grounds, Hilary is driven to show Filmer the letters
too, and to exhort him " to do justice to the living,
make amends to the living." At last Filmer sees the
light.

Order, method, regularity, natural to Annabel are not
natural to Nina. Nina may acquire them or she may not.
But whether she acquires them or whether she does not, it is
her right that she should be mistress of my house. Let us,
my wife and I [he announces to Geraldine and her parents]
let us often welcome you, here and in London, as our guests.

Thus Filmer, in the deepest sense of the words, sets
his house in order.

Two later plays in which Pinero showed much of his
distinctive power were produced by Alexander. They
were *The Thunderbolt* (May 9, 1908), with its ingeniously
paradoxical solution of a testamentary tangle ; and

Mid-Channel (September 2, 1909), with its cynical parallel between the voyage of matrimony and that from Folkestone to Boulogne, where there is a danger-point, even in the finest weather, in the middle of the crossing at the Ridge.

Theodore and Zoe Blundell have in the fourteenth year of their marriage reached the ridge, and they so mismanage the crossing that it ends with Zoe throwing herself from the balcony of a lover's lofty flat near the Albert Hall. It was all the greater shock to the audience that it was Irene Vanbrugh who thus put an end to herself. Alexander was on tour and was not in the cast, but in a letter quoted by Mr. Mason, he wrote to Pinero : " The play is a great tragedy, and will live when we are both cold." Perhaps too optimistic a prophecy, but Mr. Mason ranks *Mid-Channel* " with *Iris*, or next to *Iris*, as the most sincere and acute piece of analysis which Pinero gave to the theatre."

With 1909, when he was knighted, the most significant period of his career came to an end. But in *The " Mind the Paint " Girl*, produced at the Duke of York's Theatre in February, 1912, he was again, as in *Trelawny of the Wells*, to take his theme from theatrical life. Once more the sentimental interest lies in a love-affair between a society " swell," Lord Farncombe, and an actress, Miss Lily Parradell of the Pandora Theatre, leading lady among a group of musical comedy girls who in the words of Lily's popular ditty, " mind the paint ", or just keep on the windy side of the moral code. Pinero shows all his technical skill in manipulating and differentiating his exceptionally numerous *dramatis personæ* and in concentrating the action within the traditional unity of time.

But the raffish atmosphere of the Pandora, with its motley group of elderly hangers-on, contrasts unpleasantly with the honest if somewhat grotesque professionalism of the Wells company. And the see-saw between the " waster," Nicko Jeyes, and the somewhat milk-and-water Farncombe for Lily's hand does not deeply stir us, while there is no Tom Wrench to give the piece historical significance. *The " Mind the Paint " Girl* will always have its interest for students of Pinero's art, but Sir Barry Jackson was assuredly well advised when he chose to revive *Trelawny of the Wells* at the Malvern Festival in 1935 as a tribute to Sir Arthur.

In March, 1913, Pinero dealt with the theatre in an unusually light-hearted mood in a one-act piece at the St. James's, *Playgoers.* Here a mistress is fired with the benevolent idea of sending her domestics to the theatre. But when they are told that they will see " a play of ideas, something to stimulate your imaginations and make you think," the cook pronounces that " we're in for a preshus dull evenin'," and the result is an immediate handing in of notices.

His plays that followed, written during and after the war, including *The Big Drum* (September 1, 1915), a satirical attack on self-advertisement, and *The Enchanted Cottage* (1922), a fantasy on the marriage of a shell-shocked soldier, failed to keep his grip on the theatrical public, and this had caused him disappointment before his death on November 23, 1934.

When *Trelawny of the Wells* was revived at Malvern, *The Alchemist* was another play in the Festival programme. It was a chance combination and these two particular pieces have nothing in common. Yet taken as a whole, the careers of Arthur Pinero and Ben Jonson have much that is parallel. Each was a Londoner by birth, and drew his dramatic material from the medley of London life. Each was a minor actor before he became a playwright. Each was a dramatic craftsman pursuing his self-chosen aims in lofty independence of popular judgement. Both Pinero and Jonson saw life mainly from the satiric side. Their eyes were shut to most of its beautiful and romantic aspects.

It is notable too that both began their theatrical work in a comparatively light vein, sporting " with follies not with crimes." Jonson's early " humour " plays and comical satires may be set beside Pinero's farces of character. Each dramatist had then his period of mature and brilliant achievement, and received both popular and royal recognition, Jonson being created Poet Laureate and Pinero a knight. Each in his later years entered upon a period of decline and became out of touch with the play-going public of the day.

In Pinero's case the reasons for this are not far to seek. Bernard Shaw, Galsworthy and Granville-Barker had begun to handle on the stage political, sociological and biological problems, that were outside the range of Pinero's theatrical interest. Creative evolution would, I imagine, have meant little to him. Other Irish playwrights than Shaw, especially W. B. Yeats and J. M. Synge, were opening up novel sources of beauty and humour. Sir James Barrie had begun to mesmerize theatre-goers with his elfin fantasies.

Neither in the moral issues raised by the Great War, nor in the social issues raised by the sex-war of the feminist movement did Pinero find congenial material.

He was profoundly interested in the personal problem
of a Paula Tanqueray, an Agnes Ebbsmith or an Iris
Bellamy, but he never questioned the fundamental basis
of sexual morality. He sympathized with the revolt of
a Nina Jesson or a Rose Trelawny against the codes
of an over-ordered household, but he had no enthusiasm
for what it was then the fashion to call " the new woman."
Did he ever in his later days call to mind Telfer's words,
in *Trelawny of the Wells*, adapted from *Macbeth*, concerning Tom Wrench's play ? " And so this newfangled
stuff, and these dandified people, are to push us and such
as us, from our stools." To which Mrs. Telfer, reduced
from playing tragedy queens to being wardrobe mistress,
replies : " Yes, James, just as some other new fashion
will, in course of time, push them from their stools."
Pinero could not be exempt from this general fate of
the artist, above all, the dramatic artist. But the
whirligig of time brings in his revenges, and the reaction
against his reputation has already spent something of its
force. Let us remember, and apply to him, the words
that in his lecture he used of Robertson.

In dealing with the stage you must judge an author's work
in relation to the age in which he wrote, the obstacles he had
to grapple with in the shape of ancient prejudices and seemingly impassable barriers, and so judged it can scarcely be
denied that Robertson was a man of vision and courage.

Was not Pinero too a man of vision and courage ?
In farce, in sentimental comedy, above all in domestic
drama, he struck out fearlessly, on original lines. His
range extended from the borders of tragedy to the neighbourhood of the grotesque. And whatever its type, a

play to him was not merely a "conversation piece" but a work of constructive design.   This is evident in the extreme elaboration of his stage-directions which in the printed pages of his plays often occupy as much space as the dialogue.   This latter in its more serious flights was at times over-artificial and cumbrous.   Pinero was not by instinct a stylist; he had not the Anglo-Irish ear of a Synge or a Shaw for beautiful prose rhythm.   Yet at its best his dialogue had the finish, the fine edge, of lapidary art, and it could take on a conspicuous variety of tones.   He felt himself the inheritor of the great traditions of the English theatre.

Of his tributes to Kean and to T. W. Robertson no more need be said.   But it is characteristic of his width of outlook that in 1912 he gave a centenary lecture on Browning as a dramatist.   And in his lecture to the Royal Society of Literature on the theatre of the 'seventies he paid generous though discriminating tribute to the dramatists of that period—W. S. Gilbert, James Albery, W. G. Wills and H. J. Byron; and to the players who were then coming to the front—Henry Irving and Charles Wyndham, Madge Robertson and Ellen Terry. He himself, and it ranks high in his achievement, did much to make or fortify the reputations of most of the leading actors and actresses of his own day.   Some at least of the parts that they created from his inspiration will, I believe, endure as classic roles of the English stage. Fashions change in the theatre, but the work of a single-minded dramatic master-builder can never become wholly obsolete.

INDEX

INDEX

Achurch, Janet, 262

Addison, 18, 53, 54, 58, 59

Æschylus, 155, 159

Albery, James, 280

Alexander, Sir George, 262, 273, 274

Alleyn, Edward, 121

Anne, Queen, 57, 58

Ariosto, 199, 201

Arnold, Matthew, influences on him at Rugby and Oxford, 230–2; his debt to Greek poetry, 4, 232; *Sohrab and Rustum*, 232; *Balder Dead*, 232; *The Sick King in Bokhara*, 232; *Tristram and Iseult*, 232; *Empedocles on Etna*, 232; *Dover Beach*, 232–3; *Stanzas from the Grande Chartreuse*, 233–6; *Obermann* and *Obermann Once More*, 236–8; *The Scholar-Gipsy*, 239–40; *Thyrsis*, 239, 241–3; *Geist's Grave*, 244–5; *Matthias*, 245–6; *Rugby Chapel*, 247; *Heine's Grave*, 247–8; *The Last Word*, 249

Arnold, Dr. Thomas, 230, 231

Ascham, Roger, 152

Austen, Jane, 45

Bacon, Lord, 139

Baker, Mrs., 92, 94

Balzac, 154

Barrett, Arabel, 176

Barrett, Edward, 151, 164, 171

Barrett, Edward Moulton, 147–8, 177

Barrett, George, 167, 176

Barrett, Henrietta (Mrs. Surtees Cook), 146, 170, 175–6, 178, 180, 182

Barrie, Sir James, 278

Bartley, Mrs., 108

Bateman, H. L., 252

Beaupuy, Captain Michael, 62–3, 66

Beethoven, 66

Beggar's Opera, The, 51

Benét, William Rose, 146

Benson, Sir Frank, 85, 120

Berdoe, Edward, 127, 141

Bernhardi, 66, 79

Besier, Rudolf, *The Barretts of Wimpole Street*, 147, 154

Betty, Master, 95

Birrell, Augustine, 127

Blagden, Isabella, 125, 178

Boccaccio, 217

Booth, J. B., 119

Boswell, James, 50

Boucicault, Dion, 251

Box and Cox, 255

Boyd, H. S., 149, 151–3, 160–2, 164
Bradley, A. C., 210
Brooke, Stopford, 127
Broughton, Rhoda, 127
Brown, Mrs., 121
Browning, Elizabeth Barrett, *The Battle of Marathon*, 3, 151, 166; *Sonnets from the Portuguese*, 3, 145, 171–5, 191; *Poems before Congress*, 3, 184; *Aurora Leigh*, 3, 145, 185–91, 250; *Letters*, 146–7, 149, 151–4, 159–60, 162–5, 167, 170–1, 175–8, 181–2; *Letters of R.B. and E.B.B.*, 146, 148, 154, 165–9; *The Runaway Slave*, 148; *The Cry of the Children*, 148, 162–3, 191, *Langland of " Piers Plowman,"* 149; *Queen Anelida and False Arcite*, 149; *An Essay on Mind*, 149–50, 155; *Wine of Cyprus*, 152, 191; *Prometheus Bound*, 153; *The Seraphim*, 154–5; *The Drama of Exile*, 155–7, 190; *The Dead Pan*, 157–9, 160–1, 191; *Catarina to Camoens*, 161; *Rhyme of the Duchess May*, 161; *Lady Geraldine's Courtship*, 161–2, 165; *Cowper's Grave*, 162, 191; *Casa Guidi Windows*, 179–81; *Napoleon III in Italy*, 182–4; *A Tale of Villafranca*, 183–4; presentation of, in *The Barretts of Wimpole Street*, 147, 154; early influence of Malvern and Langland, 149, of Pope, 149–51, and of Greek,

151–3; criticisms on contemporaries, 153–4; Christianity and humanism, 154–60; a metrical experimenter, 160–1; dislike of London, 163–4; courtship, marriage and Journey to Italy, 164–71; visits to England, 176–8, and to Paris, 177–8; enthusiasm for political liberty in Italy and France, 179–84; her death, 185
Browning, Robert, *Pauline*, 3, 122–4, 127, 130, 133; *Paracelsus*, 3, 127–44, 159, 189; *Letters*, 122, 124–6, 129, 141–2, 146–7, 172; *Sordello*, 124; *Men and Women*, 130, 191; *Dramatis Personæ*, 130; *The Ring and the Book*, 127, 133, 191; *A Blot on the 'Scutcheon*, 164; *Mr. Sludge the Medium*, 179; *Prospice*, 191; honoured at Oxford, 125; the Browning Society, 125–7; phases of his reputation, 127–8; courtship and marriage, 164–9; first knowledge of *Sonnets from the Portuguese*, 171–3; later married life, 176–9; compared with A. H. Hallam, 200; centenary lecture, by Pinero, 280
Browning, Robert Wiedeman, 146, 176
Brutus, or *The Fall of Tarquin*, 115
Buckstone, J. B., 252
Bulwer-Lytton, Edward (Lord Lytton), 153, 251
Bunyan, 6

INDEX

Burbage, Richard, 121
Burdett-Coutts, Baroness, 121
Burdett, Osbert, 174
Burgess, Sir John, 108
Burke, 73, 81
Burney, Miss, 45
Butler, Samuel, 129
Byron, H. J., 251, 280
Byron, Lord, 40, 102, 109, 112, 153, 196, 235

Campbell, James Dykes, 80, 124
Campbell, Mrs. Patrick, 262–4
Carey, George Savile, 87
Carey, Henry : *Sally in Our Alley*, 86
Carey, Master (Edmund Kean), 88
Carey, Nancy, 86
Carlyle, Thomas, 47, 176, 246 ; *Heroes and Hero-Worship*, 48–9
Carter, John, 172
Cavour, 185
Cenci, The, 115
Chambers, Mary, 95 (*see also* Kean, Mary)
Chambers, Robert, 160, 207
Chambers, Susan, 95
Charles I, 252
Charles II, 239
Charles IV of Spain, 77
Chatham, Earl of, 73, 81
Chaucer, 157, 201, 217
Cherry, Andrew, 96, 99
Chesterfield, Lord, 7
Chesterton, G. K., 127
Childe Harold, 18, 80
Cicero, 10, 203
Clarke, Mrs., 87, 94
Clelia, 18

Cleopatra and Cassandra, 18
Clough, A. H., 230, 241
Cobden, Richard, 182
Coleridge, S. T., 66–7, 106, 121, 131, 206
Colman, George, Junior ; *The Mountaineers*, 86, 89, 90, 112, 119
Commeline, Miss, 164
Contrat Social, 65
Cook, Captain Surtees, 176
Cooper, Thomas, 117
Cornwall, Barry (*see under* Procter, B. W.)
Courtney, W. L., 127
Cox, Charlotte, 117
Craig, Gordon, 168
Cunningham, Allan, 123

Daily Telegraph, The, 259
Dante, 199, 201, 219, 273
Darley, George, 107, 117
Darwin, Charles, 140–1 ; *Origin of Species*, 160, 207
Das Leben der Schwedischen Gräfin, 44
Davis, Fay, 265, 272
Defoe, 6, 18
Denham, Sir John, 149
de Ripert-Monclar, Amédée, 129, 137
de Scudéry, Mdlle, 18
de Senancourt, Etienne : *Amiel's Diary*, 236, 237, 238
Dichtung und Wahrheit, 45
Dickens, 46
Dickinson, Miss E. (later Mrs. Dowden), 126
Diderot, 42, 44
Doctor Faustus, 110, 137, 144
Doll's House, The, 259, 262

Donne, W., 196
Dowden, Edward, 124
Draper, Daniel, 52
Draper, Mrs. Elizabeth, 52
Drury, Dr., 102
Dryden, 149
Dumas, 153
Du Maurier, Sir Gerald, 268
Dunciad, The, 56
D'Urfé, *Astræa*, 18

Elliston, Robert William, 101–2, 116–17, 119
Elton, Sir Abraham, 192
Emery, Winifred, 263
Enthoven, Mrs. Gabrielle, 85
Epistle to Augustus, 19
Erasmus, 140
Essay on Man, 149
Euphues, 18
Euripides, 152
Evelina, 45
Everlasting Mercy, The, 186
Examiner, The, 105

Faerie Queene, The, 213, 215
Fair Maid of the Inn, The, 129
Farr, William Windham, 194
Fielding, Henry, 41, 45–6, 53
Fletcher, John, 129
Forbes-Robertson, Sir Johnston, 259, 262, 264
Forster, John, 122, 130–1
Fotheringham, J. K., 127
Fox, Rev. W. Johnson, 123, 131
Frobenius, 140
Frohman, Daniel, 257
Froude, J. A., 124
Fyfe, Hamilton, 255, 273
Furnivall, F. J., 124–5, 127, 131, 141, 172–3

Galsworthy, John, 278
Garrick, David, 96, 105, 110, 118
Garrick, Eva, 110, 117
Gatti, the brothers, 263
Gay, John, 51
Gellert, C. F., 44
George III, 88, 108
Germ, The, 56
Ghosts, 259
Gilbert, W. S., 280
Gladstone, W. E., 193
Glanvil, 239
Godwin, William, 65
Goethe, 44, 66, 232
Goldsmith, 50, 53, 55
Gosse, Sir Edmund, 127, 171, 173
Grand Cyrus, 18
Granville-Barker, Harley, 250, 278
Grattan, T. C., 96–7, 106
Grein, J. T., 259
Grey, Lady Jane, 152
Griffin, W. Hall, 127
Gurney, Archer Thompson, 124

Hallam, Arthur Henry, his *Remains in Verse and Prose*, 4, 192, 200; his impression on Eton contemporaries, 193–4; one of "the Apostles", at Trinity College, Cambridge, 193–4; friendship with Alfred Tennyson and expedition to Spain, 195–7; engagement to Emily Tennyson, 197–8; poems addressed to her, 198–200; oration on *Italian Works of Imagination*, 200–1; *Remarks* on Gabriele Rossetti's *Disquisizioni*, 201–

INDEX

2 ; essay on *Philosophical Writings of Cicero*, 203–4 ; review of Tennyson's *Poems, Chiefly Lyrical*, 204–5 ; death in Vienna, 205 ; value of his critical work, 206 ; *In Memoriam* in its personal and wider aspects, 4, 206–9, 210
Hallam, Henry, 192, 206
Hallam, Julia Maria, 192
Hamlet, 36, 91, 96–7, 106
Hardy, Mrs. Thomas, 120, 229
Hardwicke, Sir Cedric, 110
Hare, Sir John, 254, 262, 264, 271
Harvey, Sir Martin, 119
Hawkins, F. W., 85, 109
Hawtrey, E. C., 193
Hazlitt, William, 103, 106–8, 121, 206
Hedda Gabler, 259
Heraud, J., 131
Hicks, Sir Seymour, 263
Hillebrand, Harold N., 85, 88, 91, 100, 106
Hofer, Andreas, 79
Hogarth, 47, 58
Home : *Douglas*, 92–4, 119
Home, Sweet Home, 115
Homer, 232
Hood, Thurman L., 122, 129, 172
Horne, R. H., 124, 146, 148, 151, 160
Hudibras, 129
Hughes, John, 99
Hume, David Dunglass, 179
Humphrey Clinker, 57
Hunt, J. H. Leigh, 107, 172, 204
Hutton, R. H., 127, 218, 227, 231, 243
Huxley, Leonard, 146, 170

Ibsen, Henrik, 259
Ingram, John H., 185
Irving, Sir Henry, 119, 121, 252, 280

Jackson, Sir Barry, 277
James, Henry, 127
Jameson, Mrs., 159, 169
Jane Eyre, 46, 185
Jane Shore, 92
Jerrold, Douglas, 88
Jerrold, Samuel, 88
Jew of Malta, The, 109, 110
Johnson, Dr. Samuel, 11, 50
Jones, Sir Henry, 150, 156
Jonson, Ben, 110, 129, 278

Kant, 66
Kean, Charles, 95
Kean, Edmund (the elder), 86
Kean, Edmund, centenary commemoration of, 2, 120, *Lives of*, 85 ; early London life, 86–8 ; member of travelling companies, 88–102 ; in *The Mountaineers*, 89–91, 102, 120 ; in *Jane Shore*, 92–3, in *Douglas*, 93–4 ; in other parts, 94–6, marriage to Mary Chambers, 95–6 ; as Hamlet at Waterford, 96–7 ; friendships with Grattan and Knowles, 97 ; in *Venice Preserved*, 97–9, 101 ; at Exeter and Guernsey, 99–101 ; his innovation as Shylock at Drury Lane, 103–5, 119 ; other Shakespearian parts, 105–8, 208 ; in *A New Way to pay Old Debts*, 108–9 ; in *The Jew of Malta*, 109–

287

10; in *Oroonoko*, 111–12;
in *Bertram*, 112–15; Keats
plans *Otho the Great* for him,
116; visits to America, 116–
18; intrigue with Charlotte
Cox, 117–18; his death,
118; lack of " team " spirit,
119; his passion and inten-
sity, 121; interest of Pinero
in his career, 120–1, 270
Kean, Howard, 95, 101
Kean, Mary, 96, 99, 101, 109
Keats, George, 116
Keats, John, 200, 204, 206;
Otho the Great, 116
Kemble, Fanny, 176
Kemble, J. P., 87, 103
Kendal, Dame Madge, 85, 120,
251, 280
Kendal, W. H., 254
Kenyon, Sir Frederic, 127, 146,
157, 165, 178
Kenyon, John, 165, 178, 185
King, Edward, 192
King Lear, 96
Kingsland, W. G., 127
Kingsley, Charles, 177
Knowles, James, 211, 251
Knowles, Sheridan, *Brian Bor-
oihne, Leo*, 97

La Calprenède, 18
Lamb, Charles, 108, 206
Landor, W. S., 177, 186
La Nouvelle Héloïse, 42–4
Lawrence, W. J., 85, 91, 97,
101
Le Juif Polonais, 252
Lee, Henry, 101
Lee, Nathaniel; *Alexander the
Great, The Rival Queens*, 95

Leopold, Grand Duke of Tus-
cany, 180
Lessing, *Miss Sara Sampson*, 44
Lewis, Monk, 112
Lillo, George, *The London
Merchant*, 88
Littlewood, S. R., 120
Louis XVI, 64
Lubbock, Percy, 146, 170, 179,
182
Luther, 140
Lycidas, 241
Lyly, John, 6

Mabinogion, The, 216
Macaulay, Lord, 54
Macbeth, 87, 102, 108, 279
MacColl, Norman, 123
Macready, W. C., 116, 119, 131
Malory, Sir Thomas, *Morte
d'Arthur*, 210, 211, 220, 222,
224
Marie-Claire, 44
Marivaux, 41
Marlowe, Christopher, 109, 110,
144
Martin, Mrs., 153, 159, 163–4,
167, 170, 177
Mason, A. E. W., 263, 273, 276
Massinger, Philip : *A New Way
to Pay Old Debts*, 86, 108,
112, 119; *The City Madam*,
108
Maturin, Charles Robert, *Ber-
tram*, 86, 112–15
Maude, Cyril, 263
Maugham, Somerset, *Smith*, 19
Maurice, Frederick Denison,
194
Merchant of Venice, The, 105,
109, 110

Merivale, Charles, 195
Merry Wives of Windsor, The,
87
Mill, John Stuart, 122, 123
Miller, Captain, 88
Millett, Maude, 263
Milnes, Richard Monckton,
(Lord Houghton), 195
Milton, John, 19, 67, 72, 81,
173, 175, 194, 201, 241
Mirabeau, 61, 66
Miroir Politique, 100
Misfortunes of Arthur, The, 211
Mitford, Miss, 153, 170–1, 178,
182
Modern Painters, 202
Molloy, J. F., 85
Montagu, Lady Mary, 7
Morning Chronicle, The, 104, 105
Morning Post, The, 104, 105,
120
Morris, William, 234
Morton, J. M., 255
Moxon, Edward, 161
Munden, J. S., 109
Murray, John, 192
Myers, Frederic, 74, 81

Napoleon I, 49, 60, 66, 70, 76–7,
120
Napoleon III (Louis Napoleon),
171, 182–4
Nash, Thomas, 6
Neaill, Marianne, 107
Nelson, Lord, 49, 76
Nethersole, Olga, 262
Nettleship, J. T., 127
Nietzsche, 66

Œcolampadius, 140
O'Neill, Eliza, 116

Oroonoko, 111–12
Orr, Mrs., 127, 137
Othello, 107, 110, 118
Otway : *Venice Preserved,* 86,
97, 101, 119
Our Village, 153
Oxberry, William, 104

Palafox, 78
Panizzi, Anthony, 194
Paradise Lost, 36, 213
Parsifal, 222
Patmore, Coventry, 207
Payne, J. H., 115
Pendennis, 58
Petrarch, 199, 201, 217
Phelps, 119, 266
Pinero, Arthur Wing, Sir, early
career, 250, 252–3 ; member
of Irving's Lyceum Com-
pany, 253–4 ; begins dram-
atic authorship with *The
Money-Spinner,* 254 ; his
farces, *The Magistrate, The
Schoolmistress, Dandy Dick,
The Amazons,* 254–6 ; *Sweet
Lavender,* 256–7 ; *The Pro-
fligate,* 257–9, 264 ; influence
of Ibsen, 259–60 ; *The Second
Mrs. Tanqueray,* 260–4, 266,
279 ; *The Notorious Mrs.
Ebbsmith,* 264, 279 ; *The
Benefit of the Doubt,* 264–5 ;
*The Princess and the Butter-
fly,* 265–6, 273 ; *Trelawny of
the Wells* and T. W. Robertson, 249–50, 266–71, 276–7,
279 ; *The Gay Lord Quex,*
271–2 ; *Iris,* 272–3, 279 ;
separation from Alexander,
273–4 ; *His House in Order,*

274–5; *The Thunderbolt*, 275; *Mid-Channel*, 276–7; *The " Mind the Paint " Girl*, 276–7; *Playgoers*, 277; *The Big Drum*, 277; *The Enchanted Cottage*, 277; his death, 277; some parallels with Ben Jonson, 4, 278; causes of decline of popularity, 278–9; his vision and courage, 279; interest in Edmund Kean, 120–1, 270, and in the mid-Victorian theatre, 250–1, 280

Pink Dominoes, 255

Pitt, William, 64

Poel, William, 110

Political Justice, 65

Pollard, Graham, 172

Pope, Alexander, 18, 48–9, 53, 56, 149; his *Homer*, 151, 160

Porter, Jane, 115

Powys, J. C., 127

Prévost, 41–2

Price, Mrs., 87

Procter, B. W. (Barry Cornwall), 85, 88, 91, 176

Prometheus Vinctus, 154

Quintessence of Ibsenism, The, 259

Raymond, 103, 119

Reynolds, Frederick : *The Exile*, 97

Richard II, 108

Richard III, 105, 117

Richardson, Ralph, 111

Richardson, Samuel, *Pamela*, 1, 6–8, 10–21, 25, 33, 41, 44, 46; *Clarissa*, 1, 7–9, 20–32, 42–4, 146; *Sir Charles Grandison*, 1–2, 7, 32–41, 45; *Familiar Letters*, 6; influence in France, 41–4; influence in Germany, 44–5; influence in England, 45–6

Rienzi, 153

Robertson, Thomas William, his revolution in domestic drama, 189, 251–2; adapts *David Garrick*, 251; success of *Society*, followed by *Ours*, *Caste*, *Play*, *School* and *M.P.*, 252; as Tom Wrench in *Trelawny of the Wells*, 251, 266–70

Robespierre, 64, 66

Robins, Elizabeth, 263

Robinson Crusoe, 96

Rogers, Samuel, 176

Romeo and Juliet, 108

Ronte, Heinz, 45

Roselle, Amy, 263

Rosmersholm, 259

Rossetti, Dante Gabriel, 123, 234

Rossetti, Gabriele, 201

Rousseau, 20, 42–4, 53, 62

Rowe, Nicholas, 92

Ruskin, John, 177, 202

Sand, George, 177

Schiller, *Die Götter Griechlands*, 158

Scots Magazine, The, 105

Scott, Clement, 259

Scott, Sir Walter, 45, 80, 94, 112, 153

Scottish Chiefs, The, 115

Shakespeare, William, 26, 30, 106, 119, 120, 201; his *Son-*

nets, 171–3 (*see also under the separate plays*)

Sharp, William, 123, 127

Shaw, George Bernard, 259, 278, 280

Shelley, P. B., 116, 131, 193, 200, 204, 206, 235, 248

Sheridan, R. B., *Pizarro*, 88 ; *The Rivals*, 94 ; *The School for Scandal*, 96

Shirley, 185

Siddons, Mrs. Sarah, 87, 91, 103

Sidney, Algernon, 73

Sidney, Sir Philip, 6, 73

Smollett, Tobias, 41, 46, 57

Sophocles, 152, 232

Southerne, Thomas, 111

Southey, Robert, 66

Spanish Tragedie, The, 18

Spectator, The, 18, 57

Spedding, James, 195

Spens, Janet, *Charlotte Brontë*, 46

Spenser, Edmund, 201, 215

Spurgeon, Caroline, 133

Steele, Sir Richard, 53–6, 59

Sternhold and Hopkins, version of 137th *Psalm*, 12

Sterne, Laurence, 52–3

Sullivan, Barry, 109

Swift, Dean, 6, 18, 50–2, 55

Swinburne, A. C., 84, 243

Switzerland, 115

Symons, Arthur, 127

Synge, J. M., 278, 280

Tale of a Tub, 51

Tasso, 199, 201

Tate, Nahum, 108

Tatler, The, 18

Tennyson, Alfred (Lord), Friendship with Arthur Hallam, 194–7 ; *In Memoriam*, 4, 192, 194, 198–9, 206–9, 210, 241 ; *Poems, Chiefly Lyrical* (1830), 195–6, 204 ; *Recollections of the Arabian Nights*, 205 ; *Oriana*, 205 ; *Poems* (1832), 205 ; *Idylls of the King*, 4, relation to Malory's *Morte d'Arthur*, 210–13 ; spiritual interpretation of the legend, 4, 228–9 ; *The Coming of Arthur*, 214–15 ; *Gareth and Lynette*, 215–16 ; *The Marriage of Geraint* and *Geraint and Enid*, 215–17 ; *Balin and Balan*, 217–18 ; *Merlin and Vivien*, 218–19 ; *Lancelot and Elaine*, 220–1 ; *The Holy Grail*, 221–2 ; *The Last Tournament*, 223–4 ; *Guinevere*, 224–5 ; *The Passing of Arthur*, 226–7 ; *The Two Voices*, 207 ; *The Princess*, 210 ; *Maud*, 210 ; *The Lady of Shalott*, 220 ; *Sir Galahad*, 221

Tennyson, Charles, 194

Tennyson, Emily, 197, 198–9

Tennyson, Mary, 198

Tennyson, Hallam (2nd Lord), 198

Terry, Edward, 256

Terry, Ellen, 280

Testament of Beauty, The, 186

Texte, M., *Jean-Jacques Rousseau*, 41

Thackeray, W. M., *The English Humourists of the Eighteenth Century*, 2, 47–59 ; on

Pope, 48–9, 53, 56–7; on Swift, 50–2; on Sterne, 52–3; on Addison, 53, 58; on Steele, 54–5; on Fielding, 45, 55; on Goldsmith, 55; *Esmond*, 38, 58, 266; *Vanity Fair*, 50, 58; *Pendennis*, 58
Tidswell, Miss Charlotte, 87
Times, The, 105, 117, 193
Times Literary Supplement, The, 187
Tobacconist, The, 110
Tom Jones, 55
Treitschke, 66, 79
Trench, R. C., 194, 196
Tristram Shandy, 45, 53

Vanbrugh, Irene, 268, 271, 274
Vestiges of Creation, 159, 207
Victoria, Queen, 212
Vie de Marianne, 41
Volpone, 129

Wagner, 222–3
Walker, Hugh, 127
Waller, Edmund, 149
Walpole, Horace, 7, 45, 112
Watson, I. B., 96
Webster, Ben, 263
Werther, 45
Wesley, John, 73
Whittingham, William, 12

Wieland, 44
Wills, W. G., 252, 280
Wilson, J. Dover, 97
Wilton, Marie (Lady Bancroft), 252, 270
Wise, T. J.: *Letters of Robert Browning*, 122, 124, 196
Wolfe, General, 73
Wolfe, Humbert, 160
Wood, Mrs. John, 255
Wordsworth, William, visits to France, and association with Michael Beaupuy, 60–3; revolutionary ardour, 63–4; disillusionment, 64–6; *Poems dedicated to National Independence and Liberty*, 2, 67–73, 76–80, 120, 229; *The Prelude*, 61–5; *The Convention of Cintra*, 73, 77–8, 83; *The Happy Warrior*, 74–6; interpreter of British conception of liberty, 83–4
Wyndham, Sir Charles, 280

Yates, Edmund, 126
Yeats, W. B., 278
Young, C. M., 107, 117
Young, Edward, *The Revenge*, 110

Zamick, M., 194